PENGUIN BOOKS

THE LIVING TRUST WORKBOOK

Robert A. Esperti and Renno L. Peterson are practicing attorneys who together built a major metropolitan law firm on estate planning and also cofounded the National Network of Estate Planning Attorneys and the Esperti Peterson Institute for Estate Planning. Their previous books include *Loving Trust, The Living Trust Revolution* (both available from Viking), *The Handbook of Estate Planning, Incorporating Your Talents,* and *Protect Your Estate.* They lecture on estate and business planning to professional groups nationwide.

Robert A. Esperti
and Renno L. Peterson

THE
LIVING
TRUST
WORKBOOK

How You and Your Legal
Advisors Can Design, Fund, and
Maintain Your Living Trust Plan

PENGUIN BOOKS

PENGUIN BOOKS
Published by the Penguin Group
Penguin Books USA Inc., 375 Hudson Street, New York, New York 10014, U.S.A.
Penguin Books Ltd, 27 Wrights Lane, London W8 5TZ, England
Penguin Books Australia Ltd, Ringwood, Victoria, Australia
Penguin Books Canada Ltd, 10 Alcorn Avenue,
Toronto, Ontario, Canada M4V 3B2
Penguin Books (N.Z.) Ltd, 182–190 Wairau Road, Auckland 10, New Zealand

Penguin Books Ltd, Registered Offices:
Harmondsworth, Middlesex, England

First published in Penguin Books 1995

1 3 5 7 9 10 8 6 4 2

A NOTE TO THE READER
The authors are not engaged in rendering legal, tax, accounting, or similar professional services. While legal, tax, and accounting issues covered in this book have
been checked with sources believed to be reliable, some material may be affected
by changes in the laws or in the interpretations of such laws since the manuscript
for this book was completed. For that reason the accuracy and completeness of
such information and the opinions based thereon are not guaranteed. In addition,
state or local tax laws or procedural rules may have a material impact on the
general recommendations made by the authors, and the strategies outlined in this
book may not be suitable for every individual. If legal, accounting, tax, investment,
or other expert advice is required, obtain the services of a competent practitioner.

Portions of this work first appeared, in different form, in the authors' *Loving
Trust, The Living Trust Revolution,* and *Loving Trust (revised and expanded),*
published by Viking Penguin. Copyright © Robert A. Esperti and
Renno L. Peterson, 1988, 1991, 1992, 1994.

Grateful acknowledgment is made for permission
to reprint the following material:
"Beneficiary Designation of Trustees under Revocable Trust Instrument" form.
Reprinted by permission of the American Bar Association.
Account agreements from Enterprise National Bank of Sarasota.
Used by permission.

LIBRARY OF CONGRESS CATALOGING-IN-PUBLICATION DATA
Esperti, Robert A.
The living trust workbook: how you and your legal advisors can design, fund, and
maintain your living trust plan / Robert A. Esperti and Renno L. Peterson.
p. cm.
ISBN 0 14 02.4097 7
1. Living trusts—United States—Popular works. 2. Estate
planning—United States—Popular works. I. Peterson, Renno L.
II. Title.
KF734.Z9E873 1995
346.7305'2—dc20
[347.30652] 94-18250

Printed in the United States of America
Set in New Baskerville
Designed by Victoria Hartman

This book is dedicated to the members of the National Network of Estate Planning Attorneys. These are attorneys who are committed to changing the way Americans plan their estates and who have as their primary goal helping each of their clients achieve his or her own specific planning objectives in the best way possible.

This book is also dedicated to all estate planning professionals—attorneys, financial planners, life insurance agents, stockbrokers, and accountants—who share our belief that satisfying the hopes, fears, dreams, aspirations, and goals of clients is the most important aspect of estate planning.

Acknowledgments

All books are more than the products of their authors. It takes a number of people to bring a book to life. In writing this workbook, we have incorporated many of the suggestions and forms of our colleagues, especially those who are members of the National Network of Estate Planning Attorneys. We wish to give particular thanks to the following attorneys without whose input we never would have been able to complete this work:

Richard W. Bayer, Esq.   Peter J. Parenti, Esq.
Dennis Brislawn, Esq.   Robert Saalfeld, Esq.
W. Edward Dean, Esq.   Richard L. Randall, Esq.
David B. Freyman, Esq.   Arnold L. Slavet, Esq.
Robert A. Goldman, Esq.   Bradford L. Stevens, Esq.

We would also like to thank Lisa Kane DeVitto, Esq., for her preliminary efforts in putting this book together, David K. Cahoone, Esq., for his very special efforts in writing, editing, and organizing, and Michele Griffin for spending countless hours on her word processor.

Preface

The Living Trust Workbook was written primarily for three kinds of readers:

- Those who have had estate planning done by a lawyer, but who know or suspect that somehow it is incomplete or lacking.
- Those who have purchased a do-it-yourself estate planning kit or documentation from a living trust company rather than engaging the professional services of their own lawyer.
- Those who have not yet gotten around to planning for themselves and their families, but who would like to do so.

If you have had estate planning done by a lawyer but are uncomfortable with that planning, this book will enable you to review what you have done. It will show you how to find out from your existing attorney, or a new attorney if you no longer desire to use your current attorney, whether or not it is in your best interest to make additions or changes in your planning. By reading this book, you will understand the planning you have so that you can ask your attorney to take the measures necessary to fine-tune your plan.

If you have purchased a do-it-yourself estate planning kit or documentation from a living trust company, this book will expose the major defects that are inevitably found in this kind of planning. *It is our overwhelming experience that planning done with these companies works better for the salesperson and company than it does for you!* After reading this book, you will be able to readily identify the problems in your planning and to retain an attorney and other professional advisors to take the right steps to obtain real planning to fit your particular goals.

If you have not yet accomplished any planning, we show you—from the very beginning—the right way to effectively and efficiently complete your estate plan.

This book is designed to assist you to implement a modern living trust–centered estate plan from beginning to end. It provides step-by-step advice that has helped thousands of satisfied clients over our forty-plus years of practice experience. Through countless dialogues with and teaching professional estate planning courses to accountants, lawyers, life insurance agents, and stockbrokers all over America and our leadership of the National Network of Estate Planning Attorneys and the National Network of Estate Planning Advisors, we have culled the best workable estate planning strategies and practicalities.

In Part One, we explain how you can formulate your estate planning goals, and how to work profitably with your attorney and other estate planning advisors from the beginning all the way through to the successful completion of your estate planning documentation. We explain what estate planning is and what you should expect to accomplish. We flesh out what a living trust–centered estate plan should look like so that you can clearly see a bright and crisp picture of your objectives.

Part One also explains the Esperti Peterson Planning Process. This process is the distillation of our planning and teaching experiences, and embodies precisely what you should and should not do to make your estate planning exercise effective and pleasant. It encompasses professional planning secrets and empowers you to find an estate planning lawyer with whom you can work comfortably and trust. It tells you how to take best advantage of the planning talents of your accountant, financial planner, life insurance agent, and stockbroker. In addition, Part One shares those planning matters that each of your advisors is good at and enjoys accomplishing, and those tasks which he or she is not so good at and, quite frankly, would rather delegate.

Part Two allows you to breathe life into the legal language of your plan. We originally wrote Part Two for our law practice clients to show them how they could actively participate in making sure that each of their assets and property interests was placed safely into the protection of their living trusts. Part Two discloses how we worked with our clients in "funding" their trusts, and how they and their accountants, financial advisors, life insurance agents, and stockbrokers shouldered—with pleasure—many of the tasks of completing various aspects of their trust funding.

Part Two warns you of hidden planning dangers while stepping you through the procedures for getting each of your assets into the protection of your trust. It presents you with the very same forms and instructions that we give to our clients. Our forms are the "how to" that make your trust live following your disability or death. We share them in the hope that your estate planning efforts will succeed because of proper follow-through. **These forms can substantially**

affect your property rights and should only be used in conjunction with the advice of your lawyer and other planning advisors.

This workbook was written to prompt action. It gives you a great many options every step of the way and empowers you to make the right choices at the right time, to maximize your and your family's emotional and financial successes. It is based on the simple philosophy that knowledge with action is knowledge with purpose.

Robert A. Esperti
Renno L. Peterson

Contents

Preface vii
Introduction xiii

PART ONE

Designing Your Living Trust

1 ◆ The Definition of Estate Planning 3

2 ◆ A Living Trust–Centered Plan 8

3 ◆ The Esperti Peterson Planning Process 20

4 ◆ How to Find an Estate Planning Lawyer 29

5 ◆ Creating Your Professional Team 37

6 ◆ Checklist for Designing Your Plan 46

7 ◆ Personal Information Checklist 60

8 ◆ Meeting with Your Professional Tcam 77

9 ◆ Your Second Meeting 85

PART TWO

Funding Your Living Trust

10 ◆ An Overview of Funding 91

11 ◆ The Different Types of Revocable Living Trusts 99

12 ◆ Methods of Funding 111

13 ◆ Bank Accounts and Certificates of Deposit   126

14 ◆ Publicly Traded Stocks, Bonds, and Other Securities   135

15 ◆ Personal Effects and Other Tangible Personal Property   148

16 ◆ Insurance and Retirement Plans   156

17 ◆ Mortgages, Notes, and Other Receivables   165

18 ◆ Business and Professional Interests   177

19 ◆ Real Property Interests   191

20 ◆ Miscellaneous Property   214

21 ◆ Other Important Elements of Your Living Trust–Centered Plan   217

22 ◆ A Final Word   227

Appendix ◆ Forms   229

Index   311

Introduction

A Living Trust Background

It is a fact that living trust–centered estate planning is far superior to will planning/probate and to jointly owned property planning. Up until 1992, however, there was a professional debate as to whether or not living trust–centered planning was superior to them. But that issue has now been laid to rest. Our book *The Living Trust Revolution: Why America Is Abandoning Wills and Probate* proves conclusively that a properly completed living trust plan written by a competent lawyer working in conjunction with other professional advisors is by far the most effective estate planning technique in virtually every estate planning situation imaginable.

It is also a fact that more and more Americans are demanding—and getting—living trust planning from their professional advisors. The numerous living trust books, countless newspaper and magazine articles, and an amazing array of "living trust" seminars now being held in almost every community in America have started to change the way Americans view estate planning. Today, a better informed public expects to avoid the expense and delay of the probate process.

There has also been a growing recognition by sensitive and informed lawyers that the living trust does indeed have many advantages over will planning/probate and other planning methods. However, this recognition has been slow in coming; the legal community does not readily accept change. Unfortunately, most practitioners have not been trained adequately in living trust planning methods. A vast majority of law schools are still teaching courses on wills and trusts created in wills (testamentary trusts) that offer little or no training on living trusts. But this too is changing.

In spite of a dramatic increase in the public's demand for living trust planning, living trust documents continue to be misunderstood by a great many people because of tremendous amounts of misinformation being naively disseminated by the media. This misinformation centers on two disparate groups: the fast buck hucksters who have jumped on the living trust bandwagon as part of their get-rich-quick selling schemes, and insecure probate lawyers who are clinging to their self-serving, anachronistic views.

A number of probate lawyers attacked our book *Loving Trust* because they believed that it unfairly touted living trust planning and needlessly brought emotion into their red tape–filled, bureaucratic world. They were both right and wrong. They were right in their assessment that we assumed responsible practitioners knew that living trust–centered planning was best for clients. They were wrong in assuming that *Loving Trust* was about living trust planning. In short, in their fear over a dwindling probate future, they missed the point: *Loving Trust* is not about living trust planning. It is a book about how people can put emotion and caring into their estate plans through the proper use of living trust–centered planning.

We discovered a simple but powerful truth. Estate planning is not a thing— a product or a commodity. It is a living process that can put joy into people's lives. We initially developed the Esperti Peterson Loving Trust Planning Process to describe what happens in this living process, and have refined it into the Esperti Peterson Planning Process in recent years.

Experience has repeatedly taught us that if clients and professionals alike understand our planning process, a meaningful estate planning result is assured. The process starts with the definition of estate planning. We have discovered that if a definitional agreement can be reached between clients and their advisors, significant planning can soon follow. This may not seem like a monumental breakthrough, but it is. Getting ordinary people to communicate with ordinary lawyers is no mean feat.

Most people who have estate plans appear to misunderstand the far-reaching effects of their planning documents. What they think their plans say and what those documents really say are two different things. It is our experience that once clients are taken through a "translation process," they are invariably shocked!

When the Esperti Peterson Planning Process is used, the plan fits the client's hopes, fears, dreams, values, aspirations, and financial situation. It is a warm and personal communication process that we will talk a great deal about in Part One.

The Use of Forms

The danger of creating a book that contains legal forms is that it may prove the old adage that "a little knowledge can be a very dangerous thing." The forms in this workbook are legal in nature. They can substantially affect your rights in your property and, if not used correctly, can create income tax, gift tax, and estate tax problems. However, they can also save you time and money if used in conjunction with your attorney's advice and review. They are meant to enhance and augment that advice rather than replace it, and should be used with care under professional supervision.

Never attempt to transfer property to your trust without first consulting your lawyer and your other professional advisors for their advice and general directions. Property interests that include real property, certain privately owned business interests, and some investment interests (all of which we will cover in great detail in later chapters) should only be transferred to your trust by a competent lawyer.

However, you, your lawyer, and your other professional advisors will benefit from these forms. Your lawyer will get assistance on ministerial matters that are not legally challenging and that he or she is probably not interested in doing. Your other advisors will get to contribute their professional know-how, and they usually will perform many of these services at no fee or for a much lower fee than your lawyer would charge. You will save legal fees for work your lawyer would prefer to delegate elsewhere.

PART ONE

■

Designing Your
Living Trust

∘ 1 ∘

The Definition of Estate Planning

Many people try to accomplish estate planning without knowing what it is or how to specifically define it. In our experience, it is important to define precisely what estate planning is and what it accomplishes before trying to complete it. We believe that it is equally important for you to recognize that estate planning is a *process*—with a definite beginning and end—rather than just a thing, strategy, or product.

We have reviewed a number of attempts to define estate planning over the years, but they all seemed to be devoid of any life; they were more like scientific formulas than practical definitions that the public could grab hold of and put to work in their personal situations. Conventional definitions seem to be preoccupied with death and dying rather than planning today and tomorrow for healthy people or vibrant charitable organizations.

Perhaps the greatest myth about estate planning is the perception that estate planning is confined to "death planning." We think this idea comes from the public's understandable belief that estate planning is based solely on the preparation of a Last Will and Testament. Traditionally, people viewed wills and probate as the only acceptable technique for estate planning. Since wills take their lives from the deaths of their makers—the only time that wills can work on behalf of their makers is when their makers die—estate planning has been identified as death planning; no more, no less.

Because the prospect of our own death is often difficult for many of us to contemplate or accept, it is only natural that we shy away from all death-related activities, including taking the time or making the effort to plan for the inevitable. The tragic result is that this definitional view discourages so many people from accomplishing real planning.

Done the right way, estate planning is *not* death planning. In reality, estate planning is an act of love, not an act of death. Our experience is that people who love are people who plan. People who care about themselves and others are far more likely to want to create a plan that preserves their assets and shares them with others in a kind and conscientious manner.

Once a person comes to the realization that estate planning is an act of love, it is relatively simple to define estate planning. Here is our definition of estate planning:

> I want to control my property while I'm alive. I want to take care of myself and my loved ones if I become disabled. I want to give what I have to whom I want, the way I want, and when I want and, if I can, I want to save every last tax dollar, professional fee, and court cost possible.

Our definition of estate planning has several components. Let's briefly examine each one in order to put estate planning in a proper perspective.

Control

The most important element of our definition of estate planning for almost every client we have met with over the past three decades is *control,* a theme that is emphasized throughout our definition of estate planning and in the Esperti Peterson Planning Process.

Your ability to keep control in your estate planning efforts will manifest itself in many ways. If you totally abrogate control by choosing not to have a will or a trust—or any other formal planning, for that matter—you will still have an "estate plan."

If you should become incapacitated without accomplishing formal planning for that contingency, there is nevertheless an entire set of state laws that directs how you and your wealth will be cared for. If you die without initiating formal planning steps, there is yet another whole set of state laws that directs how your property will be gathered up, inventoried, valued, and distributed. This estate plan is not exactly Orwellian Big Brotherism, but there can be no doubt that if you do not take control of your estate planning, the state—Big Brother—will fill the void for you and your family.

Your state's control also extends to other aspects of your planning. For example, the joint tenancy property that you own with your spouse or another may be tied up in the courts for both you and your other joint tenant if one of you becomes incapacitated or if one of you has creditor problems. It will be lost forever to your wishes on your death. It is immune to the provisions of your will or living trust planning!

It is important from the outset of any estate planning inquiry that you recognize that you can lose control over your property the second that you acquire it if you do not fully understand the concepts of "title" and property ownership.

To exercise estate planning control, you must take responsible action to implement and use your own estate plan, rather than leaving it to Big Brother.

Incapacity

After control, the definition of estate planning addresses *incapacity*. Insurance company statistics, called morbidity tables, show that on average the odds of suffering a debilitating disability—total mental or physical incapacity—is about six times greater in the next year than the odds of dying. This is nothing new to most of us. We know that we are living longer lives, but also that it is quite likely that in our longevity we will spend a considerable amount of time and money in hospitals and/or nursing homes.

Even if you try to control the quality of your life, there is no assurance that you will avoid the problems of incapacity. You can eat right, exercise, take vitamins, and follow the many other suggestions that have been developed to help all of us live better longer. But there is much you cannot control about your health. You cannot pick your parents and ancestors, all of whom determined your genetic makeup. You cannot completely control the environment and its effects on your health.

You can, however, to a great extent control how you are to be cared for if you become incapacitated. As part of estate planning, you can purchase long-term health care, implement savings plans, or buy disability insurance. You can also leave instructions about how you want to be cared for in the event of your incapacity. Your estate plan can clearly direct how your property and money should be used for you and your loved ones. You can prevent—to a surprisingly great degree—the state's imposing its rules about how you and your assets will be cared for if you are legally incapacitated. But you can only exercise this control if you take the time and make the effort to make it happen. A workable estate planning definition is packed with action.

Giving Your Property to Whom You Want

After you have controlled your property while you are alive and well, and after you have planned for your incapacity, then you can look forward to *giving your property to others at a time or times of your choosing*. Notice that you do not have to give your property away at death in order to plan your estate. You can give it away during your lifetime or retain it in trust for one or more persons, generations, or charities at your total discretion.

It is absolutely clear that our laws allow you to control your property, and to pass it in the manner you want to the beneficiaries you choose, with amazing latitude and flexibility. After all, it's your property and you can plan for it any way you want, assuming, of course, that you initiate the process and control it all the way through to completion.

Planning for Taxes and Expenses

The final part of our definition of estate planning addresses *taxes, fees, and costs*. One of the most famous quotations about taxes comes from a court opinion. In this opinion, Judge Learned Hand wrote:

> Anyone may so arrange his affairs that his taxes shall be as low as possible; he is not bound to choose that pattern which will best pay the Treasury; there is not even a patriotic duty to increase one's taxes.
> —*Gregory* v. *Helvering*, 69 F.2d 809 (1934).

No one is duty-bound to pay the maximum amount of taxes of any kind, unless, of course, he or she wants to—a phenomenon that we have yet to witness in our professional careers.

The same can be said of paying professional fees and court costs. If you can arrange to reduce these types of fees as part of your planning, more of your money and property will pass to those people whom you love or those charities that need your help. Good planning does everything reasonably possible to cut unnecessary expenses and costs.

Notice that this cost savings part of the definition of estate planning is at the end and not the beginning, and that it is preceded by the phrase "if I can."

For many people, it is more important to plan the way they want to plan and to take care of themselves and their loved ones than it is to try to change their planning desires in order to simply accommodate tax or cost planning.

There can be no question that most of us want to reduce taxes and costs. The question is, do we want to save these costs at the expense of compromising our control or our ability to give what we have to whom we want the way we want and when we want? Some people will say yes, but it is our experience that the far greater number will say no. If saving taxes and costs were our only motivation, we could simply leave everything we own to a qualified public charity and avoid both. The secret of good planning is to reduce taxes and costs *and* retain control.

The Definition of Estate Planning Is Your Standard of Measurement

You should measure every estate planning idea and technique that you are now using, or that is suggested to you, by our definition of estate planning. If the idea or technique does not meet the definition, then you should avoid or discard it. Planning suggestions that meet the definition of estate planning should be considered carefully and adopted in a comprehensive plan that is developed by you and a team of professional advisors who understand the definition of estate planning and who also fully understand your wishes and needs.

We believe that the type of estate plan that consistently meets the definition of estate planning is what we call a living trust–centered plan. In the next chapter, we will give you some bottom-line answers to the questions "Do I need a living trust–centered plan?" and "Do I have a living trust–centered plan?"

·2·

A Living
Trust–Centered Plan

In our book *The Living Trust Revolution*, we proved beyond a doubt that living trust–centered planning is far superior to will planning/probate and other methods of estate planning, including joint tenancy with right of survivorship and outright beneficiary designations. The facts show that everyone who wishes to accomplish estate planning objectives should consider and implement a living trust–centered plan. They also clearly show that a living trust–centered plan is the only type of estate planning that can meet all of the elements of our definition of estate planning.

What Is a Living Trust–Centered Plan?

The living trust is an ancient and venerable legal concept developed in the tradition of the English common law over a thousand years ago. It predates the Last Will and Testament by over five hundred years. The living trust, in its earliest form, was used by members of the English nobility to ensure that their property passed the way they wanted without unnecessary interference by the government. Today, living trusts are valid in all of our states and possessions. The living trust has been analyzed, studied, and favorably written about by legal scholars in definitive legal treatises, and has been used successfully by highly skilled estate planning practitioners for literally hundreds of years.

A revocable living trust, also known as an "*inter vivos*" trust, is created by a trust maker who transfers property to a trustee for the benefit of a beneficiary. A revocable living trust can be established either by declaration, where the trust maker is the sole trustee, or by a transfer of property in trust to several trustees, who can include the maker. A revocable living trust can be revoked or amended by the trust maker at any time prior to death, allowing it to be adjusted as the planning needs of its maker change.

Revocable living trusts can sometimes be difficult to conceptualize, especially for people who have not read one or seen one actually work. In our book *Loving Trust*, we used an analogy of "baby-sitter instructions" to describe a living trust. Over the years, we have found that this is the easiest way for most people to understand how a living trust works. When we left our minor children with a baby-sitter for a getaway weekend, the baby-sitter received several minutes of verbal instruction accompanied by pages of written instructions and miscellaneous notes detailing all sorts of matters that needed thought, attention, and action. We and our spouses were most always close to a telephone and were not reluctant to use it frequently to add instructions and to confirm that all was right with our children and households.

A properly drafted living trust is like a set of baby-sitter instructions for the care of loved ones. Our instructions tell our trustee—the baby-sitter—how to care for our beneficiaries—our children. The instructions are as detailed as possible to cover all of the expected—and unexpected—events that might occur. Not only do these instructions tell our trustee about how to use our money and property to care for our beneficiaries, they tell our trustee why we left certain instructions and how we want them carried out.

When you think of baby-sitter instructions, you might think that they only apply to loved ones, not to you or your spouse while you are alive. However, one of the most important features that a revocable living trust has, and that a will does not have, is its ability to provide instructions for the care of its maker. A revocable living trust is valid and operational the day it is signed. If the trust maker becomes sick or incapacitated, the living trust can control the maker's property for his or her benefit or for the benefit of others without the intervention of the probate court. By contrast, a will can only function after the death of its maker and is unfortunately subject to probate; a living trust can care for its maker immediately and avoids both a living probate and a death probate.

Living trust–centered planning is the term we use to describe an estate plan in which a living trust is used as the foundation. But the living trust is only a foundation. A total estate plan requires additional documentation to make it effective for purposes of meeting the definition of estate planning.

A living trust–centered plan must have, *at an absolute minimum*, the following important legal documents and information:

- The living trust document itself
- A "Pour-Over" Will
- Durable Special Power of Attorney for Funding
- A Health Care Power of Attorney
- A Living Will
- A Memorandum of Personal Property or some other mechanism to dispose of special personal effects
- An anatomical gift form, if applicable in your state
- Burial and memorial instructions
- Information about all of your property
- The location of all your important papers and financial information
- Lists of all your advisors and those people or institutions that should be contacted at your disability or death

If this looks like a pretty comprehensive list, it is supposed to. A living trust–centered estate plan is comprehensive. To help you understand how complete a living trust–centered plan can be, let's take a look at the documents that comprise a good plan.

The Living Trust Document

A living trust, to be truly effective and to reflect your estate planning goals, should not be a terse set of boilerplate instructions fresh from someone's forms book. The living trust document must contain your instructions about how you want your property controlled while you are alive and well, upon your disability, and after you have died. This cannot be done in just a few pages.

A good living trust document will have extensive language that relates to you and your family. It will enable you great flexibility while you are alive and able to control your property. It will define what "disability" is and how your trustees will care for you and your loved ones if you are disabled. It will have your instructions as to how your property will pass at your death. In fact, it will even allow you to name trustees, whether they be family members, friends, advisors, a bank, or a trust company, who will follow your instructions at your disability or death.

The living trust document that you get may be thirty, forty, fifty or more pages in length. If it is, don't despair. Long is not necessarily bad or complicated. In estate planning, long usually means that your lawyer has considered as many reasonable possibilities as possible and has tried to address each of them. This is the essence of good lawyering.

Pour-Over Will

For every living trust–centered plan there must be a short, single-purpose, "fail-safe" will. This special kind of will, called a "Pour-Over" Will, must be signed so that property that you do not put in the name of your trust will end up in your trust after your death.

A Pour-Over Will simply says:

> I leave any property owned by me at my death, and not already in my trust, to my trust. Please have my executor put it in my trust.

Property in your name at your death is subject to probate. If you have not left a will leaving this property somewhere, it passes to your heirs as decided by the law of your state. Since you want your revocable living trust instructions to control all your property after you die, you must provide that any property not in the name of your trust gets there through your Pour-Over Will. That's where it gets its name—any assets you forgot to put in your trust are poured over into it after your death.

Durable Special Powers of Attorney for Funding

A Durable Special Power of Attorney for Funding is an integral part of a living trust–centered plan. It allows you to give others the power to transfer your property into your trust if you become disabled and are unable to do it yourself. This is where the "durable" comes from: The power survives your disability. For example, if you have a stroke that totally incapacitates you, and you have not transferred all your property into your trust, those people to whom you have given such a power can transfer your property into your trust for you.

A Durable Special Power of Attorney for Funding avoids a potentially expensive, time-consuming, and often unnecessary court process called a guardianship or a conservatorship. If a person is mentally incompetent, he or she cannot effectively manage his or her financial affairs. That person cannot sign checks, sell property, or otherwise enter into day-to-day financial transactions. Without a Durable Special Power of Attorney, the incapacitated person must be declared mentally incompetent in a public court hearing. After being judged incompetent, the court appoints a financial guardian, called a conservator, to take control of the incompetent person's property. The conservator is paid a fee for these services. All expenses of the court proceeding and all of the conservator's expenses in taking care of the property are paid for out of the incompetent person's assets.

All assets held in a revocable living trust avoid this court-controlled process. That is a major reason why funding a living trust fully is so important. A Durable Special Power of Attorney for Funding allows other people to fund an incompetent person's trust so that the need for a conservatorship is eliminated.

We believe that a Durable Special Power of Attorney for Funding must be "special." "Special" means that whoever you name in your Durable Special Power of Attorney for Funding can only transfer your property into your trust; that person cannot sell, take, use, or give your property to anyone else. Once your property is in your trust, it can be administered pursuant to your instructions.

Some lawyers draft Durable Powers of Attorney that are general powers of attorney. **Do not sign one of these.** Limit the power of the people you name in a Durable Power of Attorney to one thing: the ability to transfer your property to your trust. Granting the holder any more power means you have lost control over your property. A general power of attorney, even if done in the guise of a Durable Power of Attorney, is dangerous and should be avoided.

Since Durable Special Powers of Attorney are limited to one function, you can give them to many people, although some states restrict them to relatives. Generally, the more you give out, the better chance there is that someone will always be available to transfer your property into your trust if you are disabled. Give one to your lawyer and one to your accountant. If you are close to your insurance agent, give one to him or her. Hand them out to relatives and to the trustees you name in your trust.

Durable Special Powers of Attorney, when limited to transferring your property into your trust, can only help you; they cannot hurt you. They are fail-safe devices to prevent court supervision of property you did not put in your trust.

Health Care Power of Attorney

A Health Care Power of Attorney is a special type of Durable Special Power of Attorney in which you give another person the authority to make health care decisions for you if you are unable to make medical decisions because of illness or injury. These decisions include:

- Choice of physician and choice of hospital or nursing home
- The power to determine, upon advice of a physician, whether you are in need of surgery or medication
- The ability to authorize or withhold surgery or medication
- Any other decision concerning your care, comfort, maintenance, and support.

A Health Care Power of Attorney is only used if you are in a coma or you are not mentally competent to make these decisions. Most hospitals now prefer that their patients have a Health Care Power of Attorney.

Living Will

A Living Will is a document that provides instructions to physicians, health care providers, family, and the courts as to what life-prolonging procedures you want if you are terminally ill or in a persistent vegetative state and are not able to communicate your wishes. By having a Living Will, you are able to state your personal views on how you wish to be treated if you are terminally ill or in a persistent vegetative state, which is a term that is intended to mean a person who is brain-dead. Perhaps more important, you are taking the pressure off of your loved ones; if you have not done a Living Will, then those people who are closest to you, such as your spouse or children, must make the difficult decisions as to your care under these tragic circumstances.

Memorandum of Personal Property

A Memorandum of Personal Property can be used in conjunction with a Pour-Over Will or a revocable living trust. A Memorandum of Personal Property is a separate written document in which you give specific items of your personal property to named individuals. We discuss this memorandum in more detail in Chapter Fifteen, "Personal Effects and Other Tangible Personal Property."

Anatomical Gift Form

If you would like to make anatomical gift after you have passed away, your desires should be included as part of your living trust–centered planning. The laws of each state control the requirements for making anatomical gifts. Because of the differing state requirements, you should consult with your attorney as to how it is done in your state. In Chapter Twenty-one, "Other Important Elements of Your Living Trust–Centered Plan," we discuss this subject in greater depth.

Burial and Memorial Instructions

Another concern of many of our clients is how they properly convey their wishes with regard to how they are to be buried, the type of funeral they would like, and any other instructions with regard to memorials. As with anatomical gifts, burial and memorial instructions vary from state to state. Your attorney will be able to advise you what your state requires. Please refer to Chapter Twenty-one, "Other Important Elements of Your Living Trust–Centered Plan," for more information on burial and memorial instructions.

Other Living Trust–Centered Plan Documents

In Chapter Seven, "Your Personal Information Checklist," we show you how to organize and furnish information about all of your property. Organization of your affairs is one of the greatest advantages of having a living trust–centered plan. If the plan is properly implemented, you should know what you own and whether it is in your trust or not. Just as important, if you become disabled or you die, your trustees and loved ones will be able to better understand your planning.

As part of the organization required in a good living trust–centered plan, you should identify the location of all your important papers and you should have a list of all of your advisors and others whom you would like to be contacted in the event of your disability or death. We have developed a Location List that does just that. In Chapter Twenty-one, you will find out the importance of the Location List and a form of Location List that we use for our clients.

Just because a living trust–centered estate plan is thorough does not mean that it has to be onerous or tedious. It just needs to be complete. In conjunction with your lawyer and other professional advisors you can comfortably do much of the necessary work yourself. The secret is to follow our planning process; it allows you to be fully prepared. It will save you time and money and allow you to have a plan that meets every one of the requirements of the definition of estate planning.

Even when we plan complex and highly sophisticated estates with documents concerning such issues as a nominee partnership, a nominee agreement for funding, or declarations for funding, land trusts, family limited partnerships, irrevocable trusts, charitable trusts, and even charitable foundations, we nevertheless anchor the entire plan with a revocable living trust; it functions as the foundation for this myriad of additional planning.

A last and most important element of a living trust–centered plan is what we call "funding." The second part of this workbook is devoted to it and its nuances, because a living trust–centered plan can only meet the definition of estate planning if it controls all of your property. In order for it to do so, your trust must acquire title to your property; this process gives you even greater control over your property while you alive and after you are disabled or gone. The process of funding your trust includes making sure that your investments, insurance, and retirement portfolios have been reviewed by your financial advisors. Your advisors will be invaluable to you in determining whether your assets are structured in a way that maximizes their benefit to you and your loved ones based on your estate planning objectives. As you plan your estate, you cannot forget about the financial side of your affairs; it is every bit as important as the loving and legal sides of your estate plan.

Your initial reaction to all of this may well be that a living trust–centered plan sounds great, but that it may cost too much for you and your modest estate.

Cost is always a valid and significant concern of most people. Our research clearly shows that a living trust–centered plan costs *far less* in the long run than other planning alternatives.

The Initial Costs of Preparing Living Trust–Centered Planning

One of the major objections to living trust planning that remains—despite the overwhelming evidence for its superiority—is cost. In fact, "How wealthy does a person or family have to be to afford a living trust–centered plan?" is one of the most common questions we are asked when appearing on radio and television programs or teaching estate planning seminars to professionals. There is no mystery in the answer. If you own assets and have loved ones or charities that you would like to help, then you are a perfect candidate for a living trust–centered plan.

The cost of probate and administration is expensive. Every valid study that has been conducted on the costs of probate, including a study that we commissioned (it was supervised by businesspeople and structured by the head of a major university's statistics department) concludes that on average probate fees for estates that require an executor are about 5 to 6 percent of a person's gross estate. Gross estate means the value of a person's estate without subtracting any mortgages, debts, fees, or expenses. People who have smaller estates lose even a larger percentage to probate costs than those who have larger estates. Studies show that smaller estates, those under $100,000, sometimes lose up to 16 to 20 percent to probate costs. Probate can also cause delay, which means that loved ones may not have access to the funds that are left for many months. If someone with a smaller estate becomes incapacitated, the costs of what we call a living probate—a guardianship or a conservatorship proceeding—can be even more expensive than a death probate. Obviously, a smaller estate cannot absorb these costs.

We believe that regardless of the size of your estate, you ought to seriously consider living trust–centered planning. You will likely pay more in the initial stages for living trust–centered planning than you would for simple will planning, but in the long run this planning will cost substantially less. The adage "You get what you pay for" is most apropos here. Even when the costs of creating, funding, and administering living trusts are taken into consideration, a living trust–centered plan is significantly more economical than will planning/ probate.

We are frequently asked how much a living trust–centered plan should cost. Given the fact that fees vary dramatically from one locale to another, that is a tough question. Through our leadership of the National Network of Estate Planning Attorneys, however, we have been able to get some idea of what lawyers are currently charging for living trust–centered plans all over America. Living trust plans that contain little, if any, federal estate tax planning generally cost $2,500 or less in many parts of the country. But if you have an estate of over $1.2 million, including the face amounts of your life insurance and your retirement benefits, your fee is going to be significantly higher than for someone with $100,000 whose objectives do not require sophisticated tax planning techniques. Living trust plans with federal estate tax planning in them can cost anywhere from $1,500 to an extreme of $50,000 or more for the humongous plan that involves tens of millions of dollars.

It is difficult to set fee parameters for this more sophisticated planning due to the cost of living and various other economic differences in different geographic areas. Also, the skills and experience of lawyers vary. It is very likely that a Wall Street or Beverly Hills trust expert is going to charge a whole lot more for his or her planning skills than a competent trust practitioner in Liberal, Kansas, or Caseville, Michigan.

Note that these fee estimates are based solely on the drafting of the living trust–centered plan documentation. They do not necessarily include the lawyer's time in transferring property into your trust. (That is the topic of Part Two of this book.)

If you need sophisticated planning, equate your lawyer's fee quote to other commodities you commonly purchase, and determine its value not only to what you are receiving, but to other ways you spend comparable dollars. For example, if you have an estate of $3 million and your lawyer quotes you a fee of $8,500 for your complete plan—including all of that important tax planning—compare your fee to the price of that new car you bought not too long ago at several times that amount. If you do, we suspect that it will make all the difference in the world as to how you feel about paying your expert's fee. Unlike that new automobile, which loses thousands of dollars of value the minute you drive it off the car lot, your estate planning should continually appreciate in value over time while initially saving your family many hundreds of thousands of dollars of unnecessary costs and taxes. And a living trust–centered plan based on our planning process should stand the test of time. It should not have to be redone in its entirety, but rather amended from time to time as you grow, change your mind, or take advantage of new tax planning opportunities that may surface.

Keep in mind that probate fees can easily exceed 16 percent of smaller estates and that they average from 5 to 6 percent of the gross value of all estates. In our professional experience and judgment, fees for living trust–centered planning are generally one of the great bargains to be found in America's law offices these days.

Please remember that you only get what you pay for. If you buy a *do-it-all-by-yourself* forms book or a computer program in order to keep your costs down, you are asking for trouble and will most likely increase your costs substantially. Living trust planning is complex, and it deals with a multitude of statutes, court rulings, and interpretations by the Internal Revenue Service and other governmental agencies.

If you mess up being your own lawyer, you and your loved ones will suffer. Your efforts can mean a living probate for you if you are adjudicated as incompetent or are otherwise incapacitated, and also death probate for your property and loved ones. Leaving a monument of extra expenses, complexities, stress, and frustration because of previous penny-wise pound-foolish judgments is not, on reflection, what most people would choose to leave their families. Do-it-yourself and stay-away-from-lawyers estate planning accomplishes just that. **However, there is much that you can do yourself if you work in conjunction with your lawyer and other professional advisors that will both reduce your costs and make them happy.**

The same can be said about seeking out nonlawyer advisors to draft your living trust. There are too many businesses—and their number appears to be growing—that sell living trusts through salespeople or through the mail. **We recommend that you avoid these companies.** Not only will they cost as much as or more than doing your planning the right way with a lawyer, they will cost your family a great deal more on your disability or death. These companies and their salespeople will not be around at that time. But let the buyer beware—*caveat emptor*—will still ring in more than a few ears in their aftermath. There can be no question that you or your family will be left holding the bag long after these people have spent your hard-earned money.

We have heard of so many bad experiences with these companies that it would take another book to relate the magnitude of the horror stories. Don't be misled with promises of living trust plans that have been reviewed by lawyers or the representation that the company will provide a lawyer just for you. All of these are empty promises to entice you to part with your money.

We can't encourage you strongly enough to work with professionals whom you seek out and hire in attempting to meet the requirements of estate planning as it applies to you, your family, and your assets by following the Esperti Peterson Planning Process.

What Is the After-Death Cost
of a Living Trust–Centered Estate Plan?

Some living trust critics argue falsely that the after-death costs of administering a trust are equivalent to average probate costs. The results of extensive research that we published in our book *The Living Trust Revolution* have proven just the opposite. They show that a properly funded revocable living trust with assets of less than $600,000 reduces after-death costs to an amount that in all likelihood will be less than one-half of one percent as compared with the 5 to 6 percent average costs associated with probate. In our experience, the after-death costs for larger estates that utilize a fully funded living trust plan are slightly higher and may approach three-quarters of one percent. Not only does all of the evidence show that a living trust–centered plan is far superior to will planning/probate, it conclusively proves that fully funded revocable living trusts cost significantly less than will planning/probate!

·3·

The Esperti Peterson
Planning Process

In our many years of planning and teaching, we have observed how numerous clients and their advisors take an "upside down" approach to estate planning. By this we mean that either the client or his or her advisors hear of a "brand-new" idea or the latest tax or planning strategy. Excited about its potential, they often implement this innovation without giving real thought to its impact on the client's overall planning objectives. The next time a new gimmick or strategy comes along, it too is implemented. Of course, there is no preconceived, coherent plan. All of these new "ideas" just get added on to whatever other "ideas" are already in place.

After this random approach to planning is repeated a few times, the whole planning process gets murky. It's hard for the client or his or her advisors to understand or remember why all these planning techniques were used. With this approach to planning, even legitimate planning ideas often make no sense in retrospect. Both clients and professional advisors alike get confused as to what has been done and why.

The Planning Pyramid

In Figure 3-1, there is a diagram of what we call the Planning Pyramid. You can readily see that there are five tiers of the pyramid. The foundation says "Me." With the Esperti Peterson Planning Process, estate planning strategies are based primarily on your needs and your desires. It recognizes that you are the most important person in the planning paradigm.

The next tier consists of family. Most of us approach estate planning wanting

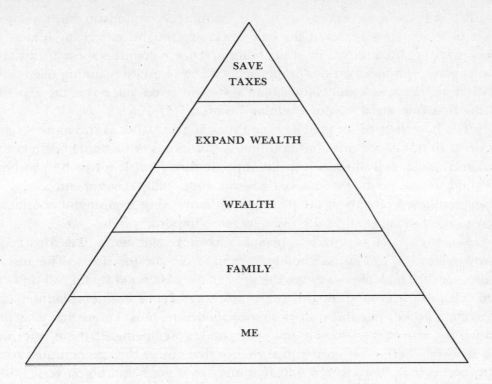

Figure 3-1. The Planning Pyramid

to provide for our families. This concern can be addressed while we are alive and well, or upon our disability or death. In any event, the planning process must address each and every one of those possibilities to be valid professionally.

After we have taken care of our needs and those of our families, most of us would like to keep what we have; doing just that is the next tier in the Planning Pyramid.

Reasonable people avoid carelessly risking their hard-earned or inherited wealth regardless of the promised return. Estate planning is, for the most part, estate enhancement and preservation, both of which are important elements in the planning process. Once we have accomplished our first three tiers of objectives, it would be nice to expand our wealth so that we have more. This is the fourth level of the Planning Pyramid. Growing our nest egg is great, as long as it doesn't interfere with our other objectives. The planning process recognizes that wealth enhancement should only work closely with wealth preservation.

At the pyramid's peak we identify our desire to save or reduce taxes and expenses. It may not be possible for you to maintain your present wealth or expand it unless taxes of all kinds are reduced. Reducing taxes, however, may conflict with the four prior goals in the Planning Pyramid; you can save your taxes by losing your money at the race track, or thoughtlessly giving it away to mercenary organizations. Sound planning practice recognizes these truths and always places emphasis on the proper sequencing of estate planning needs and motivations. **Expenses and taxes should always be saved, but not at the expense of the first four steps in your Planning Pyramid.**

Notice how the steps in the Planning Pyramid get smaller as you move toward its peak. In our experience, however, most approaches to planning begin at the pyramid's peak and work in just the opposite direction. It turns the planning pyramid upside down. Professional advisors continually recommend a bevy of strategies aimed directly at tax planning without giving meaningful consideration to the fundamental issues raised by more important tiers.

This conventional approach to planning has not made sense to us for a great many years. How can anyone build a pyramid from the top down? The answer is they can't. The higher they go, the greater the likelihood that it will tip over and crash to the ground. Before any sophisticated tax or business planning can be accomplished, you and your professional advisors must know what your priorities are with respect to you and your family's well-being. If those priorities are ignored, there is only a minimal chance that any of the tax-motivated strategies will ever coalesce into results that meet your goals and objectives.

The planning process starts with the first tier of the Planning Pyramid. That is the starting place for all tax and business planning. It starts with "Me" and what you want. The Planning Pyramid provides the planning blueprint; your desires and family wishes are its foundation. As you progress up the pyramid, the planning gets easier as the blocks get smaller. That's as it should be; planning should get easier—not harder—every single planning step of the way.

Beginning the Process

Armed with the definition of estate planning and the knowledge that a living trust–centered plan is superior to alternative planning techniques, you can confidently follow our process by building your Planning Pyramid one tier at a time from the bottom up.

There are two applications of our planning process. One is for you as the client. The other is for your professional advisors—your lawyer, accountant, financial advisors, life insurance agent, and whomever else you decide to enlist as a planning ally.

From your perspective, the planning process involves how you initiate, participate in, and complete your living trust–centered plan. For your professional advisors, it involves how they accommodate your hopes, fears, dreams, aspirations, values, and even idiosyncrasies or eccentricities while helping you to initiate, control, and complete your living trust–centered plans.

The Esperti Peterson
Planning Process from Your Perspective

From your perspective, the planning process emphasizes *control*. You immediately establish control by initiating the planning process. The Esperti Peterson Planning Process makes it clear to your advisors that you wish to be kept informed and in total control of your estate plan during each of the steps that need to be taken to make your planning a reality. If you follow our planning process step by step, you will keep total control of your affairs and planning initiatives, quickly reach planning closure, and feel good about the entire exercise.

Step One: Educate Yourself

The more knowledge that you have, the easier it will be for you to meet your estate planning challenges. There are a number of relatively painless ways to educate yourself in estate planning basics. Read or skim our books *Protect Your Estate, Loving Trust,* and *The Living Trust Revolution.* We also advise you to read other recommended planning books that catch your eye or interest you as you peruse the shelves of your bookstore. Look for books that are written to be understood and that clearly and credibly explain estate planning alternatives that are written by credentialed authors. For those of you who prefer lectures to reading, we would suggest that you attend one or more estate planning seminars hosted by professionals in your community. Over the past few years, these seminars have proliferated throughout America. If you look in the financial pages of your local newspaper or in your mail, you will likely find listings for several seminars that you can conveniently attend. We would suggest that you attend at least two seminars. Doing so will enable you to experience two different speakers and planning perspectives. Go with the idea that you are not necessarily going to work with the seminar hosts; these seminars are for your education. Stay away from those seminars that use scare tactics or which are high-pressure; find seminars that are educational.

Remember, you do not want to become an expert; that would take a law degree and decades of specialized practice experience and advanced education. Study and learn until you have enough information and understanding to comfortably participate in the planning process. Once you are there, you will know enough to understand and participate in meaningful planning dialogues with your advisors that will keep them professionally honest.

Step Two: Get Prepared

The more you are prepared, the better plan you will have and the more time and money you will save. To do so, it is important that you anticipate what you and your advisors will need in order to complete your living trust–centered plan. Much of this workbook is devoted to doing just that. Here is a synopsis of what you will need.

- Complete the checklist that is found in Chapter Six of this workbook, "Checklist for Designing Your Plan." It will help you to confront and analyze those issues that are absolutely necessary in a properly drafted living trust–centered plan. These are the trust instructions that allow you to plan using your hopes, fears, dreams, values, and aspirations for you and your loved ones. Do not skimp in terms of time and thought here; this is where the thought that will manifest the love and caring is put into your plan. Read *Loving Trust* if you want more information on these alternatives.

- Complete the personal information checklist found in Chapter Seven. This checklist allows you to organize important information about you and your family that your lawyer and advisors will need to complete your estate plan. This information is vitally important to your first meeting with your lawyer or your other advisors. **They must have this information in order to help plan your estate.** If they do not have it prior to the meeting, they will need to get it from you during the meeting, and there will be less time to discuss important planning issues. The more time your professional advisors have to use during your initial meeting to get this detailed information, the less time they will have for discussing your planning objectives.

Step Three: Create Your Professional Team

In the next two chapters, we will offer our ideas and insights into how you should go about choosing the members of your professional team. Your team may consist of only your lawyer and you; this is perfectly fine in some cases, but is generally not preferable. It is far more preferable that your professional team consist of your financial advisor, life insurance agent, accountant, and perhaps even a trust officer or estate planning specialist from your bank or full-service financial institution, and your estate planning lawyer.

Step Four: Meet with Your Professional Team

You must meet with your professional team. You can begin with your lawyer or you can begin by meeting with other members of your professional team. In Chapter Eight, "Meeting with Your Professional Team," we offer some insights on how you can determine which is the best route for you.

In these initial meetings, you will be able to see how your advisors do their part in the planning process. It is here that you will participate in the actual design of your living trust–centered estate plan. You will get different planning perspectives from each of your advisors and you will ultimately decide which of their many planning suggestions best meet the definition of estate planning for you. This is another education phase. It adds to your knowledge, and adds to your advisors' knowledge as well. The more they know about you, your family, and how you feel about all of the planning options and strategies as they apply to you and your family, the better their advice will be to you and to each other. It is here that the real planning and idea-making is accomplished.

Step Five: Complete Your Living Trust–Centered Plan

In this step, you meet with your lawyer and your other advisors to finalize your living trust–centered estate plan. You and your lawyer will review your plan in detail; the lawyer will explain every document and compare it to your planning objectives and design.

You should be absolutely satisfied that the plan meets your needs and that you substantially understand its language. You should ask questions in order to become totally familiar and comfortable with its structure. Do not sign it until you are secure in the belief that it accomplishes your overall planning goals and specific objectives.

Step Six: Fund Your Plan

A living trust plan will not avoid a living or death probate unless the living trust is properly funded. It is in this stage that living trust plans are most vulnerable to abuse and oversight. Once documentation is completed and signed, many professionals and clients seem to run out of planning steam. They don't take on the task of funding the living trust with fervor, and often ignore it completely. It's almost as if they run out of enthusiasm and energy; like a runner stopping just short of the finish line in an important race, they appear to pull up short of the completed funding process.

Stopping short of fully funding your living trust–centered plan is not the thing to do. If your trust is not funded, the assets that are left out will have to go through probate to get into your trust on your incapacity or death.

Part Two of this workbook is devoted to funding your trust. For this exercise to be accomplished easily and successfully, you must provide your lawyer and your other advisors with evidences of title to all of your assets. In Chapter Eleven we provide you with a funding checklist. In this checklist, you will find a list of assets, a designation of how they are titled, a place to determine who is responsible for getting the assets into the trust, a date by which the funding should be completed, and a place to check off as each asset is transferred into your trust.

Funding is so important that we have included for your review copies of form letters, samples of funding documents, and an explanation of the funding process for a significant number of assets. **Funding is a function for which your entire estate planning team shares joint responsibility.** You can do some, or even most, of the funding if you choose. Your lawyer can do most or all of the funding if that is your desire and he or she is willing. Your financial advisor or accountant can also accomplish a substantial amount of your funding. What each of your advisors may contribute to your funding effort is explained in detail in Chapter Ten.

Step Seven: Follow-up

The planning process does not end when you have finished designing, creating, and funding your living trust–centered plan. Experience has taught us that your life will change as the years pass. Your interests will mature and often change, including how you view loved ones and favorite charities. Your hopes, your fears, your dreams, and your aspirations are likely to change. You will buy additional property and dispose of older holdings. As you change, the laws will likely change too; government giveth and government taketh away in a seemingly endless circle of ever-changing politically motivated legislation.

Just as you have periodic medical checkups, you should have periodic estate planning checkups. They may be only for a few minutes by telephone or they may be extensive and involve a meeting or two. In any event, they should be planned for in advance and periodically scheduled, for your protection and the protection of your family.

The Esperti Peterson Planning Process
from the Perspective of Your Advisors

We teach estate planning principles and advanced planning courses to practicing professionals throughout America. As practicing attorneys and educators, we are dedicated to helping our professional colleagues. Attorneys, accountants, financial planners, life insurance agents, stockbrokers, and other advisors need ongoing advanced education so they can provide the highest quality estate planning advice and services to their clients.

To reach that goal, these professionals must understand the definition of estate planning and the planning process. **When you call upon the full resources of your professional team, you will get the best planning advice possible.**

The Esperti Peterson Planning Process does not refer to a particular kind of trust or legal document. It is a planning process that uses the revocable living trust as its foundation or center. It emphasizes the interdependence of a client and all of his or her estate planning advisors in meeting that client's specific goals and objectives.

Our planning process is based on the simple but often overlooked premise that a client's lawyer and other professional advisors work for the client. Too often it seems that the client is viewed as the person who must respond to the needs of each professional rather than the other way around. In order to truly serve clients, all professional advisors must recognize that a client's wishes must be respected above all else.

The Esperti Peterson Planning Process requires that each and every estate planning professional:

- Believes that estate planning concentrates on what clients want and need, not on what advisors tell them they want
- Takes the time to fully understand and appreciate the client's hopes, fears, dreams, values, and planning aspirations
- Has a good understanding of basic estate planning principles and is willing to continually improve his or her estate planning knowledge
- Develops effective communication techniques and understands that the estate planning lawyer must have the ability to draft documents that are both technically accurate and fully understandable to reasonable clients
- Has a willingness to take the time to listen to, educate, and motivate his or her clients and other professionals

- Has the desire and the ability to work with the client's other professional advisors on a professional and meaningful basis

If you work with professional estate planning advisors who have accepted this planning process as the foundation of their practices, you can be assured that the result will be an estate plan that meets the definition of estate planning as it applies to you. In the next two chapters, we will help you find the kind of advisors who understand and believe in this planning process and who will provide you with a living trust–centered plan that meets your planning objectives.

·4·

How to Find an
Estate Planning Lawyer

The number of lawyers who are candidates for working with you on your estate planning matters and who have adopted our planning process is rapidly growing. Trusts of all types have become a topic of great interest to the public, and lawyers throughout America are taking notice. Competition among lawyers has been increasing as our numbers have been swelling. So has their inclination to extend their legal horizons and to get heightened career satisfaction from their practices.

Many lawyers already have the know-how to draft a basic living trust. There is no reason why your lawyer cannot easily and reasonably produce a living trust plan in a reasonably short period of time by using our planning process.

The lawyers you talk with will generally fall into one of five categories:

- Those who are familiar with our planning process and who routinely prepare living trust–centered plans for their clients. These lawyers are often members of the National Network of Estate Planning Attorneys.
- Those who are unfamiliar with our planning process or the National Network of Estate Planning Attorneys but who are familiar with revocable living trusts and are favorably inclined to practice under a paradigm similar to our planning process.
- Those who regularly use traditional will planning who would like to be more involved in drafting living trust–centered plans and who would like to adopt this process of planning.
- Those who have not done a great deal of estate planning but who

would like to do so using the techniques, processes, and strategies that we and other colleagues continually teach and write about.

• Those who are convinced that wills and probate are the *only* way to plan and who dismiss revocable living trusts and the planning process out of hand.

The first two types of lawyers will absolutely meet your estate planning needs. The second two are very much worth talking to and may very well be excellent candidates for your planning team. The last will not meet your needs if you believe in our approach to estate planning.

Contacting a Lawyer Who Regularly Uses the Esperti Peterson Planning Process

We have trained many lawyers nationwide and are in the process of training many more. Our National Network of Estate Planning Attorneys is a national organization of attorneys who are devoted to our planning process. Members of the network regularly attend advanced estate planning seminars and symposia sponsored by the network, and have access to numerous practice aids designed to give them advanced cutting-edge professional tools to accomplish state-of-the-art estate plans.

You can get a list of these network attorneys by writing the National Network of Estate Planning Attorneys, 410 Seventeenth Street, Suite 1260, Denver, CO 80203. Please enclose a check for $2 to cover shipping and handling.

Contacting a Lawyer You Know but Have Not Used

Knowing a lawyer you like and in whom you have confidence will give you a head start in getting your estate plan prepared. As you know by now, estate planning based on our process is highly personal. Your lawyer will need to know what you own, how much you owe, and how all of your property is titled. He or she will also be privy to your hopes, fears, dreams, and aspirations for yourself and your loved ones. It is therefore very important that you like and have much confidence in the lawyer you ultimately select.

If you have a friend who is a lawyer whom you like and respect, call and let him or her know that you are interested in using his or her services. Tell your friend that you want help preparing your estate plan and ask the following questions:

- Would you be interested in helping me plan my estate?
- Are you familiar with the Esperti Peterson Process of estate planning?
- Have you read Esperti/Peterson's best-selling book *Loving Trust*?
- Have you read *The Living Trust Revolution* or *Protect Your Estate*?
- Do you have experience in drafting revocable living trusts?
- Do you have expertise in federal estate tax planning? (You would ask this only if your estate approximates $600,000 or more.)
- Will you charge for our first meeting? If yes, What will your charge be?

Give your friend the opportunity to expand upon and explain his or her answers. Resist the temptation to ask your questions in machine-gun fashion; take your time. Most lawyers are happy to talk with a client for whom they can do additional work. Let your friend share his or her knowledge and capabilities; they may be considerable.

We believe that since you are simply exploring whether or not you will be using your lawyer friend's professional services, good taste—and good business—should prevent him or her from charging for the first hour or so of your meeting and for your exploratory telephone call. If your friend does charge for an initial consultation, you must make the decision whether or not you are willing to pay for it. Your friend may convince you that he or she is the perfect lawyer for you and that your initial meeting will be so productive it will be worth the cost.

Whether or not you decide to proceed is up to you. However, you will not have the opportunity to make that decision unless you first ask the question, "Do you charge for the initial consultation?" More problems are created between lawyers and their clients over miscommunication about fees than in any other area. Make sure you agree on the billing arrangement for your first meeting and for all other meetings or services.

Your telephone conversation may not go well. The lawyer could very well become defensive about your requests. He or she may say:

- A living trust is not in your best interests, or
- It does not fit your particular situation, or
- It can't be done, or
- You don't need a living trust plan; all you need is a will, or

- Probate is not as bad as it is made out to be, or
- Probate is different in your state and can be accomplished with streamlined efficiency at little expense.

These are responses that we hear about all too often as we travel America. We believe that they are absolutely wrong. We wrote *The Living Trust Revolution—Why America Is Abandoning Will and Probate* to put these arguments to rest. If the lawyer resists your request for living trust planning done generally in accordance with the principles of our planning process, you will have to make a choice. You can politely end the conversation, take the time to share your knowledge and our books with him or her, or engage the lawyer to proceed with a conventional will planning/probate plan.

However, if the lawyer is not adamantly against preparing a living trust–centered estate plan and would like to discuss his or her own view in the privacy of his or her office so you can decide what is best for you, we recommend you make an appointment. The lawyer is showing that he or she is professionally unbiased and cares about meeting your objectives.

Your friend may want to help you, but may admit that he or she is not as familiar with living trust–centered estate planning as he or she would like to be. Sophisticated professionals will not, as a general rule, attack what they do not know. If the lawyer seems genuinely interested in preparing your plan, suggest that he or she review *The Living Trust Revolution, Loving Trust,* and *Protect Your Estate.* You might also suggest that your lawyer look into membership in the National Network of Estate Planning Attorneys or a number of other fine organizations dedicated to advancing cutting-edge estate planning strategies.

Do not waste time; find out as quickly as possible if your friend is interested in working with you. If not, thank him or her, ask for a professional recommendation, and move on. You can either initiate the process with yet another lawyer friend or utilize one or more of the techniques we describe in this chapter.

Contacting a Lawyer You Have Used

If you already have a lawyer, you should not assume that he or she knows a great deal about living trust–centered estate planning or our approach to planning. You should use the same direct approach that we have previously discussed and ask all of the essential questions.

Your lawyer may refer you to his or her partner or associate. If that is your case, you should treat this colleague as if he or she were a complete stranger. You would approach this lawyer in the same manner you would approach a lawyer you do not know.

You Do Not Know a Lawyer

We can help you find a member of the National Network of Estate Planning Attorneys or a lawyer who practices under a similar philosophy that embraces our planning process techniques. Other than writing for a list of members in the National Network of Estate Planning Attorneys, there are at least four other good sources for finding one of these lawyers:

- Ask friends, relatives, and business associates.
- Ask your other professional advisors.
- Contact your bank's trust department.
- Contact your community's local estate planning council.

We are confident that you will find either a member of our national network or a responsible lawyer who practices with a similar philosophy.

Ask Your Friends

Despite the fact that lawyers are not always popular with the public, those who are members of the National Network of Estate Planning Attorneys usually rank high with their clients. They are perceived as professionals who can work with other professionals in a team environment. They are client oriented and work hard to communicate complex legal strategies in understandable language. Ask your friends if they have either a revocable living trust–centered estate plan or if they have used a member of the National Network of Estate Planning Attorneys. If they have, ask them for the name and telephone number of the lawyer who prepared it.

You may have friends, relatives, business associates, and colleagues who have revocable living trust plans with which they are delighted. Question them about how they found their lawyer and what they did to check out his or her credentials. Ask them how the lawyer conducted all meetings and on what basis he or she charges. Ask them *how long it took for their trust to be completed.* We emphasize this because lawyerly delay in producing work seems to be a common public complaint that has even found its way into bar ethics committee agendas.

Ask Your Advisors

Accountants, bankers, financial planners, life insurance agents, and stockbrokers frequently deal with lawyers. They are part of the professional community and are usually knowledgeable about who is doing what and how well they are doing it. Most advisors are more than happy to direct you to other professionals with whom they have worked and whom they respect.

We realize, however, that you might not know or work with any of these advisors. If you are in this situation, we suggest that at a minimum you contact your insurance carriers and ask them for the names of a few of their better insurance agents who do business in your community. You could also ask your friends if they have a top-notch agent whose services they are happy with. In any case, insurance agents are generous with their time and in most cases should be most helpful in helping you find the right lawyer. Don't be surprised if they try to sell you some insurance. That is their job, and the good ones are always on the lookout for new clients. However, do not be put off if they are professionally aggressive. Take the time to listen to them; the good ones usually have much to say.

Plan to involve your other professional advisors in designing and implementing your living trust–centered plan (we explain how to do this at length in the next chapter); their collective recommendations can be highly profitable to you and your family. Don't be afraid to ask your advisors whom they would recommend as an estate planning lawyer. Your advisors are there to help you; they will be flattered and will usually go to great lengths to help you find just the right lawyer for you.

Contact a Trust Officer

Almost every city or town in America has a bank with a trust department. Larger cities also have trust companies. By law, trust departments and trust companies and their employees cannot prepare trust documents. These institutional trustees administer trust documents that are prepared by lawyers engaged in the private practice of the law.

Before a trust department will accept the trusteeship of any trust, its officers will review the trust document to see if it meets minimum standards of clarity and legality. Some trusts are rejected because they are legally defective, others because their instructions are too vague or unclear.

Because trust officers continually review large numbers of trust documents, they are in constant contact with lawyers who prepare them. Some trust officers have the sole task of calling on lawyers and selling them on the idea of using the trust department as the trustee for the trusts they draft on behalf of their clients. In addition, the officers of bank trust departments and trust companies often provide assistance to lawyers who wish to prepare trusts.

Contact the trust departments of your local banks or your local trust companies and make an appointment with one of their trust officers. Share this workbook with them and ask for a list of lawyers who have such a practice; it is likely that you will be given several names. If you ask, it is also likely that your trust officer will help you set up an appointment with your first choice and act as a facilitator for subsequent meetings.

If your bank has a trust department, ask your personal banker for an introduction. He or she will be glad to accommodate you. If your bank does not have a trust department, set aside a few hours and go trust-department shopping. If you arrive at their reception desk, the receptionist will usually be pleased to arrange for you to meet immediately with a trust officer without a prior appointment. Remember, you are a potential client for that trust department and the officer you meet with. In addition to helping you find a lawyer to meet your needs, he or she will want to explain to you why you might wish to choose that trust department as a trustee in your estate plan.

It has been our experience that you will not be charged for this referral service. Trust departments provide much information as a public service and are a wonderful source of lawyer recommendations.

Contact an Estate Planning Council

Most major cities have an estate planning council. Members of the estate planning council include accountants, financial planners, lawyers, and life insurance agents. These professionals meet on a regular basis to discuss trends in estate planning, new laws, and new planning ideas and strategies. They are the professionals who spend much of their time planning estates.

Look in your telephone book to find the phone number of the estate planning council in your area. If you cannot find it, call your local bank's trust department for information on how you can make contact with its officers.

Meeting a Lawyer You Do Not Know

Once you have the names of lawyers who prepare revocable living trust–centered estate plans and whose philosophy is consistent with the planning process, you need to make contact with them. We are advocates of the direct approach. Call the lawyer. However, this may not be as easy as it sounds. Lawyers are often unable to take calls and may not be able to return your call immediately. You may not receive a return call at all unless you leave the proper message.

When a lawyer sees a telephone message from someone whose name does not look familiar, he or she may very well put your call slip on the bottom of the stack assuming that you may be selling something. If you are unable to make contact, leave a message that you are interested in using his or her services and would appreciate a prompt call back. Most lawyers want new clients. When they see your "I'm a potential new client" message, they will likely put your slip on top of their stack.

When you talk with the lawyer, mention who gave you his or her name and state your business. Ask the questions and use the techniques that we described earlier in this chapter under the heading "*Contacting a Lawyer You Know but Have Not Used.*" If you feel good about your conversation, set an appointment; if not, cut the conversation short with a polite but firm thank-you and go to the next name on your list.

Many lawyers leave instructions with their secretaries as to how new clients are to be handled. If this is the case, listen to the secretary and follow his or her procedure. You can take the opportunity to ask about how the lawyer works, the charge for the initial meeting, and any other information you are offered. Secretaries often are better at explaining office procedures than their lawyer bosses. If you still want to talk to the lawyer, it is your right to insist on it.

Not all lawyers will promptly return your telephone call. If a lawyer or his or her secretary does not call you back within a reasonable period of time, we would not dissuade you from going to the next name on your list; professionals who are not prompt in returning their phone calls are usually not prompt in getting their work out.

Confirm in Writing

Neither you nor the lawyer wants to start off on the wrong foot. A great way to do so is for either of you to miss the time or day of the first meeting. Communications can go awry; confirm your appointment in writing. It is doubtful that the lawyer's office will do so. Form 401 in the Appendix is a sample letter for you to use.

Once you find a lawyer you want to use, you will most probably wish to continue building your professional team. In the next chapter, we take a look at the other advisors you will want to spend some time with in order to design, implement, and finalize your living trust–centered estate plan.

° 5 °

Creating Your
Professional Team

We advocate an interprofessional or "team" approach to our clients when we are called upon to design a living trust–centered estate plan based on the Esperti Peterson Planning Process. Unfortunately, on first blush, some of our clients are uneasy or even distrustful of this planning approach because they view it as potentially putting too many professionals on the same planning shovel. These suspicions or fears are not generally well founded and dissipate when we convey how important it is for each professional to communicate his or her expertise and observations to the planning opportunities at hand.

Knowing how and when to use each of your advisors in the planning process is a key to saving time and money rather than spending it.

Why Use Other Advisors?

Reading books and learning about estate planning will make you knowledgeable. It will not make you an expert. You will very likely have many questions that they raise but do not answer. No one can anticipate and write about every conceivable method of designing and implementing specifically tailored estate planning strategies. No one!

If you have a relatively uncomplicated planning situation and you understand planning basics, you may only need a lawyer to answer a few of your questions, to draft your trust documentation, and to help you put property into your trust by *funding* it. But there is often a whole lot more to estate planning than mere basics.

If you have a considerable number of questions, you should talk with your life insurance agent or accountant. You may also wish to talk with your stockbroker or financial planner. You may wish to seek the services of your bank's trust department, or the estate planning specialist at a full-service financial institution you are doing business with before you meet with your lawyer. By receiving their advice, you may be able to better communicate your needs and desires to the lawyer.

Different advisors offer different planning perspectives. In our experience, professional advisors have a tendency to present a limited number of planning strategies to their clients. This is not done out of laziness or incompetence. It is the product of their education, experience, and background; it is what makes them professionally unique. By asking questions of all your advisors, you will elicit different perspectives and opinions and get the benefit of many points of view. This will allow you to expand your planning horizons and give you greater insight into the estate planning strategies and alternatives that are best for you. Many nonlawyer advisors have a remarkably strong working knowledge of trusts. Remember, professional advisors who are not lawyers cannot give you legal advice; they can, however, share their knowledge and better prepare you for meeting with your lawyer.

Before we go on, we would like to emphasize that no matter how knowledgeable your nonlegal advisors may be, do not allow them to draft your estate planning documents. Only lawyers may draft legal documents. Anyone else who does—other than yourself, of course—is breaking the law. Drafting legal documents without a license is a crime in every state. Doing it all by yourself is not a crime, it's just criminal.

Which Advisors to Involve

There are a number of professionals who are available to help you with the process of designing your estate plan. These are basically the same advisors who can help you put your property into your trust. They are your:

- Accountant
- Financial planner
- Life insurance agent
- Stockbroker
- Trust officer

They each have a specific professional function and perspective that, if properly utilized, can offer you much help in the design of your estate plan.

Any one of these advisors may also be a member of a national organization called the National Association of Estate Planning Advisors. This organization was created to offer training and other educational services pertaining to estate planning for nonattorney advisors. As you determine which advisors you would like on your team, ask each one if he or she is a member of the National Association of Estate Planning Advisors. If you find an advisor who is, consider using that advisor for your estate planning team. Usually an advisor who is a member of this organization has taken extra time and energy to learn as much as he or she can about estate planning and the planning process.

Your Accountant

If we could realistically do it, we would require that all of our clients have an accountant. An accountant's objectivity, knowledge, and skills are very useful when confronting the financial problems and dilemmas that life offers. We have always encouraged our clients' accountants to get involved with us as early as possible in the planning for our clients.

Accountants invariably charge by the hour, and their rates are usually very reasonable for the services they provide. The hourly rates charged by all but the most sophisticated accountants are usually well below that charged by lawyers for similar services.

Accountants understand the need for proper estate planning. They have been advocates of living trust–centered estate plans for many years and traditionally have been major advocates of our planning process. An accountant is invaluable to a successful estate planning experience. This is because the accountant usually knows far more about his or her client's financial affairs than anyone else, including the client. If you have an accountant, it is our experience that you spend more time with him or her than your other advisors combined.

If you are single and you are worth in excess of $600,000 or if you and your spouse have property worth more than $600,000, we strongly suggest that you have an accountant as one of your estate planning team members. Accountants are usually well versed in the income, estate, and gift tax aspects of estate planning.

We have a great deal of favorable practice experience in dealing with accountants and also have a high regard for their academic training. As the authors of the American Institute of Certified Public Accountants' course on *Estate and Gift Taxation*, we gained a healthy respect for their professional prowess.

Having an accountant who can "run the numbers" will help you and your other professionals to save time and money.

Your accountant can be of great assistance in helping you and your lawyer transfer property to your living trust. Our clients' accountants have been invaluable in helping both us and our mutual clients to fully fund their living trust plans. Accountants are used to keeping good records, and they keep wonderful track of a multitude of transactions in great detail. They are invaluable to your professional team when it comes to knowing the specifics of your financial life.

Your Financial Planner

There is a great deal of confusion as to what a financial planner is and what one does. We do not expect the confusion will dissipate until this relatively new breed of advisor is more generally understood by the marketplace.

A lack of licensing with regard to the "financial planner" has made the selection and use of those who hold themselves out as financial planners somewhat risky. Our advice is look for the CFP (certified financial planner) or ChFC (chartered financial consultant) designations; they are both respected and credentialed. Certified financial planners and chartered financial consultants are both backed by very selective and highly competent professional associations. They respectively go through a rigorous qualification process. However, the generic term *financial planner* is used indiscriminately by some salespeople who are in truth just aggressive salespeople.

Generally, credentialed financial planners analyze and make recommendations about almost every aspect of their clients' financial lives. Some of the services they provide include family budgeting, choosing and managing investments, creating ways and means of building wealth, and preserving wealth through business, tax, and estate planning strategies. Financial planners may also be accountants, life insurance agents, lawyers, or stockbrokers.

You must be as cautious in selecting a financial planner as you would be in hiring any other professional. Even the hearty recommendations of friends or other advisors should be subject to your usual careful scrutiny. Make sure that the planner is certified or chartered and that he or she has the background and experience to assist you. Always ask for a résumé and a list of references. Do not retain anyone until you have thoroughly checked his or her references.

As soon as reasonably practical, you should inquire as to how that financial planner charges for his or her services. Financial planners generally charge for their services in one of three ways:

- Some charge solely on a fee or hourly basis, much like a lawyer or an accountant. If that is the case, you should ask what the fee is and how it is determined. Your first consultation should be at no charge.
- Other financial planners receive their compensation from commissions generated by the products they sell. These include annuities, life insurance, stocks, bonds, and investments of all types. These planners make money only if you buy, so they would like your business only if you are a serious buyer, planner, or investor. It is not uncommon for these types of financial planners to charge a minimal fee for the preparation of your master financial plan. Their initial planning effort will have suggestions as to what investments you ought to make and sometimes even the amount of life insurance you need. The financial planner will then offer to sell you the products that your plan suggests you need. This is commonly accepted practice and should be respected.
- Some financial planners charge both a fee and take commissions. Many of them will offset their fee by the commissions they earn, in effect giving you a fee rebate if you buy their products.

Like an insurance agent, your financial planner can help you create and design your living trust–centered planning. Even though oriented to the financial side of planning, good financial planners are people oriented. It is not by accident that some of the better financial planners are also members of the life insurance profession.

Your Life Insurance Agent

Estate plans work better when they have real-dollar fuel in them. Insurance proceeds represent real-dollar fuel that provides the cash it takes to support and care for your loved ones in the case of your disability or death. Because of this, we have always gladly included our clients' insurance agents in the planning process. It would be wise for you to involve your life insurance agent in designing your living trust–centered plan.

Many life insurance agents have had formal training in the Esperti Peterson Planning Process or in estate planning in general. For years, life insurance companies have traditionally offered excellent estate planning training programs for their agents. In addition, national organizations like the American College of Life Underwriters offer extensive and sophisticated courses to life insurance professionals on all aspects of trust and estate planning. Those life insurance agents who have graduated from the American College are allowed to use the letters CLU (chartered life underwriter) after their names, indicating that they have graduated from a thorough and rigorous planning curriculum. They know their business!

Many life insurance agents do not have a CLU designation but are nevertheless highly skilled practitioners who are a pleasure to work with. Many of them are trained in the Esperti Peterson Planning Process. Ask your agent what his or her skills are and about the courses he or she has attended. You may be pleasantly surprised at just how much expertise your agent has.

You should interview your life insurance agent much as you would your lawyer. It would be helpful if you could work with an agent who has some expertise in the planning process or who has access to insurance company home-office experts who have been trained in it. You should contact your agent early in the design stage of your estate plan. When you meet with your agent, tell him or her exactly what you are doing and that you would like him or her to help you and your lawyer with the design of your estate plan. If you do, it is likely he or she will ask for sensitive personal and financial information. By giving him or her good information, you will make it easier for your agent to help you. Give him or her a copy of your personal information checklist. If you are uncomfortable doing so, you should start searching for another agent.

By far the most important input your life insurance agent can give you—other than the amount and type of life insurance that you need—is his or her ideas on providing for your loved ones. We have taught a number of America's finest life insurance professionals sophisticated estate planning techniques over the years, and believe one of their greatest strengths is their capacity for knowing their clients and their needs; we have been impressed with not only their product knowledge, but also with their feeling for, and knowledge of, their clients.

If you have confidence in your agent, you can enlist him or her as part of your estate planning team and benefit from his or her planning knowledge and efforts without having to pay hourly rates.

If you do not have an agent you are comfortable with, take the time to interview others. Find one you like and in whom you have confidence. Together with your other advisors, you can design a living trust–centered plan that meets your needs and specifications, and that has the proper amount of real-dollar fuel—with the right octane—to power your estate planning mission through to its successful completion.

Sometimes we have clients whose life insurance is part of an employee benefits package. These clients often do not have any other life insurance coverage and do not have a life insurance agent. We always encourage these clients to seek out a life insurance professional or financial planner to review their benefits and make suggestions as to how they should be structured and complemented with other coverage. Our experience has been that most employee benefit plans, while certainly worthwhile and valuable, do not always meet all of a client's needs. Even if the insurance agent or financial planner charges for this service, it is a worthwhile endeavor.

Some companies have a particular department that has full information about employee benefits. If questions arise about benefits and how they relate to estate planning, this department can be contacted for information. Also, the agent who helped implement the employee benefit plan can often help in the estate planning process; if the agent cannot help, he or she can direct you to someone who can. For information about your benefit plan's agent, contact your benefits department.

Your Stockbroker

Many brokerage firms offer free estate planning seminars that include presentations and discussion on wills and trusts, as well as related investment areas including life insurance. These seminars can prove to be the perfect opportunity to give you the answers to many of your generic living trust and estate planning questions.

Local lawyers are frequently the guest speakers at these seminars. They offer their views on estate planning, trust planning, probate avoidance, and related planning areas. While some of these lawyers may not have been exposed to our planning process, you nevertheless should be able to ask meaningful questions of them at the meeting. This forum will allow you to receive some "free" education and facilitate your planning understanding.

Most stockbrokers work for full-service financial institutions that provide wonderful financial planning services for their clients. The knowledge of their staffs of specialists goes well with their overall financial acumen and products. These specialists will often assist the broker and his or her client with living trust design and overall estate planning strategies.

The services offered by stockbrokers may or may not be free of charge. When fees are charged, they are sometimes hourly and sometimes a set or fixed fee. Make sure you know in detail what services are provided by your stockbroker and his or her firm and how much they cost before agreeing to an engagement. They are almost always clearly spelled out and reasonable.

Your Trust Officer

Like full-service financial institutions, trust companies and banks with trust departments are wonderful sources of estate planning advice. Trust officers are well versed in trust law and in the day-to-day practicalities of estate planning. They are competent to answer most of your estate planning questions.

Trust officers offer a unique planning and design perspective. Where a life insurance agent will encourage planning for loved ones and will emphasize that love in your planning, trust officers will view your estate planning more from an administrative or operational perspective. They will be concerned with the complexities of administration, investment strategy, and liability issues.

Trust officers are in the business of operating and administering trusts. You do not have to bank at an institution in order to use its trust services or consult its trust officers. Institutional trustees offer a unique public service and they want your business, which is why they will be more than willing to meet with you to discuss your estate planning thoughts without charge. Trust officers want you to name their institution as a trustee. You represent new business to the trust officer and his or her financial institution, and will be treated with professional courtesy.

When you meet with a trust officer, please keep in mind that trust officers have many trusts to administer, and also that they have a limited amount of time. Prepare for the meeting by writing down the questions you wish to ask. Explain that you are in the process of designing a living trust and that you are considering naming a financial institution as one of its trustees. Be sure to bring your copy of this workbook; it may help to expedite the communication process.

Trust officers are highly specialized professionals—most have law degrees—who can answer questions concerning trust law. A trust officer can be of service to you in several ways. He or she can help you understand how a living trust–centered plan works and what you can do to provide for loved ones. He or she can offer invaluable experience about how a living trust operates and how it can be administered. A trust officer can help you locate a competent lawyer whom you would enjoy working with in your community. A trust officer can also help you transfer many types of property into your revocable living trust.

Traditionally, banks and trust companies—corporate fiduciaries—have not charged a fee for these services. They are rendered as both a public service and as an inducement to you to name their bank as one of your trustees. Banks and trust companies make money by *serving* as trustees. By helping potential customers in any way they can, trust officers can show you how efficient and knowledgeable they could be if their institution were acting as a trustee of your trust. When designing your living trust–centered plan, do not overlook their valuable services.

You do not always need a full team of professional advisors to design and implement your living trust–centered plan. You and your lawyer can successfully complete it together. However, we have found over decades of experience that by using other advisors you can make the process of designing and implementing your estate planning much more effective, efficient, and a great deal more fun. By properly using your various advisors' talents, you can maximize your estate planning results and also keep your time and dollar outlays to an absolute minimum.

·6·

Checklist for Designing Your Plan

One of the greatest frustrations that professional estate planners experience is not being able to get their clients to communicate fully with them. Your hopes, fears, dreams, values, aspirations, and even your eccentricities are critically important to every member of your estate planning team. The purpose of this chapter is to help you to organize your thinking about a number of rudimentary but critical estate planning questions and issues, and to prepare you for meeting with your estate planning lawyer and other advisors.

All of us have certain feelings and ideas about how we want to be cared for, and about how we would like to provide for our loved ones. Sometimes our feelings and ideas are not clearly defined or are hard to express. It often takes the input of others for us to define and articulate our feelings. We would like to offer you a planning structure that will enable you to come to grips with your desires and motives for the care and well-being of yourself and your loved ones.

In our law practice we have been able to assist thousands of clients in planning for their loved ones. To our amazement, most of our clients continually express remarkably similar feelings and planning motives for their loved ones. As a result, this chapter contains a comprehensive checklist that contains a variety of practical and loving planning solutions based on those desires and motives that we have repeatedly identified during our planning careers.

We are confident that you can accomplish significant planning results consistent with the planning process by selecting the particular desires and motives that best fit you and your loved ones. This checklist is a shortened version of the one found in Part 2 of our book *Loving Trust*. In *Loving Trust*, there is a complete and lengthy explanation of these alternatives. We strongly suggest that you read *Loving Trust* if you have any questions about them.

For your convenience, we have designed the Checklist for Designing Your Plan to reflect *your* desires and *your* planning alternatives. If you are married, your spouse should also check those alternatives that best fit his or her objectives.

These alternatives represent the loving portion of your living trust–centered plan. It is here that you will have the opportunity to examine how you feel about your well-being and the needs and requirements of your spouse, children, grandchildren, parents, and other loved ones; it is where you can record your charitable feelings as well. It is this process of self-examination, and the thoughts behind it, that are so often neglected in the typical lawyer's office and in the boilerplate drafting books sold by living trust companies.

In our experience, it is difficult for many of our clients to visualize a revocable living trust. Earlier in this workbook, we described a revocable living trust as a set of baby-sitter instructions. A revocable living trust is a complete set of instructions that tells the trustees what to do when certain events occur. Certain "subtrusts" are then created. For example, when you become disabled, the living trust defines what disability is and then makes sure that your trustees use your property to care for you the way you want.

Imagine, if you will, a chest of drawers. When you need a pair of socks, you open the sock drawer. When you need a sweater, you open the sweater drawer. A revocable living trust works the same way. Instead of having drawers, your living trust document creates subtrusts. When you die, your trustee looks to the trust document and may "open" a Pocketbook Trust for your spouse or a Family Trust for your spouse and children. After your spouse dies, your trustee will "close" the Pocketbook and Family subtrusts and open new subtrusts for your children, grandchildren, or charity.

All of these subtrusts are created within a master document, which is your revocable living trust. As you can see, the more extensive your "chest of drawers" is, the more instructions you can leave. That is why using a very good lawyer and surrounding yourself by other competent professionals will assure that your revocable living trust document reflects all of the instructions that you must leave to care for yourself and your loved ones no matter what happens.

This master checklist for designing your own estate plan with the Esperti Peterson Planning Process is your estate planning blueprint. When completed, it should significantly help your lawyer to prepare your estate plan efficiently and at the lowest cost possible.

How to Provide for Yourself

If you are like most of our clients, the odds are pretty good that you have never planned for your disability. We understand when people tell us that it doesn't seem practical to plan for themselves. Most of us have the attitude that no matter how bad things are for others, those things could never happen to us. As a result, we are usually taken by complete surprise when those things do indeed happen to us.

Over the years, we have seen a remarkable pattern of motives that clients express when planning for their disability. Following are the five most commonly requested planning motives from our practice files and from our book *Loving Trust*, along with a place for your uniquely special motive. Read through these motives and check the one that reflects your wishes.

( ) Take care of me and nobody else.

( ) Take care of my needs first and then my spouse's needs.

( ) Take care of my needs first, then my spouse's and then my children's or dependents', in that order.

( ) Take care of me, my spouse, and my children based solely on our needs, without any priorities among us.

( ) Take care of me and my children based solely on our needs, without any priorities among us.

( ) My own motive:

_____

_____

_____

How to Provide for Your Spouse

In the case of your death, you can provide for your spouse by leaving some or all of your property in a special trust for your spouse that we call a Pocketbook Trust. This trust is sometimes called a Marital Trust.

If you leave some or all of your property in trust for your spouse, your planning motives will determine how much control you would like your spouse to have over the property that you leave to him or her in the Pocketbook Trust. Place a checkmark at the appropriate motive.

( ) I want my spouse to have total control over my property.

( ) I want my spouse totally taken care of, but I want to limit my spouse's right to leave my property on his or her death.

( ) I want my spouse totally taken care of, but I will decide where my property goes on my spouse's death.

( ) My spouse can have only the income my Pocketbook Trust earns and nothing more; I will say where my property goes on his or her death.

( ) My spouse will get only whatever my state's laws require that I must leave him or her.

( ) My own motive:

_____

_____

_____

How to Provide for Your Family

You may decide that you would like to leave some of your property in a Pocketbook Trust for your spouse and some of your property in another trust called a Family Trust for the benefit of your spouse, children, grandchildren, or others.

A Family Trust is ordinarily used for two reasons. The first is when your estate is greater than $600,000 and you wish to accomplish federal estate tax planning. Here, you would create both a Pocketbook Trust and a Family Trust. A second reason you might want to use a Family Trust is when you do not necessarily have a federal estate tax problem, but you do not want all of your property to pass directly to your spouse. There are several situations in which this motive may arise. In second marriages, there is often a real concern that the surviving spouse will not care for the deceased spouse's children. By allocating some property to the Family Trust, the spouse who dies first can be assured that some property will pass to his or her children.

Another situation in which a Family Trust can be used is when a person is not confident in his or her spouse's emotional stability or his or her ability to make prudent decisions. For example, your marriage may be a very good one —the first for you and your spouse—and your spouse may be an excellent parent to your children. But what if your spouse is extraordinarily emotional and easily taken in by the guile of others? You would be understandably concerned that if you left all your property to your spouse, he or she could easily leave it to a new spouse or to someone else who entered his or her life. Your dilemma could be easily solved with a Family Trust that provides instructions to the contrary. For example, the Family Trust could provide that your spouse is to be the primary beneficiary of the Family Trust and that your children are the secondary beneficiaries. The Family Trust would then care for your spouse and children as long as your spouse was alive, but the trustee would make all decisions with regard to investments and distribution of the property. After the death of your spouse, the Family Trust would end and your children would then be entitled to the property.

You may have other family members such as parents, nieces, or nephews that you wish to care for. In that event, you may want to leave some property in a Pocketbook Trust for your spouse, but leave other property in trust for these extended family members. A Family Trust can be designed to do just that.

There are a myriad of other reasons to leave property in a Family Trust. If for any reason you do not want to leave all or part of your property directly to your spouse, then a Family Trust can be designed to accomplish your objectives.

When you establish your Pocketbook and Family trusts, you must make the decision as to how much of your property will be allocated between the two trusts. If saving federal estate tax is one of your motives for designing and creating your trust, the section in this chapter under the heading "How to Save Federal Death Tax" will help you determine how you should allocate your property in conjunction with federal estate tax planning.

If your estate is valued at less than $600,000—as are the majority of all Americans' estates—the only restraint on how you divide your property between the two trusts will be your spouse's right under your state law to a certain percentage or dollar amount of your property. Put another way, the minimum amount that you can allocate to your Pocketbook Trust is the amount that your state's law requires you to leave your spouse. Most states' laws require that surviving spouses get a portion of their deceased spouse's property. To find out what the law is in your state, you will have to ask your lawyer or refer to the appendix in our book *Protect Your Estate*, which briefly explains each state's law concerning spousal rights. Once you know the "magic" minimum, you can thereafter allocate as much as you like to your Family Trust.

This part of the checklist will allow you to decide how you are going to allocate your property between the Pocketbook Trust and the Family Trust after you have died. Once you have decided how to allocate your property, you must then determine what the terms of your Family Trust will be. Place a checkmark at the appropriate motive.

( )   I want all my property to pass to my spouse in my Pocketbook Trust, so I don't need a Family Trust.

( ) I want my spouse to receive whatever he or she is entitled to under state law with the balance passing to my Family Trust.

( ) I want my property equally divided between my Pocketbook and Family trusts.

( ) I want _____ percent to pass to my Pocketbook Trust and _____ percent to my Family Trust.

( ) I want all my property to pass to my spouse in my Family Trust.

( ) I want to have maximum federal estate tax planning because my estate is in excess of $600,000.

( ) My own motive:

_____

_____

_____

Once you have decided to allocate property between your Pocketbook Trust and your Family Trust, you then must determine what the terms of the Family Trust are going to be. The following motives will help you to decide how to distribute income and principal out of the Family Trust. Again, place a checkmark by the appropriate motive.

( ) I want primarily to care for my spouse by providing him or her with as many benefits and as much control as possible.

( ) I want to provide for my spouse and my children based on their respective needs, while giving priority to the needs of my spouse. I want my children and grandchildren to get what is left after my spouse's death.

( ) I want to provide for the respective needs of my spouse and my children, but if my spouse remarries, I want to provide only for my children.

( ) I want to provide for the respective needs of my spouse and my children, except that I want my spouse taken care of during any period of time that he or she is single.

( ) I want to provide for the respective needs of my spouse, children, and other loved ones, and will set forth my priorities.

( ) I want to provide for loved ones other than my spouse.

( ) My own motive:

_____

_____

_____

How to Provide for Your Minor Children

We may love our children the same, but we do not treat them the same. If your children are still minors after you and your spouse die, they need special care and attention. The cornerstone of this care and attention is called a Common Trust. The Common Trust is based on the philosophy that when it comes to minor children, need is more important than equality. The Common Trust's purpose is to provide for all of your children's needs from a common source just as if mother or father were living and doing just that until your youngest child reaches adulthood or achieves certain goals. Place a checkmark by the motive which reflects your aims and desires.

( )   All my children are adults. I do not want a Common Trust.

( )   I want my Common Trust to end when my youngest child is twenty-one years of age.

( )   I want my Common Trust to end when my youngest child is twenty-three or completes college, whichever happens first.

( )   I want my Common Trust to end when my youngest child is _____ years of age.

( )   My own motive:

_____

_____

_____

How to Distribute Your Children's Property

After the Common Trust ends, or if you do not want a Common Trust, then you may want your property to be divided among your children or other beneficiaries. Many times, it is best to leave this property in Separate Trusts for each of your children or beneficiaries rather than give it to them outright. The size of your estate, the age of your children or other beneficiaries, their ability to handle money, their health, state of their marriage, and other factors will determine whether you should hold your property in trust.

If you do decide to hold your property in Separate Trusts, how do you want it distributed to your children or other beneficiaries? There are an almost in-finite variety of methods to distribute property. Here are a few of the more common alternatives from which you might choose.

( )   I want my property distributed to my children immediately.

( )   I want my children to have total and complete access to the property from their Separate Trusts.

( )   Make two distributions to my child, one-half at a minimum age, the re-mainder at another stated age.

( )   Make two distributions to my child, the first at a minimum age, or im-mediately if that age has been met, the second to occur five years from the date of the first distribution.

( )   Make four distributions to my child, the first to occur at a minimum age, or immediately if that age has been met, the second through the fourth to occur every five years.

( )   Make multiple unequal distributions, the first to occur at a minimum age, or immediately if that age has been met, the others at stated ages.

( )   Make no mandatory lifetime distributions to my child, but take care of my child in whatever way he or she needs, whenever he or she needs it from the trust funds.

( )   Make entirely different distribution patterns for each of my children.

( )   My own motive:

_____

_____

_____

If you leave your property in trust, you must first determine whether or not discretionary distributions from each of the Separate Trusts for your children will be made on a liberal basis or based on higher standards of need. For ex-ample, let's say that you have decided to create a Separate Trust for one of your children. The first mandatory distribution of principal is to be made. Upon the death of the survivor of you and your spouse, you direct your trustee to pay the child one-half of the principal of the Separate Trust. The remainder of the principal is to be paid out five years later. During the period of time that the principal is held in trust, do you want your trustee to be liberal or conservative? Are there special circumstances under which you would allow your trustee to give principal to your child? These types of instructions should be in your living trust.

( )   I want my trustees to liberally provide for each of my children.

( )   I want my trustees to provide only for the health, education, support, and maintenance of each of my children.

( )   My own motive:

_____

_____

_____

If one of your children dies while property is being held in a Separate Trust for that child, there must be a way for that property to be distributed. There are several different alternatives for this type of distribution.

( )   I want my child's trust property to pass pursuant to my child's directions.

( )   I want my child's trust property to pass to my child's children or, if none, to my other children.

( )   My own motive:

_____

_____

_____

How to Give to Charity

Giving to charity through a properly designed plan can generate significant income, estate, and gift tax benefits. Many of us are charitable. We make meaningful gifts to our churches, synagogues, and other charities. We care about others and involve ourselves in charitable activities by contributing our resources and time. Unfortunately, many of us give little or no thought to continuing our charity after we are gone. Here are some ideas that you may want to incorporate as part of your living trust–centered plan.

( )   I want to give specific assets to my favorite charities on my death.

( )   I want to give cash gifts in specific amounts to my favorite charities on my death.

( )   I want to make cash gifts that represent specific percentages of my estate's value to my favorite charities on my death.

( )   I want to make cash gifts of specific amounts that cannot exceed a certain percentage of my estate's value to my favorite charities on my death.

( ) I want to create a special subtrust in my trust that will make gifts in perpetuity to my favorite charities after my death.

( ) I want to create a charitable foundation in my trust that will make gifts according to my charitable philosophy to public charities that agree with that philosophy.

( ) I want to give my home or farm to charity, but live in it during my life.

( ) I want to create a special separate trust for charity to which I can transfer some or all of my assets that will give me a lifetime income.

( ) I want to create a special separate trust that will give its income to charity during my life, but which will give its assets to my loved ones on my death.

( ) I want to purchase life insurance in order to meet my charitable desires.

( ) My own motive:

_____

_____

_____

How to Ultimately Distribute Your Property

Something that every living trust–centered plan should contain is a provision that distributes your property upon the very unlikely event that everyone in your immediate family dies in the same accident. Obviously, the larger your family, the smaller the risk. Good planning dictates that, no matter the risk, a plan should be made. Over the years we have found that these "ultimate remainders" generally fall into one of four alternatives.

( ) I want one-half of my property to pass to my heirs and one-half of my property to pass to my spouse's heirs under my state's laws.

( ) I want all my property to pass to my heirs under my state's laws.

( ) I want my property to pass to certain individuals.

( ) I want all my property to go to charity.

( ) My own motive:

_____

_____

_____

How to Select Your Trustees

Selection of trustees for your living trust can sometimes appear to be difficult. While choosing your trustees is certainly important and will involve serious deliberation, we suspect that many professionals have so muddied the trustee waters that choosing a trustee is often viewed as a much harder process than it really needs to be. By using the following checklist, your task will likely be less daunting than you think.

The first alternatives deal with naming your trustees while you are alive and well.

( ) I will act as my sole trustee.
( ) My spouse and I will act as my co-trustees.
( ) I will act as a co-trustee along with: _____
( ) My own alternative:

_____

_____

_____

You need to name successor trustees on your disability.

( ) In the case of my becoming disabled, the following individuals or institutions will act as my successor trustees in the order I have set out (if I do not name an institution, at least two individual trustees must always serve):

_____

( ) In the case of my becoming disabled, the following individuals or institutions will *replace all my initial trustees* and will act in the order I have set out (if I do not name an institution, at least two individual trustees must serve):

_____

( ) In the case of my becoming disabled, my initial co-trustee must choose a major institutional trustee to serve as successor co-trustee. When my initial co-trustee can no longer serve, this institutional trustee can serve alone.

The trustees you name after your death may be the same as those trustees you named to serve after your disability. Often, however, they are not.

( )   After my death, my disability trustees will continue to serve. If one (or more) of my trustees resigns, is terminated, or cannot serve for any other reason, then that trustee will be replaced by the following individuals or institutions in the order I have set out (if I do not name an institution, at least two individual trustees must serve):

_____

_____

( )   After my death, my disability trustees will be replaced by the following individuals or institutions in the order I have set out (if I do not name an institution, at least two individual trustees must serve):

_____

_____

( )   After my death, my initial co-trustee must select a major institutional trustee to serve as co-trustee. When my initial co-trustee can no longer serve, this institutional trustee can serve alone.

We think that it is extremely important that your beneficiaries can remove your trustees after you are disabled or after you have died. Here are some alternatives that can be used to effectuate that planning strategy.

( )   Should I become disabled and/or after my death, my spouse can terminate any of my successor trustees. After my spouse is no longer a trustee, a majority of my beneficiaries can terminate any of my successor trustees. When all my successor trustees have either been terminated or are no longer available, my beneficiaries must choose a major institutional trustee.

( )   Should I become disabled and/or after my death, a majority of my beneficiaries can terminate any of my successor trustees. When all my successor trustees have either been terminated or are no longer available, my beneficiaries must choose a major institutional trustee.

( )   Should I become disabled and/or after my death, my own alternative is:

_____

_____

_____

How to Save Federal Death Tax

For many of us with larger estates, saving federal estate tax is important. There are a number of ways to plan for federal estate tax savings. Different alternatives are used based on the size of an estate and the importance that you give to minimizing federal estate taxes.

If your estate is between $600,000 and $1.2 million, here are some federal estate tax saving alternatives.

( ) I want my first $600,000 to pass to my spouse in my Pocketbook Trust and the remainder to go to my Family Trust.

( ) I want my first $600,000 to pass to my Family Trust and the remainder to go to my spouse in my Pocketbook Trust.

( ) I want my property equally divided between my Pocketbook and Family trusts.

( ) I want my spouse to receive whatever he or she is entitled to under our state law, with the next $600,000 of my property passing to my Family Trust, and whatever is left—if any—passing to a Pocketbook Trust Two, which is for the benefit of my spouse, but, after my spouse dies, any property left in Pocketbook Trust Two will pass to my children.

If the value of your estate is over $1.2 million, then the following alternatives should be considered for federal estate tax savings.

( ) I want to save federal estate tax and thereafter care for my spouse as much as possible with a single Pocketbook Trust.

( ) I want to save federal estate tax; I also want to take care of my spouse and to be assured that my children will have one-half of what's left of my property on my spouse's subsequent death.

( ) I want to save federal estate tax, while giving as much of my property to my children as possible.

Once you have finished these checklists, you should have a much better picture of how you want to plan and some of the issues that are important in estate planning. Perhaps you will even have a better appreciation for the definition of estate planning. These alternatives are far from all of the ideas that clients come up with. They are a sampling of the most commonly used alternatives. While not all of them may necessarily fit you, it is on this underpinning that you can build your own plan.

When you meet with your professional team and talk with them, different ideas will surface. Your thoughts may very well change after hearing about the experiences of your advisors. You will, however, have a solid basis on which to discuss your planning objectives. The next step is for you to complete your personal information checklist. This will give your advisors information about your financial affairs and will help them tailor your financial and tax planning needs to fit you and your family's needs.

· 7 ·

Personal Information Checklist

The purpose of your Personal Information Checklist, which is found at the end of this chapter, is to help you get your financial information organized for your lawyer and your other professional advisors. It will allow them to better understand your situation and to help you to plan your estate in an efficient and effective manner.

Your Personal Information Checklist is divided into three parts. The first part elicits important family information. It is here that you write down important facts that are necessary for your attorney to draft your living trust–centered plan. Proper legal names, addresses, phone numbers, social security numbers, children's names, and other personal family information are all necessary so that proper legal documentation can be prepared. When you do this detailed legwork for your attorney and other advisors, it saves them the time of having to carefully question you to ascertain this information. It allows them more time to talk with you about your and your family's planning needs.

The second part of the Personal Information Checklist is a series of questions. These questions are designed to discover any other information that may be relevant to your planning needs. If even one of these questions applies to you, your lawyer and other advisors will have necessary input on information which will be important to the success of your overall estate plan.

The last part of the Personal Information Checklist is financially related. Knowing what you own and how you own it is absolutely vital for your lawyer and other advisors in helping you plan. Your living trust planning will be designed to use your money and property to take care of you and your loved ones. Your planning cannot control property that is not properly owned. **Any property that your living trust–centered plan does not control will very likely be subject to probate and may not pass to whom you want in accordance with your instructions.**

Before you begin filling in your Personal Information Checklist, here are some suggestions that should make your task a little easier.

Locate the Titles to Your Property

For every type of property, there is a method of identifying who owns it. The word *title* is a sort of general, catchall term used to describe how property is owned. The term *evidence of title* is the actual document that shows title. For example, a car title is the piece of paper you look at to decide who owns a particular car. The document itself is the evidence of title. The name on the car title determines the car's ownership. Like a car title, there is some document or other evidence that identifies how most property is owned. If the document that evidences title cannot be found, neither you nor your lawyer will be able to determine ownership.

Ascertaining the title to your real estate, cars, and investments can be easy. If you have real estate, your deed is your title. Read the deed to determine whose name your real estate is in. For a car or other licensed vehicle, like a boat or a truck, look at your title. It works the same as a deed. The person named on the title is the owner. For stocks, your stock certificate is your title. For bonds, the bond itself is the title.

To locate the title to most of your property, you need only remember one thing: **Your title to property is whatever document or documents you received when you bought the property and would need if you were to sell it.**

If you made investments in partnerships, real estate trusts, or other more exotic property, you signed documents when you made your investment. These documents are your evidence of title. If you handle your investments through stockbrokers and they hold your investments, then your brokerage account is your evidence of title. Whatever paperwork you signed to set up the account is what you will need to ascertain your ownership.

There are some types of property that are sold without legal documents passing hands. Let's use a bicycle as an example. When you sell a bike, you either get cash or a check. No one asks about title. If you buy a bike from a store, however, you are given a bill of sale, called a receipt. That is your title to your bike. If you later sell your bike, you really should give the buyer a bill of sale, but most of us treat our possession of the bike as proof of our ownership. Almost all personal property like bikes, clothes, and furniture are bought and sold using a bill of sale. That is what is used to transfer them from one person to another.

The same is true of collections, such as artwork or stamps, and most other forms of personal property. Sometimes you keep the bill of sale (receipt), sometimes you do not. If you do not, then your canceled check is your receipt and your proof of title to the property. If you pay cash, then "possession is nine-tenths of the law.'' The fact that you have the property in your possession means you probably own it.

To determine title to your property for which you do not have a receipt or a canceled check, you need to look to who paid for it. If you paid for it out of your money, it is yours. If the money came from a joint account, then the property is owned jointly with the other joint tenant on the account.

Bank accounts, savings accounts, certificates of deposit, and other cash investments are created by signing a signature card or other document establishing the account. Whatever you signed to set up the account is your evidence of title to that account.

Life insurance policies, disability policies, and retirement plans differ from most types of property when you are looking for the particulars of ownership. You will need to locate your life insurance policies and disability policies, along with the application you originally signed and any changes in the policies, called endorsements. It is on the application—not the policy—that you will find who owns it and who will receive the proceeds; they are not necessarily the same people.

You must find the beneficiary designations for your insurance policies and your retirement plans. They are needed so that the proceeds can be directed into your trust. Again, please locate your application, almost always inserted at the end of the policy; it contains the information you are looking for.

To help you locate the title to your property, each category of property in your Personal Information Checklist explains what document is your evidence of title. The checklist has spaces for you to mark how your property is titled.

Types of Ownership

When you begin the task of listing what you own and how you own it, you will likely find various types of ownership on your deeds, bank accounts, car titles, and other assets.

There are several ways in which a person can hold title to property. These include fee simple, tenancy in common, joint tenancy, tenancy by the entirety, and community property. Let's briefly look at each type of ownership. If you would like a more detailed discussion of the various forms of joint ownership and the numerous pitfalls created by joint ownership, you should read *Protect Your Estate*, Chapters 3, 4, and 13; and *The Living Trust Revolution*, Chapter 24.

Fee Simple

Property owned in fee simple is owned entirely by one person. The fee simple owner is the sole and absolute owner. Absolute ownership means the owner can give the property away, sell it at any time, and devise it at his or her death.

Tenancy in Common

Property owned in tenancy in common is owned by more than one person at a time. Each person owns a part of the property as determined in the deed or other evidence of ownership. Typically, the ownership interest will be in direct proportion to the number of owners. Therefore, if John, Jim, and Stanley own JJS Ranch as tenants in common, each of them owns one-third of the property, unless the deed states otherwise. However, the tenancy in common deed could provide that the property is owned 50 percent by John and 25 percent each by Jim and Stanley.

Even though each tenant in common owns a specific interest in the property, each tenant has the right to use the entire property. Absent a specific written agreement to the contrary, a tenant can sell his or her interest, give it away, or leave it at death.

Joint Tenancy with Right of Survivorship

This form of ownership is similar to tenancy in common ownership in that two or more individuals concurrently own the property. However, unlike tenancy in common, each joint tenant is considered to own 100 percent of the property. Upon the death of a joint owner, because of the "survivorship" feature, the deceased joint tenant's interest in the property "disappears" and the property is owned entirely by the remaining living joint tenants. For example, if Mark, Mary, and Joan own a house as joint tenants with rights of survivorship and Mark dies, Mary and Joan would own the entire property as joint tenants. If Mary then dies, Joan would be the sole owner of the property; she would own the property in fee simple.

A joint tenant can sell or give his or her interest away during life, but *has no ability to dispose of it at death.*

Tenancy by the Entirety

This type of joint ownership is available in many states for property titled in the names of husbands and wives only. Property owned in tenancy by the entirety is exempt from the claims of creditors of either spouse individually. A judgment against both spouses is necessary before any tenancy by the entirety property can be taken by a creditor.

During the lifetime of both spouses, the property can only be transferred with the consent of both spouses. It cannot be transferred by one spouse acting alone. When one spouse dies, the survivor owns the entire interest in the property in fee simple, just like joint tenancy with right of survivorship.

Community Property

Under community property ownership rules, each spouse owns one-half of all "marital property." Marital property in community property states is generally defined as all property acquired during a marriage. Exceptions to community property include property acquired prior to marriage, gifts made to a spouse, and inheritances received by a spouse. Separate property can become community property if it is commingled with community property.

Estate planning for community property interests is on the rise because of the increased number of couples owning community property. Presently over 25 percent of the U.S. population lives in states where community property principles apply. The community property states are Arizona, California, Idaho, Louisiana, Nevada, New Mexico, Texas, Washington, and Wisconsin.

Married couples who move from a community property state to a separate property state can retain the community property nature of their property by continuing to treat it as such. Therefore, it is imperative for your lawyer to determine if you own any community property even if you live in a common-law state.

By looking at the various titles to your property, you should have little trouble figuring out who legally owns what. If you cannot, don't worry about it. Bring to your lawyer the documents that you think show title and get help. There is no reason for you to agonize over title. It takes three years of law school and a few years of experience for a lawyer to begin to understand title. Do not expect to be an instant expert. It takes a lot of training to understand the intricacies of property ownership.

Your other advisors can be of great assistance in locating title to your various assets and property interests. If you cannot find the deed to your house or to your investment properties, contact the broker or lawyer who handled the purchase for you, the bank who provided the mortgage money, or the title company that helped close the sale. One or the other will likely have the deed or a copy of it. For stock or bond investments, contact the broker who sold them to you.

For life insurance, contact your life insurance agent. For your group insurance, go to your human resources or benefits office.

If you devote a little thought to how you acquired your property, you should be able to think of someone who can help you. Don't be shy in asking your advisors to do this. They will likely not mind doing it, and their efforts will save you much time and money.

Value of Your Property

For purposes of your Personal Information Checklist, you do not need to agonize over the exact value of each of your assets. An appraisal of real estate or of a business is not, at least initially, necessary for your lawyer and other advisors to make recommendations as to your living trust–centered planning. It may be that as the planning process progresses, appraisals will be needed for more sophisticated planning, such as for charitable remainder trusts, irrevocable trusts, or grantor retained income trusts; they are not ordinarily needed for basic living trust planning.

For bank accounts, publicly traded securities, and other assets that are easily valued, you should make an attempt to ascertain a realistic value. Include your latest bank statement or statement from your brokerage firm. For real estate and other hard-to-value assets, make a realistic and informed guess. For your personal effects or other personal property that are very hard to value, lump them together and put them in a category that we call "Other Personal Property." However, for valuable personal property such as jewelry, collections, antiques, or the like, list them separately with your best informed guess as to their value.

Decades of experience in working with clients has taught us that many people believe that if they provide their lawyer and other advisors with values that are contrived to be very low, they will somehow save taxes or even professional fees. **This is not the case. Inaccurate or distorted values will only cause your professional team to prescribe planning strategies that are inappropriate and potentially injurious to you and your family's well-being.**

PERSONAL INFORMATION CHECKLIST

Full Legal Name _____

Signature Name _____ Nickname: _____

Home address _____ City _____ County _____ State _____ Zip ____

Home telephone _____ Birth date _____ Social security number _____

Employer _____ Position _____

Business address _____ City _____ State _____ Zip _____

Business telephone _____

Married ( )   Divorced ( )   Widowed ( )   Single ( )

Spouse _____

Signature Name _____ Nickname: _____

Birth date _____ Social Security number _____ Business Telephone _____

Employer _____ Position _____

Business address_____ City _____ State _____ Zip _____

Date of Marriage _____

Children (*Use full legal name*)   Parent(s)*   Birth date

_____	_____	_____
_____	_____	_____
_____	_____	_____
_____	_____	_____
_____	_____	_____
_____	_____	_____

* Use JT if both spouses are the parents, H if husband is the parent, W if wife is the parent, S if you are a single parent.

Other Dependents (Friends or relatives who are dependents)   Relationship

_____	_____
_____	_____
_____	_____

Advisors   **Telephone**

Attorney _____ _____

Accountant _____ _____

Primary personal bank _____ _____

Life Insurance Agent _____ _____

Stockbroker _____ _____

IMPORTANT FAMILY QUESTIONS

1. Do you have a child with a learning disability? _____

2. Do any of your children receive governmental support or benefits? _____

3. Do you have adopted children? _____

4. Do any of your children have special educational, medical, or physical needs? _____

5. Are any of your children institutionalized? _____

6. Are you or your spouse receiving social security, disability, or other government benefits? ____

7. Do you wish to disinherit any of your children, grandchildren, or other relatives? _____

8. If you have minor children, whom do you wish to be their primary guardian? _____

9. Whom do you wish to be the contingent guardians if your primary guardians are unavailable? _____

10. Have either you or your spouse been divorced? _____

11. Are you making payments pursuant to a divorce or property settlement agreement? *(Please furnish a copy)*

12. Have you been widowed? *(If a federal estate tax return or a state death tax return was filed, please furnish a copy)*

13. In what states have you lived while married to your current spouse? During what periods of time did you reside there? _____

14. Have you or your spouse ever filed federal or state gift tax returns? *(Please furnish copies of these returns)*

15. Have you or your spouse completed previous will, trust, or estate planning? *(Please furnish copies of these documents)*

16. Did you and your spouse ever sign a pre- or post-marriage contract? *(Please furnish a copy)*

17. Are both you and your spouse United States citizens? *(If either or both of you are not a U.S. citizen, please specify if you are a resident alien or a nonresident alien)*

HOW PROPERTY IS OWNED

This checklist is designed to help you list all the property you own, how it is titled, and what it is worth. You may own more property than can be listed on this checklist. If so, use extra sheets of paper to list your additional property.

Immediately after the heading for each kind of property is a brief explanation of what document or documents you will need as evidence of title to your property. Remember, having these documents is essential in transferring property to your living trust. By collecting this documentation yourself, you will save substantial professional fees.

How you own your property is extremely important for purposes of properly designing and implementing your living trust–centered plan. For each property category, there is a column titled "Owner." When filling in this column, use the following abbreviations:

If you are single and you own property in your name only, use	I
If you are married and property is owned in the husband's name, use	H
For property owned in the wife's name, use	W
For property owned in joint tenancy with a spouse, use	JTS
For property owned in joint tenancy with someone other than a spouse, use	JTO
For property owned in tenancy in common with a spouse, use	TCS
For property owned in tenancy in common with someone other than a spouse, use	TCO
For community property, use	CP
If you can't determine how the property is owned, use	?

CASH ACCOUNTS

Evidence of title: signature card or the document you signed to set up the account.

Name of Institution	Type*	Acct. Number	Owner	Amount
				Total _____

* Checking Account (CA), Savings Account (SA), Certificates of Deposit (CD).

Note: If Account is in your name (or your spouse's name) for the benefit of a minor, please specify and give minor's name.

INVESTMENT ACCOUNTS

Evidence of title: the documents you signed to set up the account, account statement.

Name of Brokerage Firm	Type*	Acct. Number	Owner	Amount
				Total _____

* Specify if a money market, investment, cash management, or other account that is in a street name.

STOCKS

Please list all stock ownership in publicly owned corporations *(stock traded on an exchange or over the counter)*. Stock owned in family or nonpublicly traded companies should be listed under the corporate business section; stocks held in a street name or investment account should be listed under Investment Accounts.

(continued on following page)

Evidence of title: stock certificate.

Company	Owner	Number of Shares	Fair Market Value

Total Value _____

BONDS

Evidence of title: bond instrument.

Description (*U.S. Savings Bonds, corporate, municipal, etc.*)	Owner	Face Value
_____	_____	_____
_____	_____	_____
_____	_____	_____
_____	_____	_____
	Total Value	_____

PERSONAL EFFECTS

Itemize major personal effects such as motor vehicles, boats, jewelry, collections, antiques, furs, and all other valuable nonbusiness personal property. Give a lump sum value for miscellaneous, less valuable items.

Evidence of title: Registration or title issued by your state, bill of sale, receipt, canceled check, or source of cash to purchase property, gift tax return, or inheritance tax return if you received property by gift or inheritance.

Description	Owner	Value
_____	_____	_____
_____	_____	_____
_____	_____	_____
Miscellaneous, less valuable personal effects:	_____	_____
	Total Value	_____

RETIREMENT PLANS

Evidence of title: summary plan description, documents you signed to set up the plan, account statement, beneficiary designation.

Type of Plan*	Company	Beneficiary Upon Your Death	Percent Vested	Value
_____	_____	_____	_____	_____
_____	_____	_____	_____	_____
_____	_____	_____	_____	_____
_____	_____	_____	_____	_____
			Total Value	_____

* Pension (P), Profit Sharing (PS), H.R. 10, IRA, SEP, 401(K)

LIFE INSURANCE POLICIES AND ANNUITIES

Evidence of title: the policy itself, including all endorsements and amendments, and the original application you signed.

Policy Number and Company _____

_____

Type* _____ Insured _____
Owner _____
Primary beneficiary _____ Secondary _____
Who pays premium† _____ Cash value _____
Amount of loans on policy _____ Face amount _____

—

Policy Number and Company _____

_____

Type* _____ Insured _____
Owner _____
Primary beneficiary _____ Secondary _____
Who pays premium† _____ Cash value _____
Amount of loans on policy _____ Face amount _____

—

Policy Number and Company _____

_____

Type* _____ Insured _____
Owner _____
Primary beneficiary _____ Secondary _____
Who pays premium† _____ Cash value _____
Amount of loans on policy _____ Face amount _____

—

Policy Number and Company _____

_____

Type* _____ Insured _____
Owner _____
Primary beneficiary _____ Secondary _____
Who pays premium† _____ Cash value _____
Amount of loans on policy _____ Face amount _____

* Term, whole life, split dollar, group life, annuity.
† Husband (H), Wife (W), Jointly (JT), Tenants in Common (TC), or Community Property (CP).
Note: If stock is owned either JT or TC with someone other than spouse, please furnish name and relationship.

MORTGAGES, NOTES, AND OTHER RECEIVABLES

Evidence of title: promissory note, written contract, or other documents creating right to receive payment.

Name of Debtor	Date of Note	Date Note Due	Owed to	Current Balance Owed
___	___	___	___	___
___	___	___	___	___
___	___	___	___	___
___	___	___	___	___

Total Value _____

PARTNERSHIP INTERESTS

Evidence of title: partnership agreement, certificate of partnership, or any documents you signed when purchasing the partnership interest. Include any buy/sell agreements.

Percentage of Partnership Interest*

Partnership Name	General Partner	Limited Partner	Owner*	Value
___	___	___	___	___
___	___	___	___	___
___	___	___	___	___

Total Value _____

* Please state the percentage interest you have in the partnership when you list your interest as a general or limited partner.

CORPORATE BUSINESS AND PROFESSIONAL INTERESTS

Privately owned *(nonpublicly traded)*
Evidence of title: stock certificate, minute book.

Company	Number of Shares	Buy/Sell Agreement*	Percentage Ownership	Owner†	Value
___	___	___	___	___	___
___	___	___	___	___	___
___	___	___	___	___	___
___	___	___	___	___	___

Total Value _____

* Please state if a Buy/Sell Agreements exists.
† Husband (H), Wife (W), Jointly (JT), Tenants in Common (TC), or Community Property (CP).
Note: If stock is owned either JT or TC with someone other than spouse, please furnish name and relationship.

SOLE PROPRIETORSHIP BUSINESS AND PROFESSIONAL INTERESTS

Evidence of title: balance sheet, depreciation schedule, registration or title issued by your state, bills of sale, fictitious name or trade name affidavit. Since a sole proprietorship is an amalgamation of assets, each asset must have an evidence of title.

Name of Business	Description of Business	Owner*	Value
_____	_____	_____	_____
_____	_____	_____	_____
_____	_____	_____	_____
_____	_____	_____	_____
_____	_____	_____	_____
		Total Value	_____

* Husband (H), Wife (W), Jointly (JT), Tenants in Common (TC), or Community Property (CP).

FARM AND RANCH INTERESTS

Evidence of title: If your farm or ranch is not owned by a corporation or partnership, you need to treat it as a sole proprietorship. Describe each asset.

Description *(livestock, machinery, leases, etc.)*	Owner*	Value
_____	_____	_____
_____	_____	_____
_____	_____	_____
_____	_____	_____
_____	_____	_____
_____	_____	_____
	Total Value	_____

* Husband (H), Wife (W), Jointly (JT), Tenants in Common (TC), or Community Property (CP).

OIL, GAS, AND MINERAL INTERESTS

Evidence of title: lease agreement, deed, royalty agreement, farmout agreement, pooling agreement or other agreement you signed to create your oil, gas, or mineral interest.

Description *(lease, overriding royalty, fee mineral estate, working interest, pooling agreement, etc.)*	Owner*	Value
_____	_____	_____
_____	_____	_____
_____	_____	_____
_____	_____	_____
	Total Value	_____

* Husband (H), Wife (W), Jointly (JT), Tenants in Common (TC), or Community Property (CP).

REAL PROPERTY

Evidence of title: deed or land contract (do not use mortgage or tax assessment).

Where you have either a deeded or land contract interest *(land or buildings that you own in partnership with someone else should be listed under the partnership section)*:

General Description and/or address	Owner	Fair Market Value	Mortgage
_____	_____	_____	_____
_____	_____	_____	_____
_____	_____	_____	_____
_____	_____	_____	_____
_____	_____	_____	_____

Total Value _____

* **Note:** If two or more names are on deed or contract without stating type of ownership, please use "?".

ANTICIPATED INHERITANCE, GIFT, OR LAWSUIT JUDGMENT

Evidence of title: copies of wills or trusts, copy of lawsuits or judgments, or any other document that evidences your anticipated interest.

Description _____
_____
_____
_____
_____
_____

Total estimated value _____

OTHER ASSETS

Other property is any property that you have that does not fit into any listed category.

Evidence of title: documents you signed to purchase the property, documents you received when you received the property, or any other document you have that shows you own the property.

Description	Owner	Value
_____	_____	_____
_____	_____	_____
_____	_____	_____
_____	_____	_____
_____	_____	_____

Total estimated value _____

SUMMARY OF VALUES

ASSETS	Amounts*	
	Husband/ Single Person	Wife
Cash	$	$
Investment Accounts		
Stocks		
Bonds		
Personal effects		
Retirement plans		
Life insurance and annuity face amounts		
Mortgages, notes, and other receivables		
Partnership interests		
Corporate business and professional interests		
Sole proprietorship business and professional interests		
Farm and ranch		
Oil, gas, and mineral		
Real property		
Anticipated inheritance, gift, or lawsuit judgment		
Other assets		
Total Assets		

* Joint Tenancy (JT), Tenancy in Common (TC) and Community Property (CP) values go half in husband's column, half in wife's column.

LIABILITIES	Amounts*	
	Husband/ Single Person	Wife
Loans payable	$	$
Accounts payable		
Real estate mortgages payable		
Contingent liabilities		
Loans against life insurance		
Unpaid taxes		
Other obligations:		
_____		
_____		
Total liabilities		
Net Estate		

·8·

Meeting with Your Professional Team

Once you have identified the members of your professional team and you have completed both your Checklist for Designing Your Plan and your Personal Information Checklist, you need to retain the initiative to make sure that your living trust–centered plan is completed. You retain the initiative by meeting with your lawyer and your other advisors so that you can begin the final design, creation, and implementation of your living trust–centered plan.

Which Team Member Do You Meet with First?

There are three ways that you can approach your initial meeting with your professional team.

- You can meet with your lawyer.
- You can meet with your other team members.
- You can meet with your lawyer and other team members all at once.

Meeting with Your Lawyer First

If you feel confident about your estate planning knowledge and you are well prepared, meeting with your lawyer before meeting with your other team members can be productive. In this first meeting, you will need to cover much ground in finding out:

- Whether to hire him or her
- How much he or she will charge
- Whether you wish to modify or embellish your living trust instructions
- When the lawyer's work will be completed

Your first meeting should generally take between one and two hours. Many people are surprised at this. You might expect it to be longer, but if you follow some of the simple procedures that we will explain, you can generally get your estate planning business efficiently communicated in this time.

You should do most of the spadework ahead of time so that your lawyer can concentrate on drafting your estate planning documents without having to waste time on rudimentary information gathering and other ministerial functions. Your advance work will make it easier for you to accomplish the objectives of the first meeting and will facilitate your lawyer's grasp of what you want done.

What to Bring to the First Meeting

- **Come with your spouse.** If you don't, you can only plan for your own estate and speak for yourself. Your spouse has the right to plan his or her own estate. If you and your spouse want to plan together, you will waste a great deal of time and create unneeded conflict if you do not plan together from the very outset.
- **Bring this workbook with you.** It will help you and your lawyer to stay on track.
- **Complete the checklists.** Even if you cannot complete all of them, do the best you can. (You should have sent copies of both of these checklists with your confirmation letter to your lawyer to give him or her a head start in preparing for your meeting.)
- **Bring in as much information as you can.** Try to have copies with you of as many of your title documents and evidences of title as you can. If you do not have a copier, bring the originals and request that the attorney's staff make copies for their files.
- **Bring other team members if you wish.** If you are close to your other professional advisors, you may want to invite them to the initial meeting.

The First Meeting with a Lawyer

You should be able to quickly determine if the lawyer is someone whose demeanor and style will encourage you to go further in ascertaining his or her credentials and planning expertise. Ask yourself these preliminary questions:

- Are you comfortable with how the reception room is kept up, the attitude of the receptionist, and the manner in which you are greeted?
- Is the lawyer on time? You should not have to wait longer than ten or fifteen minutes before you are ushered into the lawyer's office, unless you are told of an unavoidable delay.
- Is the lawyer courteous? Does he or she seem to be caring?
- Is the office organized? Do you have a sense of well-being, or are you put off by the atmosphere or attitude of his or her staff?

If any of these areas are of concern to you, then you may not want to spend much time with the lawyer. Remember, you must retain a lawyer you like and respect.

The initial meeting should proceed something like this:

- Be pleasant, but try to minimize the small talk; get down to business. Both your time and your lawyer's time are valuable.
- Your first order of business should be to confirm how the lawyer is charging for your meeting. If you do not like or accept how the lawyer bills and you cannot reach an agreement, then your meeting is at an end.
- You and your lawyer should discuss your Checklist for Designing Your Plan and your Personal Information Checklist. Emphasize any information you think is particularly helpful to your lawyer's understanding of your desires.
- This is your time to talk; your lawyer should listen to you first before making any recommendations so that he or she has a clear picture of what you want, how much preparation you have done, and what your hopes, fears, dreams, aspirations, values, and special wishes are. This is a critical aspect of the planning process.
- After you are done, let your lawyer talk. Let your lawyer address any issues that he or she sees in your planning. Allow the lawyer to educate you in areas that you may not understand or where he or she sees opportunities or problems. Find out if he or she understands your needs and your family's needs, and whether or not they are viewed as the core of his or her planning objectives and strategies.
- Finalize your plan. Agree with your lawyer as to what plan you want and how it will be designed. **Make absolutely sure that your planning meets the definition of estate planning. If it does not, don't do it.**

Find another lawyer who will give you a plan that meets the definition.

- Your lawyer should be able to tell you how much your plan will cost and when it will be done. We advise you to get a set fee; hourly rates generally create ill will and confusion. Most seasoned clients avoid them if they can.

- It is imperative that you and your lawyer schedule your next meeting before you leave his or her office. Keep the momentum going; get in the habit of setting planning deadlines.

- Unless you have a real need or desire to see a draft of your documents, make it clear to your lawyer that you *do not* want to see a "draft agreement" prior to your next meeting. Your lawyer should review your entire living trust–centered plan with you at the next meeting. You will then have the opportunity to ask your questions and to point out errors, if any, and take it home for further review if you wish.

- You should confirm your agreement in writing within a few days after your meeting. In Form 801 in the Appendix, we have included a sample letter for you to pattern your letter after.

Meeting with Your Other Advisors First

Often, your other advisors can be quite valuable in helping you learn more about proper estate planning. They can offer their experiences and their knowledge, and they can give you fresh new ideas and planning concepts. Financial advisors have a vital role in estate planning and in the planning process. Here are some suggestions about how you can best work with your financial advisors when meeting with them first.

- If you have attended a seminar that was hosted by a financial advisor, you may want to meet with the advisor. You may have determined that the advisor is competent and caring, and you would like to have more information about that advisor. We encourage you to make the appointment—you have everything to gain and nothing to lose. Depending on whether you meet with a fee-based or commission-based financial advisor, you may or may not have to pay for the advice you receive during this meeting.

- If you have a financial advisor or you know one, it may be worth your time to meet with him or her and find out more about how that advisor works and what he or she can do for you.

- When meeting with a nonlawyer estate planning advisor, remember that your purpose is to gain knowledge about your planning. Your purpose is not to have the financial advisor draft documents or give you legal advice.

- Commission-based financial advisors who are well trained and who are professional in their practice habits will be far more interested in helping you get the best estate planning advice possible than in making a quick sale. These professionals know that the best client is the client who is well educated in the planning process and with whom the advisor has established a relationship built on trust, respect, and planning expertise.

- Professional financial advisors work hard to provide their clients with products that meet their planning needs and that are competitively priced. These advisors are only paid if you purchase a product and they are rewarded further the longer the product is kept on the books, so it is in their best interest to serve their clients well.

- Fee-based financial advisors are paid for their expertise and advice. They are not paid on making a sale, so there is no potential conflict of interest between the advice they give and any products that are sold. In many cases, a fee-based financial advisor will offset the fee against any products you purchase from him or her.

- Sometimes it is difficult to decide whether to use a commission-based or a fee-based financial advisor. The bottom line is that if you would feel more comfortable with someone who has no ax to grind in terms of self-interest, you should consider a fee-based advisor. On the other hand, if you would like to have advice without being obligated to pay, then perhaps a commission-based advisor is better.

- Your accountant is an excellent advisor to meet with in terms of your estate planning needs. Many accountants are knowledgeable in estate planning, especially as it relates to tax issues. Meeting with your accountant first can get you educated in the more technical aspects of estate planning.

- Some accountants are also very knowledgeable in the people-planning aspects of estate planning. If you are very close to your accountant and he or she knows about your family, then your accountant can help you design the dispositive or people part of your planning.

After you have met with another team member or members prior to meeting with your lawyer, you should then meet with your lawyer. Conduct your meeting with your lawyer in the same manner as described earlier. If you can—and you feel good about it—bring your advisor or advisors to the first meeting with the attorney. The more you involve your advisors, the better your estate plan will be.

The Team Meeting

If you have a lawyer and other advisors whom you are comfortable with, you may consider having an initial meeting with all of your professional team members. In our experience, this is the preferable approach. There are many advantages for doing this. First and foremost, it assures that each team member is involved from the beginning. This promotes effective understanding and communication. Also, each team member listens to you at the same time, so there can be no confusion or miscommunication of who said what to whom. With this approach, the final product that is developed is truly the result of the knowledge, effort, and advice of all of your professional advisors.

The disadvantage of the team meeting approach is that if the meeting is not well organized and everyone is not prepared, it can waste everyone's time and potentially your money. To be effective, the meeting must be organized. One advisor must take the lead in terms of "chairing" the meeting. The meeting should be just as described in our section on the first meeting with the lawyer. The only addition is that you will have the input and ideas of your lawyer and your other advisors, all of which can be valuable.

In most planning situations, the first meeting is not the time when your advisors should make specific recommendations about funding the trust with financial products. The first and foremost objective of this initial meeting is to design your estate plan. Once this is done, the fee is quoted and agreed upon, and a time is set to sign the plan. Then it is time to discuss the need, if any, for financial products.

Very often in the initial meeting, your lawyer and other advisors will find that your particular planning objectives require life insurance, disability insurance, long-term health care insurance, annuities, or even the sale and reinvestment of some of your existing assets. These issues should be addressed generally in the first meeting. Your advisors should then determine a plan of action so at a subsequent meeting a presentation will be made of specific recommendations.

In our lectures to lawyers, accountants, and financial advisors, we have long made the analogy of creating an estate plan to that of designing and building an automobile. In this analogy, the attorneys design and build cars. The type of car that is built depends on who wants the car and how simple or complex the driver's needs appear to be. Some people need basic transportation because their estates or objectives are modest. Other people may need—or want—a top-of-the-line luxury car loaded with all of the options. Whatever type is needed, the lawyer is the one to design and build it.

Once the car is built, it needs gas to get it where it is going. The car also needs to be periodically serviced along the way so that it can complete its journey. Financial products are often needed to assure that your living trust–centered plan has the gas, oil, grease, and other fluids to keep it going in the right direction at the right speed. It also needs appropriate maintenance to assure that it will reach its ultimate destination as intended.

Imagine, if you will, buying a beautiful new car without the ability to purchase gasoline. Imagine yourself pushing it off the dealership lot down the highway to your home. Exhausted, you set the brake. Your car sits where you left it because you have no fuel.

On the other hand, imagine going to the gas station holding two five-gallon gasoline cans. You fill them with gas and run home along the highway, gas spilling out as you lumber along. When you get home with the gas that is left, you store it in the garage or backyard with cans of gas bought on previous trips. Eventually, the older cans have evaporated and are empty. You purchased the fuel but have never owned a vehicle that could efficiently and effectively use it in meeting your transportation needs.

In both cases, you paid good money to buy something that you thought you needed that was worthless without the other. In both cases, your purchases turned out to be a waste of time, energy, and money.

We feel strongly that you need to have a car *and* have the fuel and the maintenance to keep it going. Now, this may be a very simple analogy, but it sums up decades of professional experience that leads to the conclusion that if you take the time to get a car—your living trust–centered plan—you absolutely need to take the time to explore what kind of gas, oil, and maintenance—financial products and services—that you and your family will need to get you and them where you want to go.

Your Lawyer and
Financial Products and Services

If you meet with your lawyer first and you do not involve other advisors, you should ask your lawyer to point out any needs for financial products or liquidity that he or she sees. However, this may be a futile exercise. Most lawyers are not trained in financial affairs or have no interest or knowledge of them. If this is true for your lawyer, it is especially important that you seek out a financial professional to look at your affairs. This can be done after the initial meeting with the lawyer or after the second meeting. In any event, you should do it without hesitation.

For most people seeking to get their estate planning affairs in order, it is difficult to meet the definition of estate planning without at least exploring the possibility of using financial products and services.

Preparing for the Second Meeting

The purpose for your second meeting with your lawyer is to review your living trust–centered plan, decide if it meets the goals and objectives as agreed upon in your first meeting, and sign the documents. It is also the time for you to hear any recommendations made by your other advisors, and lastly, it is the time to start funding your plan. In the next chapter, we give you advice about how your second meeting should be orchestrated.

· 9 ·

Your Second Meeting

In our book *Loving Trust* we chose to call this second meeting with your attorney the "last meeting." We continue to believe as a general rule that, except in extraordinary circumstances, no more than two meetings are necessary to discuss, agree to, and sign your estate planning documents, or to give your lawyer specific instructions on necessary changes that will allow you to sign your planning documents shortly thereafter. If the Checklist for Designing Your Plan and your Personal Information Checklist are completed fully and shared with your lawyer, two meetings are all that should be needed to get the job done in most circumstances. Two meetings also conserve your lawyer's time and keep fees to a minimum.

In some cases, an additional meeting may be called for if you need help funding your estate plan so that your property will avoid both a probate at your death and a financial guardianship if you become disabled. Funding may also encompass the purchase of financial products or services. However, for many people, two meetings with your attorney will be sufficient in terms of actually designing and building your estate planning "car."

Your second meeting should take no longer than two or three hours. It is likely to be somewhat longer than your first meeting because it will be devoted to reviewing your finished documents. Your lawyer should take you through all the documents, answer your questions, and make needed corrections at that time. You shouldn't leave without signing your estate planning documents.

You may wish to invite your individual trustees to attend this meeting. The learning experience will be invaluable and will make them much better trustees. They can ask questions and become real participants.

You should also consider inviting your other advisors to this meeting. Many times we have had second meetings in which an insurance agent, accountant, or other advisor attended. These meetings were invariably successful because of these advisors' participation. Whether or not your other advisors attend the second meeting is clearly up to you. However, it would be sound and sensible practice for you to make the necessary invitations to them; if they do not believe they can add anything, they will decline your invitation.

Reviewing and Signing
Your Living Trust Documents

Here is pretty much how the reviewing and signing of your living trust documents should proceed:

- Your lawyer should go through your living trust–centered planning with you. The review ought not to be a reading of the document word for word, but your lawyer should explain each paragraph in simple and easy-to-understand terms.
- As your lawyer reaches each part of your plan that presents one of your design alternatives, your lawyer should refer to your Checklist for Designing Your Plan and explain exactly how your desires have been incorporated into the trust agreement.
- Do not hesitate to ask questions. Some of your plan's legal phrases and terms may confuse you or be foreign to you. We have found that you should try to hold your questions until after your attorney has gone through the entire plan because it is very likely that most of your questions may be answered as he or she proceeds through the document.
- If mistakes are found or you change your mind, they should be corrected while you are in the lawyer's office. With computers, this is not a significant problem.
- After you and your lawyer have reviewed your documents and you are comfortable with what they say, you should sign them. We have met with some clients who wanted to take them home to study first. We have tried to encourage our clients to sign their documents while mulling the "fine points" by making a statement coupled with a question: "You have a simple will now. If these documents are only ninety-five percent of where they should be—and they are far closer than that—they are still many, many times better than what you have now. Wouldn't you like to have their added protection as you check the details and nuances of your plan at your convenience?"
- Sign a minimum of two living trusts. Unlike a will, which should have

only one original, a revocable living trust can have many duplicate originals. For your protection, you should have one of the originals. Who gets the other original or originals is up to you, but consider leaving one with the lawyer or giving one to your successor trustees.

- You will also sign, at a minimum, a Pour-Over Will, Durable Special Power of Attorney, a Health Care Power of Attorney, a Living Will, and the other documents that constitute a full living trust–centered plan.

Finishing the Second Meeting

Once you have reviewed and signed all your living trust–centered plan documents, there are still a few more matters to take care of.

- Discuss how your trust is going to be funded with both your lawyer and your other advisors. **In Part Two of this workbook, we explain just how that should be done.**
- If your other advisors are attending the meeting, encourage them to present any recommendations that they may have. Your accountant may have relevant input on administrative procedures or forward tax planning. Your financial advisor, life insurance agent, stockbroker, or trust banker may want to take this opportunity to make specific recommendations or to suggest a procedure for researching product planning options before reporting back to you and his or her fellow team members.
- Make sure that any remaining tasks are agreed upon and deadlines are set so that a definite end to your planning process can be determined.
- Pay your lawyer. Your commitment is to write a check for the services you received. You should also give him or her a sincere Thank-you. This is just as important as being prompt in your payment. Your lawyer will very much appreciate your thanks. Many lawyers work for more than money, and this is especially true of lawyers who are dedicated to the Esperti Peterson Planning Process.

If the Law Changes

You should ask your lawyer what happens if there is a subsequent change in the law that affects your planning. We are strong advocates of the position that by taking you on as a client, your lawyer should also assume the responsibility for contacting you if there is a change in the law that affects your planning.

There have been very few changes in trust law as compared to other legal areas. While changes in trust law are uncommon, changes in the federal income, gift, and estate tax laws have been more frequent. Even so, these changes have largely affected people with large or sophisticated estates; they have not had such a far-reaching impact on the great majority of the population as to be a burden to most lawyers.

Your lawyer should contact you if there is a change in the law that affects your planning. He or she should also explain how it affects your trust, what needs to be done to make it current, and what the charge will be to complete the amendments. Send your lawyer a letter confirming that he or she will contact you should changes in the law affect your living trust estate planning. We have included a sample letter in Form 901 in the Appendix for you to use for this purpose.

Tune-ups

Our world is built around change. Circumstances change, people change, laws change. We cannot prevent change from occurring in our lives. When changes occur that may affect your estate planning, it is quite simple to change or amend your revocable living trust and the documents that accompany it to adapt to those changes. Unlike a will, a revocable living trust is made to readily accept change. Your lawyer can make such a change easily and quickly by preparing an amendment to your trust.

In most cases, a short letter to your lawyer explaining the change will enable the lawyer to draft it and send it back to you in a short period of time. There is generally no reason for a formal visit unless you want to redesign your planning on a massive scale. It is a good idea, however, to periodically review your planning and changes in your circumstances with your attorney and other advisors. Plan to meet at least every three years, or more often if your financial or family situations change significantly.

If you take the time and make the effort to locate a lawyer, accountant, and financial and insurance advisors whom you both like and trust, and if you adequately prepare for your meetings with them while creating an atmosphere of cooperation and trust, your planning time should be kept to a minimum while your planning results are maximized.

PART TWO

■

Funding
Your Living Trust

· 10 ·

An Overview of Funding

Do you know why a living trust avoids probate? Most people do not have the slightest idea. In fact, we have found that many people believe that just because they have a living trust, they have avoided probate. Unfortunately, this is not the case. A living trust avoids probate because trusts don't die and they don't become incapacitated. People do. Probate and financial guardianships are designed to provide court-imposed supervision of the property of an incapacitated or deceased person. This is done so that creditors may be paid and so that the property may be held for the benefit of the disabled or distributed to the heirs of the deceased. If a person dies without owning property, there is no probate, because there is no property over which the probate system could take jurisdiction. In the case of incapacity, the court can take control of the person and appoint a guardian to make decisions about that person's well-being, but the court will not appoint a financial guardian if there is no property to "guard."

If you put all of your property into a revocable living trust, you control that property 100 percent because you can amend or revoke the trust anytime you want. In addition, the instructions in the trust are based on your desires, so the trust's main job is to protect you and your loved ones the way you determined that ought to precisely happen. If you are a trustee of the trust while you are alive and well, you interpret your own trust instructions and operate the trust on a daily basis.

If you become disabled or die, your trust is considered to be separate and apart from you for purposes of probate and incapacity. You—as an individual person—own nothing in your name. You—as the maker and beneficiary of your trust—*control* your trust, but it owns your property in its name. This simple legal fiction means that, because you do not own property in your name, there is no court jurisdiction of your property if you become incapacitated and there is no court jurisdiction of your property upon your death.

The one inescapable conclusion is that if you wish to avoid probate or a financial guardianship, you must make sure the title to your property is put in the name of your trust. Those assets that are left out of your living trust will be subject to financial guardianship and probate proceedings.

When you put property into your trust, you are in effect probating your own estate. It is a lot easier and less expensive to probate your estate while you are alive and well than it is to have someone else do it after you are disabled or dead. The secret to putting property into your trust is to get it done *quickly* and *correctly* at the lowest possible cost.

Who "Funds" Your Trust?

The term that is used by estate planning professionals to describe the process of getting property into a living trust is *funding*. Funding a trust can be quite easy in many cases, but it can also present some significant legal and practical challenges. How easy or difficult it is to fund a trust depends on the kinds of assets that are funded into the trust and the level of expertise and training that the person doing the funding has.

There are many assets you can easily put into your trust. All it takes is some training, knowledge, and at times a touch of perseverance. On the other hand, there are some assets that only trained professionals should transfer into your trust. Because these assets are governed by special laws or are particularly sensitive to legal rules, you should not attempt to fund your trust with these assets without close professional guidance. To do otherwise may create unexpected income tax results or may engender catastrophic ownership issues that may only get undone through expensive proceedings.

It is imperative that you, your lawyer, and your other estate planning advisors understand who is responsible for transferring which assets into your trust. You should also know which assets you are capable of transferring into your trust so that you can make the decision whether you would like to fund the trust with those assets yourself or pay one of your advisors to do it for you.

If you prefer to hire your advisors to fund your trust, then your lawyer and your other advisors must determine who is going to transfer each and every asset. It is critical that they understand the allocation of responsibility and that they will stand accountable for their portion.

It is important that you understand that professionals differ as to their enthusiasm for the funding process. There are some lawyers who take special delight in funding their clients' trusts, and there are others who would just as soon delegate that responsibility to their clients or their clients' other advisors.

Many accountants, financial advisors, and life insurance agents take particular pride in participating in funding their clients' living trusts, while others wish to have nothing to do with the process. Some full-service financial institutions view transferring securities to a living trust as a pain in the computer, while others openly advertise that they take special delight in doing so free of charge as a special service to their clients.

The Master Funding Tracking Checklist that follows will allow you to determine who is funding what assets into your trust, the deadline that has been agreed upon, and date that each asset transfer is completed. When this checklist is completed, so is your funding.

You should list all of your assets on this checklist and have it ready for your second or funding meeting. As you discuss funding, you, your attorney, and your advisors should decide who is going to fund which assets into your trust and when they can realistically complete the task. If you use this checklist, it will allow you to supervise and control the funding process. You will clearly know your funding responsibilities and you can follow up with each advisor to keep track of his or her progress.

Regardless of who does the funding, we strongly suggest that your lawyer review the completed file and that as you acquire new assets, you send your lawyer copies of documentation that show how they have been placed in the trust name.

What You Need to Know About the Income Tax Aspects of Your Living Trust

As you fund your trust, whether with the help of your lawyer or with your other advisors, you will likely run into some people or institutions that will not understand living trusts and how they operate. In the chapters that follow, we attempt to provide forms and letters that will help you to overcome those obstacles that are a product of a simple lack of living trust knowledge.

Questions frequently arise concerning the federal income tax ramifications of funding a revocable living trust. Revocable living trusts have long been recognized as legitimate title-holding entities under the Internal Revenue Code. In fact, a revocable living trust is called a "grantor trust" in the Internal Revenue Code.

Generally, a grantor trust is any trust over which a trust maker has control. Because the maker of a living trust has complete control over the trust, a re-

MASTER FUNDING TRACKING CHECKLIST

ASSET	Me	Atty	FA	CPA	Other	Deadline	Done
Real Property							
Residence	___	___	___	___	___	___	___
Vacation Home	___	___	___	___	___	___	___
Time-share	___	___	___	___	___	___	___
Rental property	___	___	___	___	___	___	___
Oil Interests	___	___	___	___	___	___	___
Mineral Interests	___	___	___	___	___	___	___
Gas Interests	___	___	___	___	___	___	___
Cemetery Plot	___	___	___	___	___	___	___
Personal Property							
Automobile #1	___	___	___	___	___	___	___
Automobile #2	___	___	___	___	___	___	___
Automobile #3	___	___	___	___	___	___	___
Airplane	___	___	___	___	___	___	___
Boat	___	___	___	___	___	___	___
Mobile Home	___	___	___	___	___	___	___
Business Interests							
Sole Proprietorship	___	___	___	___	___	___	___
Section 1244 Stock	___	___	___	___	___	___	___
General Partnership	___	___	___	___	___	___	___
Limited Partnership	___	___	___	___	___	___	___
Livestock	___	___	___	___	___	___	___
Farm Equipment	___	___	___	___	___	___	___
Liquor License	___	___	___	___	___	___	___

(continued on following page)

Intangible
Promissory Note
Mortgage
Land Sale Contract
Installment Sale Contract
Checking Account
Savings Account
Certificates of Deposit
Money Market Account
Stocks
Bonds
U.S. Treasury Bills & Notes
Flower Bonds
Stock Options
Life Insurance
Disability Insurance
Annuities
Retirement Benefits
Safe Deposit Box
Memberships
Judgments

vocable living trust is not considered to be a separate taxable entity for federal income tax purposes. Because a trust is not a separate entity for tax purposes, its maker is responsible for all the income, deductions, and credits the trust property generates. In essence, a revocable living trust and its maker are one and the same for the purposes of federal income tax law.

If a trust maker is the sole trustee or a co-trustee of the trust, all of the income, deductions, and credits generated by the trust property are reported on the maker's personal income tax return. The maker's Social Security number is used as the Federal Taxpayer Identification Number of the trust. If the trust maker is not a trustee, a separate taxpayer identification number must be obtained for the trust, but the maker still reports all income, deductions, and credits on his or her personal income tax return. In this case, the trust is required to file an information return. A revocable living trust does not become a separate taxable entity until the death of its maker.

This information is important for you to know when you set up any type of bank account for your trust. Your bank or other financial institution will ask you for the Federal Identification Number of your trust and will require that you complete and sign a W-9 form to be submitted to the IRS. A completed Form W-9 is shown in Figure 10-1. You will not have to worry about getting a Form W-9; your bank or other financial institution will furnish one to you.

As mentioned earlier, if you are trustee or co-trustee of your trust, you will use your Social Security number for your trust. If you have a joint trust, either spouse's Social Security number can be used. In either case no separate trust tax return is required. Sometimes people do not act as their own trustee. When this occurs, a new Federal Identification Number is required. It is not difficult to get one of these numbers; all you need to do is fill out Form SS-4. In Figure 10-2, there is a filled-in Form SS-4. If you need this form, either write or call your local IRS office or ask your accountant or lawyer for one.

We also suggest that you have a letter of explanation that you can use if any financial institution has questions about your trust. Form 1001 in the Appendix is a sample letter explaining the income tax ramifications of a revocable living trust. This letter assumes that you or your spouse are acting as a trustee of your living trust.

In the chapters that follow, we are going to help you and your advisors determine which assets you put into the trust yourself and which assets your other advisors should transfer into it. We will provide you with specific forms and examples of how that task can be accomplished properly.

Figure 10-1

Form **W-9**
(Rev. January 1993)
Department of the Treasury
Internal Revenue Service

Request for Taxpayer Identification Number and Certification

Give this form to the requester. Do NOT send to IRS.

Please print or type

Name (If joint names, list first and circle the name of the person or entity whose number you enter in Part I below. See Instructions on page 2 if your name has changed.)
John Doe and Jane Doe, Trustees, or their successors in trust, under the John Doe Living Trust dated March 11, 1995 and any amendments thereto.

Business name (Sole proprietors see instructions on page 2.) (If you are exempt from backup withholding, complete this form and enter "EXEMPT" in Part II below.)

Address (number and street)
111 Main Street

List account number(s) here (optional)

City, state, and ZIP code
Your City, Anywhere   00001

Part I Taxpayer Identification Number (TIN)

Enter your TIN in the appropriate box. For individuals, this is your social security number (SSN). For sole proprietors, see the instructions on page 2. For other entities, it is your employer identification number (EIN). If you do not have a number, see How To Obtain a TIN below.

Note: *If the account is in more than one name, see the chart on page 2 for guidelines on whose number to enter.*

Social security number
0 1 2 3 4 5 6 7 8

OR

Employer identification number

Part II For Payees Exempt From Backup Withholding (See Exempt Payees and Payments on page 2)

▶

Requester's name and address (optional)

Certification.—Under penalties of perjury, I certify that:

1. The number shown on this form is my correct taxpayer identification number (or I am waiting for a number to be issued to me), and

2. I am not subject to backup withholding because: (a) I am exempt from backup withholding, or (b) I have not been notified by the Internal Revenue Service that I am subject to backup withholding as a result of a failure to report all interest or dividends, or (c) the IRS has notified me that I am no longer subject to backup withholding.

Certification Instructions.—You must cross out item 2 above if you have been notified by the IRS that you are currently subject to backup withholding because of underreporting interest or dividends on your tax return. For real estate transactions, item 2 does not apply. For mortgage interest paid, the acquisition or abandonment of secured property, contributions to an individual retirement arrangement (IRA), and generally payments other than interest and dividends, you are not required to sign the Certification, but you must provide your correct TIN. (Also see **Signing the Certification** on page 2.)

Sign Here   Signature ▶ **John and Jane Doe as Trustees**   Date ▶

Section references are to the Internal Revenue Code.

Purpose of Form.—A person who is required to file an information return with the IRS must obtain your correct TIN to report income paid to you, real estate transactions, mortgage interest you paid, the acquisition or abandonment of secured property, or contributions you made to an IRA. Use Form W-9 to furnish your correct TIN to the requester (the person asking you to furnish your TIN) and, when applicable, (1) to certify that the TIN you are furnishing is correct (or that you are waiting for a number to be issued), (2) to certify that you are not subject to backup withholding, and (3) to claim exemption from backup withholding if you are an exempt payee. Furnishing your correct TIN and making the appropriate certifications will prevent certain payments from being subject to backup withholding.

Note: *If a requester gives you a form other than a W-9 to request your TIN, you must use the requester's form.*

How To Obtain a TIN.—If you do not have a TIN, apply for one immediately. To apply, get Form SS-5, Application for a Social Security Card (for individuals), from your local office of the Social Security Administration, or Form SS-4, Application for Employer Identification Number (for businesses and all other entities), from your local IRS office.

To complete Form W-9 if you do not have a TIN, write "Applied for" in the space for the TIN in Part I, sign and date the form, and give it to the requester. Generally, you will then have

60 days to obtain a TIN and furnish it to the requester. If the requester does not receive your TIN within 60 days, backup withholding, if applicable, will begin and continue until you furnish your TIN to the requester. For reportable interest or dividend payments, the payer must exercise one of the following options concerning backup withholding during this 60-day period. Under option (1), a payer must backup withhold on any withdrawals you make from your account after 7 business days after the requester receives this form back from you. Under option (2), the payer must backup withhold on any reportable interest or dividend payments made to your account, regardless of whether you make any withdrawals. The backup withholding under option (2) must begin no later than 7 business days after the requester receives this form back. Under option (2), the payer is required to refund the amounts withheld if your certified TIN is received within the 60-day period and you were not subject to backup withholding during that period.

Note: *Writing "Applied for" on the form means that you have already applied for a TIN OR that you intend to apply for one in the near future.*

As soon as you receive your TIN, complete another Form W-9, include your TIN, sign and date the form, and give it to the requester.

What Is Backup Withholding?—Persons making certain payments to you after 1992 must withhold and pay to the IRS 31% of such payments under certain conditions. This is called "backup withholding." Payments that could be subject to backup withholding include interest,

dividends, broker and barter exchange transactions, rents, royalties, nonemployee compensation, and certain payments from fishing boat operators, but do not include real estate transactions.

If you give the requester your correct TIN, make the appropriate certifications, and report all your taxable interest and dividends on your tax return, your payments will not be subject to backup withholding. Payments you receive will be subject to backup withholding if:

1. You do not furnish your TIN to the requester, or

2. The IRS notifies the requester that you furnished an incorrect TIN, or

3. You are notified by the IRS that you are subject to backup withholding because you failed to report all your interest and dividends on your tax return (for reportable interest and dividends only), or

4. You do not certify to the requester that you are not subject to backup withholding under 3 above (for reportable interest and dividend accounts opened after 1983 only), or

5. You do not certify your TIN. This applies only to reportable interest, dividend, broker, or barter exchange accounts opened after 1983, or broker accounts considered inactive in 1983.

Except as explained in 5 above, other reportable payments are subject to backup withholding only if 1 or 2 above applies. Certain payees and payments are exempt from backup withholding and information reporting. See Payees and Payments Exempt From

Cat. No. 10231X

Form **W-9** (Rev. 1-93)

1/11/93   Published by Tax Management Inc., a Subsidiary of The Bureau of National Affairs, Inc.   W-9.1

Figure 10-2

Form **SS-4** (Rev. April 1991) Department of the Treasury Internal Revenue Service	**Application for Employer Identification Number** (For use by employers and others. Please read the attached instructions before completing this form.)	EIN OMB No. 1545-0003 Expires 4-30-94

Please type or print clearly.

1 Name of applicant (True legal name) (See instructions.) John Doe and Jane Doe, Trustees, or their successors in trust, under the John Doe Living Trust dated March 11, 1995 and any amendments thereto.

2 Trade name of business, if different from name in line 1

3 Executor, trustee, "care of" name Jane Doe

4a Mailing address (street address) (room, apt., or suite no.) 111 Main Street

5a Address of business (See instructions.) Same

4b City, state, and ZIP code Your City, Anywhere 00001

5b City, state, and ZIP code

6 County and state where principal business is located

7 Name of principal officer, grantor, or general partner (See instructions.) ► John Doe, Grantor

8a Type of entity (Check only one box.) (See instructions.)
- ☐ Individual SSN _____
- ☐ REMIC
- ☐ State/local government
- ☐ Other nonprofit organization (specify) _____
- ☐ Other (specify) ► _____
- ☐ Estate
- ☐ Plan administrator SSN _____
- ☐ Personal service corp.
- ☐ National guard
- ☐ Other corporation (specify) _____
- ☐ Federal government/military
- If nonprofit organization enter GEN (if applicable) _____
- ☒ Trust
- ☐ Partnership
- ☐ Farmers' cooperative
- ☐ Church or church controlled organization

8b If a corporation, give name of foreign country (if applicable) or state in the U.S. where incorporated ►
Foreign country | State

9 Reason for applying (Check only one box.)
- ☐ Started new business
- ☐ Hired employees
- ☐ Created a pension plan (specify type) ►
- ☐ Banking purpose (specify) ►
- ☐ Changed type of organization (specify) ► _____
- ☐ Purchased going business
- ☒ Created a trust (specify) ► Grantor is no longer a trustee, or/grantor died
- ☐ Other (specify) ►

10 Date business started or acquired (Mo., day, year) (See instructions.) date of occurrence of #9 above

11 Enter closing month of accounting year. (See instructions.) December 31

12 First date wages or annuities were paid or will be paid (Mo., day, year). Note: If applicant is a withholding agent, enter date income will first be paid to nonresident alien. (Mo., day, year) . . . . ► n/a

13 Enter highest number of employees expected in the next 12 months. Note: If the applicant does not expect to have any employees during the period, enter "0." . . . . ►

Nonagricultural	Agricultural	Household
0	0	0

14 Principal activity (See instructions.) ►

15 Is the principal business activity manufacturing? . . . . ☐ Yes ☒ No
If "Yes," principal product and raw material used ►

16 To whom are most of the products or services sold? Please check the appropriate box. ☐ Business (wholesale)
- ☐ Public (retail)
- ☐ Other (specify) ►
- ☒ N/A

17a Has the applicant ever applied for an identification number for this or any other business? . . . . ☐ Yes ☒ No
Note: If "Yes," please complete lines 17b and 17c.

17b If you checked the "Yes" box in line 17a, give applicant's true name and trade name, if different than name shown on prior application.
True name ► | Trade name ►

17c Enter approximate date, city, and state where the application was filed and the previous employer identification number if known.

Approximate date when filed (Mo., day, year)	City and state where filed	Previous EIN

Under penalties of perjury, I declare that I have examined this application, and to the best of my knowledge and belief, it is true, correct, and complete | Telephone number (include area code)

Name and title (Please type or print clearly.) ► Names of Trustees

Signature ► Trustees' signatures | Date ►

Note: Do not write below this line. For official use only.

Please leave blank ►	Geo.	Ind.	Class	Size	Reason for applying

For Paperwork Reduction Act Notice, see attached instructions. | Cat. No. 16055N | Form **SS-4** (Rev. 4-91)

·11·

The Different Types of Revocable Living Trusts

Living trusts usually have one trust maker. The trust maker puts his or her property in the living trust, which has instructions that determine how the property is to be used by the trustee for the benefit of the beneficiaries. There is no requirement that a living trust has to have one trust maker. In many states, married couples use a single "joint trust" to plan both of their estates.

The Joint Trust

A joint trust is a revocable living trust in which both husband and wife are the makers and generally also the initial trustees. Joint Trusts have been used by husbands and wives for many years in community property states and are now also being used in common-law jurisdictions. Using a joint trust in a community property state can offer significant planning advantages by allowing the spouses to continue community property ownership, with its inherent protections, while at the same time enjoying the advantages of having their property owned by a living trust. There are no legal advantages per se to a married couple having a joint trust instead of separate trusts in a common law state. However, if you and your spouse own all of your assets jointly, the joint trust can be an excellent planning tool for you even if you reside in a common-law state.

The overriding reason for using a joint trust in common-law states is because it is psychologically comforting for the couple. Typically, in many marriages the couple views all their endeavors as a joint venture with the collective fruits of their labor contributing to wealth accumulation for the family unit. Often the very idea of a separate trust for each spouse, with the need for separate ownership of trust assets, causes concern that "what once was ours is now yours and/or mine." Using a joint trust allows you to engage in proper estate planning and at the same time provides the psychological comfort achieved through the perceived continuation of the joint venture.

Joint trust planning is new to most lawyers who do not practice in one of the nine community property states. Therefore, they often have reservations about preparing such trusts for their clients. This is understandable. If your lawyer is uncomfortable with them and would like to know more about how to use joint living trusts, we suggest that he or she read our article entitled "The Joint Revocable Living Trust: An Effective Planning Tool for Married Couples" in the May/June 1993 issue of *Estate Planning* magazine.

Joint Trusts and Joint Tenancy Property

When funding a joint trust with joint tenancy property, it is important to eliminate the "right of survivorship" feature so that the property passes under the terms of the trust on the death of the first spouse. The mere transfer of joint tenancy property to the joint trust may not necessarily sever the property's survivorship feature in some states. Since state law controls the methods by which joint tenancy is severed, your lawyer must determine how joint tenancy is effectively severed in your state before it can be safely placed in a joint trust.

In order to absolutely eliminate the survivorship feature, joint property should be severed or changed to tenancy in common by written agreement between the spouses. The written agreement may take several forms. Sometimes, language in a joint trust severs joint tenancy property. You should ask your lawyer if your trust has this language.

A separate "Tenancy Agreement" can be used to convert property that is owned jointly with rights of survivorship to tenancy in common property. See Figure 11-1.

If joint tenancy property is not properly severed to eliminate its survivorship feature, the Internal Revenue Service may take the position that on the death of the first spouse, all joint property will pass outright to the surviving spouse. This could mean adverse federal estate tax consequences including underutilization of the deceased spouse's exemption equivalent amount. In the worst case, this could cost an extra $235,000!

Figure 11-1

TENANCY AGREEMENT

This Tenancy Agreement is entered into on March 11, 1995, in the County of Junction, State of Anywhere, by and between:

JOHN DOE
and
JANE DOE

FACTUAL SUMMARY

Husband and Wife were married on June 6, 1965, and since that date have acquired title to property as joint tenants with right of survivorship or tenancy by the entirety.

Husband and Wife have created an estate plan using a revocable living trust and companion Pour-Over Wills, and they now wish to convert all or part of their joint tenancy property and tenancy by entirety property into tenancy in common property.

Husband and Wife are aware that they may by agreement convert their jointly owned property into tenancy in common property so that they may better control their respective interests in the property on each of their deaths.

AGREEMENT TO CHANGE JOINTLY OWNED ASSETS
TO TENANCY IN COMMON

Husband and Wife hereby grant, convey, and transfer their respective interests in their jointly held property to themselves as tenants in common.

Husband and Wife intend this agreement to be binding on themselves and on all others as to property held in joint tenancy with right of survivorship or tenancy by the entirety as of the date of this agreement regardless of the manner or form of the written title.

Husband and Wife have signed this agreement the day and year first written above.

Witnesses as to both:

_____   _____
John Doe   Witness

_____   _____
Jane Doe   Witness

STATE OF ANYWHERE   )
) ss.
COUNTY OF JUNCTION   )

    On March 11, 1995, before me, the undersigned Notary Public in and for said County and State, personally appeared JOHN DOE and JANE DOE, as Husband and Wife, personally known to me, (or presented _____ as identification) to be the persons who executed the foregoing Tenancy Agreement, and acknowledged executing the same for the purposes herein contained.

WITNESS my hand and official seal.

_____

Notary Public

My commission expires:

Separate Trusts and Jointly Owned Property

When spouses' joint tenancy property is used to fund each spouse's separate trust, typically a one-half interest in the property is transferred to each trust. Transferring the property to the trust, by itself, should eliminate the survivorship feature and convert the property to tenants in common ownership between the two trusts.

There are two different methods that are used to transfer real property that is held in joint tenancy into separate trusts. One method, which is the more conservative approach, requires three deeds. The first deed transfers each joint tenant's interest in the real property to each owner in tenancy in common. This clearly dissolves the right of survivorship feature. The second and third deeds then transfer each tenant's interest to his or her separate trusts. Figures 11-2 and 11-3 show examples of the first deed, which converts the joint tenancy to tenancy in common and a subsequent deed transferring each tenancy in common interest to the respective separate trusts of each tenant.

The second type of transfer is from jointly held property directly into the name of the trust. Figure 11-4 shows this approach.

Your lawyer will make the decision as to which method is better in your jurisdiction. Real estate is one of the assets that you want your lawyer to transfer to your trust. Even though many assets can be readily transferred into a trust by you or your estate planning advisors, real estate is not one of them. **We caution you to always use a lawyer when attempting to convey title to any real estate interest into your trust.**

Tenancy-by-the-Entirety Property

In view of the preferred status given to tenancy-by-the-entirety property that protects it from the creditors of either individual spouse, you and your spouse may not want to jeopardize this preferred status by transferring the property to a trust. Transfer of property owned as tenants by the entireties to a trust could end the protection from a creditor of either spouse, but this too varies from state to state.

For example, in Missouri there is a court case in which a creditor had an enforceable court judgment against a man. In order to collect on his judgment, the creditor tried to force the sale of some real estate formerly owned by the

Figure 11-2

WARRANTY DEED

JOHN DOE and JANE DOE, husband and wife as joint tenants with right of survivorship, GRANTORS, of Junction County, State of Anywhere, for and in consideration of TEN DOLLARS ($10.00) and other good and valuable consideration, in hand paid, receipt of which is hereby acknowledged, CONVEY AND WARRANT to JOHN DOE and JANE DOE, husband and wife as tenants in common, GRANTEES, whose address is 111 Main Street, Your City, Anywhere, 00001, the following described real estate, situate in the County of Junction, State of Anywhere, hereby waiving and releasing all rights under and by virtue of the homestead exemption laws of the State of Anywhere, to-wit:

Legal Description of Property:

WITNESS our hands on March 11, 1995.

Witnesses as to both parties:

_____   _____
John Doe   Witness

_____   _____
Jane Doe   Witness

STATE OF ANYWHERE   )
) ss.
COUNTY OF JUNCTION   )

On March 11, 1995, before me personally appeared JOHN DOE and JANE DOE, Husband and Wife, known to be the persons described in and who executed the foregoing instrument, and acknowledged that they executed the same as their free act and deed.

WITNESS my hand and official seal.

_____

Notary Public

My commission expires:

Figure 11-3

WARRANTY DEED

JOHN DOE and JANE DOE, husband and wife as tenants in common, GRANTORS, of Junction County, State of Anywhere, for and in consideration of TEN DOLLARS ($10.00) and other good and valuable consideration, in hand paid, receipt of which is hereby acknowledged, CONVEY AND WARRANT to JOHN DOE and JANE DOE, Trustees, or their successors in trust, under the JOHN DOE LIVING TRUST, dated March 11, 1995, and any amendments thereto, as to an undivided one-half (½) interest, and to JANE DOE and JOHN DOE, Trustees, or their successors in trust, under the JANE DOE LIVING TRUST, dated March 11, 1995 and any amendments thereto, as to an undivided one-half (½) interest, GRANTEES, whose address is 111 Main Street, Your City, Anywhere, 00001, the following described real estate, situate in the County of Junction, State of Anywhere, hereby waiving and releasing all rights under and by virtue of the homestead exemption laws of the State of Anywhere, to-wit:

Legal Description of Property:

WITNESS our hands on March 11, 1995.

Witnesses as to both parties:

_____   _____
John Doe   Witness

_____   _____
Jane Doe   Witness

STATE OF ANYWHERE   )
) ss.
COUNTY OF JUNCTION   )

On March 11, 1995, before me personally appeared JOHN DOE and JANE DOE, as Husband and Wife, known to be the persons described in and who executed the foregoing instrument, and acknowledged that they executed the same as their free act and deed.

WITNESS my hand and official seal.

_____
Notary Public

My commission expires:

Figure 11-4

WARRANTY DEED

JOHN DOE and JANE DOE, joint tenants with right of survivorship, GRANTORS, of Junction County, State of Anywhere, for and in consideration of TEN DOLLARS ($10.00) and other good and valuable consideration, in hand paid, receipt of which is hereby acknowledged, CONVEY AND WARRANT to JOHN DOE and JANE DOE, Trustees, or their successors in trust, under the JOHN DOE LIVING TRUST, dated March 11, 1995, and any amendments thereto, as to an undivided one-half (½) interest, and to JANE DOE and JOHN DOE, Trustees, or their successors in trust, under the JANE DOE LIVING TRUST, dated March 11, 1995, and any amendments thereto, as to an undivided one-half (½) interest, GRANTEES, whose address is 111 Main Street, Your City, Anywhere, 00001, the following described real estate, situate in the County of Junction, State of Anywhere, hereby waiving and releasing all rights under and by virtue of the homestead exemption laws of the State of Anywhere, to-wit:

Legal Description of Property:

WITNESS our hands on March 11, 1995.

Witnesses as to both parties:

_____   _____
John Doe   Witness

_____   _____
Jane Doe   Witness

STATE OF ANYWHERE   )
) ss.
COUNTY OF JUNCTION   )

On March 11, 1995, before me personally appeared JOHN DOE and JANE DOE, as Husband and Wife, known to be the persons described in and who executed the foregoing instrument, and acknowledged that they executed the same as their free act and deed.

WITNESS my hand and official seal.

_____
Notary Public

My commission expires:

husband and wife as tenants by the entirety, but which had been transferred to their revocable living trust. The court held that the property was protected because the trust contained special provisions that treated the property as if it were still tenancy-by-the-entirety property.

If creditor protection is important in your planning, tenancy-by-the-entirety property should be treated very carefully. You must talk with your lawyer about the ramifications of making direct transfers of this property into any type of living trust. There are very sophisticated legal techniques that may be used to accomplish this feat, but they are outside the scope of this book and should be left to the legal skills of your lawyer.

Transfers of Community Property to Your Trust

A joint trust rather than separate trusts for each spouse is typically used for holding community property so that the property will retain its character as community property. Notwithstanding the use of a joint trust, community property may be inadvertently converted into tenancy-in-common property or separate property if it is improperly transferred into a joint trust.

Community property transferred to a joint trust will retain its community property status if the trust clearly establishes the following requirements:

- The trust makers' intend that the trust property will continue to be community property.
- All income derived from the community property will be community property.
- If the community property is withdrawn from the trust, it will retain its community property status.

Community property status is an important feature to maintain since community property receives a 100 percent step-up in basis upon the death of the first spouse to die. "Step-up in basis" means that when a person dies, property that is included in his or her estate for federal estate tax purposes gets a new cost basis that is equivalent to its date of death fair market value. For example, if a person bought stock for $1,000 during his or her life and sold it for $5,000, there would be a $4,000 taxable gain. However, if the person died owning the stock and the stock was worth $5,000 when he or she died, the decedent's heirs would receive a new cost basis of $5,000. If the stock was subsequently sold by the heirs for $5,000, there would be no taxable gain.

For property held in tenancy in common between spouses, the surviving spouse only receives a step-up in basis for one-half of the property:

- Joe and Martha bought a commercial lot as an investment. They paid $20,000 for it and titled it in tenancy in common. Joe subsequently died. For federal estate tax purposes, the property was valued at $50,000.
- The cost basis for Martha's half of the property (which was not included in Joe's estate) is $10,000, representing one-half of the original cost of the lot. The stepped-up basis for the half that was included in Joe's estate is $25,000, one-half of its federal estate tax value. By adding the original cost basis of Martha's half of the property—$10,000—and the stepped-up basis of Joe's half of the lot—$25,000—we see that Martha's new cost basis in the property is $35,000.
- If Martha sells the property for $50,000, her taxable gain is $15,000 ($50,000 minus her $35,000 basis).

The result is far different for community property. Upon the death of the first spouse, all community property receives a 100 percent step-up in basis even though only one-half of the property is included in the deceased spouse's estate. Contrast the following example to the example earlier for tenancy in common property.

- Joe and Martha bought a commercial lot as an investment in a community property state. They paid $20,000 for it and titled it in both of their names. Joe subsequently died. For federal estate tax purposes, the property was valued at $50,000, even though only half of it was included in his estate for federal estate tax purposes.
- Martha's new cost basis in the property is $50,000. If Martha sells the property for $50,000, she has no taxable gain.

It is important to retain this 100 percent step-up in basis benefit. Inadvertently severing the community property when funding a trust will eliminate this important tax benefit. If, in the example just given, the community property is improperly transferred to a living trust, converting it into tenancy in common rather than community property, only one-half of the property would receive a date-of-death step-up in basis. This action would result in a *$15,000 taxable gain*.

As is readily apparent, the specific terms of a properly drafted joint trust must state that any community property transferred to the joint trust shall remain community property. Additionally, the trust agreement should state that the proceeds from the sale of any joint trust community property continue to be community property.

It is prudent for both spouses to enter into a community property agreement prior to funding a joint trust. This agreement should clearly explain that the spouses' intent is not to sever the community property, but to retain its character as community property. For a sample of this type of document see Figure 11-5, Community Property Agreement.

Choosing a Joint Trust or a Separate Trust

If you live in a community property state and all of your property is community property, a joint trust is the most commonly accepted way to plan. It is easy and convenient, and does not create a great deal of change in ownership, at least conceptually. The primary reason that a joint trust would not be used by a married couple in a community property state is if one or both spouses have a considerable amount of sole and separate property. In order to keep that property sole and separate, separate trusts would make much more sense.

For those who live in the other forty-one states, separate trusts are customarily and almost always used. However, there are several reasons why a joint trust may be superior to a separate trust even in these states. If a married couple owns all of their property in joint tenancy, tenancy by the entirety, or tenancy in common, a joint trust makes all the sense in the world. Why separate property that spouses consider to be owned equally by each other? A joint trust is not only better psychologically, it is easier to understand and fund. A joint trust can also be used when a married couple owns property in many different ways, but they believe that this property is really owned equally. This occurs in many marriages in which no particular attention has been paid to how title is owned so that some property is owned jointly, some is owned by the wife, and some is owned by the husband. If the intent for equal ownership is there, then a joint trust is the way to go.

Some companies that sell living trusts use joint trusts as a matter of course. These boilerplate forms are almost invariably drafted incorrectly and so create unnecessary federal gift and estate tax problems for gullible and unsuspecting couples who may have taxable estates. If you have one of these plans, it is imperative that you immediately have it reviewed by a competent estate planning attorney. Failure to do so may result in catastrophic tax consequences on the death of either spouse.

Figure 11-5

COMMUNITY PROPERTY AGREEMENT

This Community Property Agreement is entered into on March 11, 1995, in the County of Junction, State of Anywhere, by and between:

JOHN DOE
and
JANE DOE

FACTUAL SUMMARY

Husband and Wife were married on June 6, 1965, and since that date have acquired title to property as joint tenants with right of survivorship.

Husband and Wife have created an estate plan using a revocable living trust and companion Pour-Over Wills.

Husband and Wife wish to convert their joint tenancy property to a form of ownership that will give each of them control over their respective property interest on each of their deaths.

Husband and Wife are aware that they may by agreement convert their joint tenancy assets to either tenancy in common or community property, and that either of those two forms of ownership will allow them to control their respective interests in the property on each of their deaths.

Husband and Wife understand that the main benefit of choosing community property is that on the death of either spouse, the entire community property interest will receive a step-up in basis rather than a 50 percent step-up in basis under tenancy in common.

AGREEMENT TO CHANGE JOINT TENANCY ASSETS TO COMMUNITY PROPERTY

Husband and Wife hereby grant, convey, and transfer their respective interests in their joint tenancy property to themselves as community property.

Husband and Wife intend this agreement to be binding on themselves and on all others as to property held in joint tenancy with right of survivorship as of the date of this agreement regardless of the manner or form of the written title.

(continued on following page)

The parties have executed this agreement the day and year first written above.

Witnesses as to both:

_____   _____
John Doe   Witness

_____   _____
Jane Doe   Witness

STATE OF ANYWHERE   )
)   ss.
COUNTY OF JUNCTION   )

   On March 11, 1995, before me, the undersigned Notary Public, in and for said County and State, personally appeared JOHN DOE and JANE DOE, personally known to me, (or presented _____ as identification) to be the person who executed the foregoing instrument, and acknowledged executing the same for the purposes herein contained.

WITNESS my hand and official seal.

_____
Notary Public

My commission expires:

   We must caution you that your lawyer should counsel you on whether it is better for you to have a joint trust or a separate trust. An improperly drafted joint trust or a joint trust that is funded with some property from each spouse that is not equal in value may create gift and estate tax nightmares.

· 12 ·

Methods of Funding

This chapter provides a broad overview of the various methods available for funding a living trust. It also has examples of general transfer forms for these funding methods. In subsequent chapters, we discuss which of these methods can and should be used with specific types of property, and who should be responsible for funding those assets into your trust.

We cannot stress enough the importance of coordinating your funding process with both your lawyer and your other advisors. Directly ask your lawyer which assets he or she would prefer to transfer to your trust and which assets can be responsibly delegated to your other advisors or to you.

How Does a Trust Take Title to Property?

Most of the time, the title to your assets will be held directly in the name of your trust. However, there are different funding methods that can be used other than funding property directly in the name of your trust. There is not necessarily a single best method to use when funding your trust. Often it is more convenient or more practical to combine several funding methods. In order to make the correct funding decision, it would be helpful if you understand the arsenal of different funding methods available to you so that you can pick the one that is best under the circumstances for each particular asset. Your lawyer can also give you advice about which funding method best fits you.

Some of the funding methods in this chapter are conventional in nature; they are tried and true and can be used without confusion or risk. Other methods are less conventional either because they are relatively new and innovative or because they are not readily accepted in some jurisdictions.

Whenever you have heirs who may want to contest the way you leave property at your death, or if you have significant creditors, conventional funding methods should generally be used. Funding a trust using a conventional method assures that the assets will be treated as trust property in all circumstances. If a creditor or disgruntled heir successfully defeats an unconventional method of funding, the asset in question will typically be subject to the probate process. In probate, the asset will ultimately be transferred to the living trust because of the Pour-Over Will. However, when the asset is in probate, it is subject to creditor claims and may be reached by your heirs in a will contest.

You and your lawyer should select the best funding method for your particular situation, based on the type of asset, local law governing property transfers, and your special needs. Prior to using an unconventional funding method, you should ask your lawyer to explain the potential problems if the funding method is later contested by a creditor or unhappy heir.

Always remember that funding is not a rote process that should be left to chance. It should be accomplished with every bit of the professionalism and care that was put into the design, creation, and execution of your living trust–centered estate plan. Neglecting to fund your living trust will ultimately result in probate fees on your disability or death and the delay and aggravation that go along with the probate process.

Holding Title Directly in the Name of Your Trust

The most conventional approach and best assurance that a living trust will control your property is to place title to property directly in the name of the trust. This method of funding is done in several ways depending on the jurisdiction in which the assets are situated and the type of assets to be transferred into the trust.

Title in the Name of the Trustee

Strictly speaking, a living trust is not a separate entity that has the capacity to hold title to assets. The trustee of a living trust takes title in its capacity as trustee. The "trustee" designation following the trustee's name identifies the fact that the trustee is holding title on the behalf of trust beneficiaries. Title taken in the name of the trustee generally appears as follows:

JOHN DOE and JANE DOE, Trustees, or their successors in trust, under the JOHN DOE LIVING TRUST, dated March 11, 1995, and any amendments thereto.

This wording almost always assures that local laws governing how trustees must hold title have been satisfied.

Such a lengthy designation of ownership can be cumbersome. In fact, in some instances a brokerage firm or other entity will shorten this title to something like this:

> *JOHN and JANE DOE, Trustees, U/A dated March 11, 1995.*

Generally, this form of title designation is sufficient for purposes of holding title in the name of a trust because it identifies the current trustees and refers to the particular trust document. The "U/A" in this form of title stands for "Under Agreement." This tells the world that the trustees are serving subject to a particular trust instrument. You will find that with the advent of the computer age, many computer systems have a limited number of characters that can be entered. This is particularly true of motor vehicle title registration with the Department of Motor Vehicles and other government agencies, where it may be necessary to use this short-form title designation.

Sometimes attorneys shorten a trust's name to:

> *The JOHN DOE LIVING TRUST dated March 11, 1995.*

This "shorthand" designation is primarily appropriate for informal use, such as referring to the trust in correspondence. However, it may be sufficient for title holding for personal property. Whether this short form can be used to identify the trust for purposes of title to other assets usually depends on state law. In some states, a trust is regarded as a separate and distinct entity for purposes of owning property; in these states, this short form may be sufficient for purposes of holding title. In many states, however, a trust is regarded as a *relationship or contract*, and property must be owned in the name of the "trustee" or "trustees." Where this is the case, using the short form for purposes of title holding may not be sufficient. In general, it is better to use the long form of trust title, placing property in the name of the trustees and their successors.

Establishing the Authority of the Trustee

When property is titled in the name of a trust, third parties dealing with the trust will sometimes seek assurance that the trustee has the power and authority to deal with the trust property. In this case, the objective is to reassure the third party without disclosing private provisions of the trust. This disclosure problem occurs most frequently when you attempt to change your bank account to the name of your trust, when you go to your stockbroker and change your brokerage account into your trust's name, or when you change title of real estate into the name of your trust and you notify the mortgage holder of the change.

Twenty-six states have adopted laws that provide that a third party need not inquire into the authority of a trustee to transfer trust property. These states are Arizona, California, Colorado, Florida, Hawaii, Idaho, Illinois, Indiana, Kansas, Kentucky, Louisiana, Maine, Maryland, Mississippi, Missouri, Montana, Nebraska, New Hampshire, New Jersey, New Mexico, Oklahoma, Oregon, Tennessee, Texas, Utah, and Wyoming.

Your lawyer should be familiar with your state's position on how third parties view trustees acting on behalf of a trust. Your lawyer can then counsel you about how to respond to any third party who is reluctant to cooperate with a trustee for fear of incurring liability. Many times, making reference to a law that permits a trustee to act without further inquiry will end the need for the third party to see your trust document.

Affidavit of Trust

Occasionally, a bank, stockbrokerage firm, or other third party may ask to see a copy of your trust before they will transfer the title of an asset to it. This is because they want to make sure that there is a trust in existence, and that its trustees have the power to deal with the account's assets.

In our experience, there is almost never a necessity to show them the whole trust. After all, it's your trust with your private instructions in it, and its provisions should remain confidential. One way you can avoid showing the whole trust to these third parties is to use an Affidavit of Trust. An Affidavit of Trust —which should be prepared by your lawyer as part of your living trust planning—does not reveal private information regarding the disposition of trust property. The affidavit contains only the information relevant to the concerns of third parties. This information includes:

- The names of the trustees
- The trustees' powers over trust property
- Evidence the trust has been properly signed
- Provisions appointing successor trustees

Form 1201 in the Appendix is a sample Affidavit of Trust.

Attorney's Certificate

The Attorney's Certificate is similar to an Affidavit of Trust, and is another means of proving the existence of the trust and the authority of the Trustees. Form 1202 is an example of an Attorney's Certificate.

The difference between an Affidavit of Trust and an Attorney's Certificate is that your attorney, rather than the trustees, declares, under penalty of perjury, the accuracy of the trust information found in the affidavit. Occasionally, when a third party seeks assurances regarding the trust's existence and trustees' authority, a certification from a lawyer carries more weight than assurances from layman trustees, especially when the trust maker is acting as a trustee.

Surviving or Successor Trustees

A trustee's duties may end due to death, termination, disability, or resignation. When a surviving or successor trustee is acting, third parties may want to establish the continuing existence of the trust and the successor trustee's legitimacy.

A successor trustee can establish its authority through an Affidavit of Successor Trustee. Your lawyer should prepare an Affidavit of Successor Trustee that sets out the facts and circumstances leading to the change in trustees. This affidavit should refer to the trust provisions that name the successor trustees, and should state the circumstances in which a successor trustee is to be named. Documentation should be attached which demonstrates that the conditions have taken place.

When a successor trustee is serving as a result of the resignation or termination of a previous trustee, a letter of resignation or termination should be attached to the affidavit. If the change in trustees is due to the death of a trustee, a certified copy of the trustee's death certificate should be attached. Form 1203 in the Appendix is an example of an Affidavit of Successor Trustee.

Alternatives to Placing Assets Directly in the Name of the Trust

In some instances, placing legal title in the name of the trustee is not convenient or may, in rare circumstances, require disclosing the dispositive terms of the trust. Local title standards for real estate and statutes dealing with conveyancing may require recording the trust document when title to property is held in the name of a trustee. If this occurs, it eliminates the privacy of your trust agreement. However, this problem can be avoided if legal title is not placed directly in the name of the trustees.

There are several acceptable and easy-to-arrange methods of placing property in a trust other than placing title in the name of the trustees. The concept of a nominee has been a long-standing practice to achieve nondisclosure of the trust and to facilitate the ability of the trustees to engage in commerce with trust assets.

The term *nominee* is another word for "agent." When a nominee arrangement is used, title to trust assets are titled in the name of an entity or person other than the trustees. The nominee, as holder of title, agrees in a separate and private document that the nominee will hold the property on behalf of the trust. This agreement is not disclosed, so parties dealing with the nominee do not know they are really dealing with trust assets.

The Nominee Partnership

The Nominee Partnership is the more commonly used entity for holding title to trust assets. It is an entity created solely to hold title to trust property and to act as an undisclosed agent for the trustees of a living trust. A Nominee Partnership is used so that the trustees do not have to disclose the existence of a trust or its terms. Such an arrangement facilitates commerce because most third parties are more familiar with partnerships than with trusts and find it easier to deal with the partnership concept.

The genesis of the Nominee Partnership concept comes from the financial industry. Full-service financial institutions and commercial banks have traditionally created nominee devices by which they administer client accounts. When an institution invests on behalf of its trust accounts, it transacts its trust business in the name of a nominee rather than in the specific names of the various trusts. The use of a nominee simplifies the transactions and eliminates paperwork and overhead.

A Nominee Partnership is not a true partnership because it has no capital. It is, in reality, no more than an agency agreement that is called a partnership.

The Nominee Partnership has the following advantages:

- It simplifies financial transactions and property transfers by using a partnership to hold title to trust assets.
- The trust is not disclosed, eliminating the need to record the trust or show the trust provisions to third parties who have no reason to know about the trust's terms.
- It permits the division of a single asset, such as a ranch, between two or more separate trusts without having to have each trust own a part of the property.
- It equalizes the assets of the separate trusts of a husband and wife for estate tax planning purposes; an undivided one-half interest is managed for each trust.

A Nominee Partnership has a potential disadvantage. Because a Nominee Partnership holds itself out as being an actual partnership, it entitles third parties to treat it as a partnership, which raises potential partnership liability issues between the nominee partners. If one of the partners becomes insolvent or has a judgment against him or her, it is possible that the trust assets held in the name of the nominee will be subject to the claims of creditors. However, in our experience, this is a theoretical argument; we have no knowledge of this actually taking place.

The documents necessary for nominee ownership include a Nominee Partnership Agreement and a Nominee Agreement. A Nominee Partnership must have:

- At least two partners
- A partnership agreement reciting the purposes of the partnership, which is chiefly to hold title to property for the trust
- A partnership agreement that provides for succession of partners if one is disabled, dies, or can no longer serve for any other reason
- Its own Federal Tax Identification Number
- No capital of its own
- A purpose that is not entered into for profit

The partners of a Nominee Partnership are always the trustees of the revocable living trust. Married couples can each have a nominee for their respective trusts or they can use a single nominee that serves their joint trust. There always will be a Nominee Agreement between the partnership and each trust for which it holds assets.

If a title company or other third party requires recording of the partnership, then either a trade name affidavit, fictitious name certificate (as appropriate under state law), or the Nominee Partnership agreement will be sufficient.

Various states have different requirements for drafting partnerships and for creating agency relationships. If your lawyer determines that a Nominee Partnership is right for you, then make sure that your lawyer drafts the documents.

A Nominee Partnership is not engaged in a trade or business if it acts as an agent for a trust or trusts to hold title to property and collect income on behalf of the trusts. The partnership is not taxed on income; the maker of the living trust is generally responsible for all income, deductions, and credits. For these reasons, a Nominee Partnership does not file its own tax return. Nonetheless, a Nominee Partnership must have a separate Federal Tax Identification Number. The partners must file a federal income tax informational return for all income paid to the trust.

At least three states—Arizona, New York, and Louisiana—have some restrictions on the use of nominees for purposes of holding title to a trust. Because of the complexities of nominee ownership, it is always necessary to consult with your lawyer and your accountant before using a Nominee Partnership. Your lawyer can draft a Nominee Partnership and Nominee Agreement that fit your situation and meet the requirements of your state's laws.

The Nominee Corporation

Corporations should not be used as a nominee for a trust. Even though it is possible for a corporation to act as a nominee, there are many potential income tax pitfalls that make this alternative inappropriate when compared to other far safer alternatives. Stay away from the nominee corporation unless you are interested in lots of paperwork and potentially adverse income tax results.

Land Trusts

A land trust makes an excellent funding vehicle for a living trust, especially for interests in real property. The most widely used type of land trust is called the Illinois Land Trust, not because you can use it only in Illinois, but because that is where it was first used.

The Illinois Land Trust is a special trust that is designed to hold title to all types of property without disclosing the beneficiaries of the trust. In an Illinois Land Trust, property is conveyed to a trustee under a written trust agreement in which the trust beneficiaries maintain full power over the property, including the right to use it in any manner they want. At least one state—Massachusetts—requires that a land trust be recorded. For the most part, the other states do not require that the trust be recorded. Even if the land trust is recorded, there is no requirement to disclose the beneficiaries, making their identity fully confidential.

Land trusts are relatively well known by people who deal in real estate. They have long been used by developers who do not want their identities known as they acquire property. Because land trusts are well known, third parties dealing with them, including title companies, readily accept them without needing to know who the beneficiaries are.

When used in estate planning, the beneficiary of the land trust is the living trust. Ordinarily, the living trust's maker is the trustee of the land trust. All of the maker's property, real and personal, can be placed in a land trust. Since the living trust is not disclosed as the beneficiary, the trustee can freely deal with the property in the land trust without the inconvenience or trouble of having to disclose the living trust or explain its existence.

Another advantage of using the land trust in the context of living trust planning is that one land trust can be used for more than one living trust. If you and your spouse each have a separate trust, both trusts can be the beneficiaries of a single land trust, even though the value of your trusts may differ. If only one land trust is used, then it is easier to fund the trust because only one transfer is needed. For example, if you and your spouse own real estate in both of your names and you have separate trusts, that real estate can be put in the name of the land trust.

An Illinois Land Trust is, in many respects, similar to a Nominee Partnership. It is used to keep a living trust confidential so that third parties who have no need to know how you have planned your estate have no right to see your trust planning. But because a land trust is such a specialized document, we have not included one in this workbook. For more information about a land trust, you must consult with your lawyer.

The "Magic Wand" of Frederick Keydel

The Magic Wand is an alternative to a Nominee Partnership. This type of trust ownership is new and untested. You should only use it with the advice of your attorney. This retains the convenience of joint ownership while at the same time transferring property into a living trust. It is a device that can be used by married couples for their joint tenancy property when both spouses are trustees of their respective individual trusts or of a joint trust created by both of them. The innovator of this method of title holding, Frederick Keydel, a well-known estate planning attorney, refers to the Magic Wand as "joint tenancy undisclosed title holding."

To create Magic Wand ownership, four things are required:

- The husband and wife must be trustees of each of their individual revocable trusts or trustees of their joint trust.
- Their individual trusts or joint trust must authorize the trustees to hold title to trust property in their individual names without disclosing their capacity as trustees.
- The husband and wife must sign a document stating that all of the property held in their joint names belongs to their respective living trusts equally, or in whatever proportion they wish. An example of this declaration is found in Figure 12-1.
- The husband and wife must title all property to which they wish the agreement to apply in their names as joint property.

Figure 12-1

THIS FORM MUST BE TAILORED TO CONFORM WITH THE RECORDING REQUIREMENTS OF YOUR PARTICULAR STATE.

JOINT DECLARATION OF TRUST OWNERSHIP

The undersigned hereby declare that, solely as the Trustees of:

JOHN DOE and JANE DOE, Trustees, or their successors in trust, under the JOHN DOE LIVING TRUST, dated March 11, 1995, and any amendments thereto; and

JANE DOE and JOHN DOE, Trustees, or their successors in trust, under the JANE DOE LIVING TRUST, dated March 11, 1995, and any amendments thereto,

they are, pursuant to the applicable provisions of each trust, holding and will hold solely exclusively for and in behalf of each trust, having an undivided one-half share as tenants in common, the following:

Any and all properties of all kinds, whether presently owned or hereafter acquired (regardless of the means by which acquired), including without limitation, all cash, checking and savings accounts, money market accounts, certificates of deposit, notes receivable, bonds, stocks, real estate, partnership interests, furniture, household furnishings, automobiles, and any other personal property of whatever nature

which now and at any time after the date of this instrument are registered in their joint names with right of survivorship or in their names as tenants by the entireties (whether that survivorship or entireties aspect is specifically mentioned in the title or is implied in law by the circumstances and regardless of whatever variation of their names may be employed).

The undersigned hereby further affirm and declare that, from and after the date hereof:

1. All properties of any kind appearing to be owned by them jointly or by the entireties are in fact held and will be held by them solely and exclusively for and in behalf of said trusts as true owners (subject to any and all instructions from the then Trustee(s) of said trusts);

2. They will not hold title to any such properties in their joint names or as tenants by the entireties except those which in fact belong to said trusts;

3. Any and all properties now or hereafter held by them in their names as joint or entireties properties shall and will belong to said trusts and not to the undersigned or either of them individually;

4. Except to the extent of beneficial interests provided to them under the terms and provisions of said trust agreements (as now written and as the same may in the future be amended), they have and shall have no personal interest in any such properties now or hereafter held in their joint or entireties names; and

(continued on following page)

5. All liabilities which relate in any way to the acquisition of or which are a lien upon any of the properties governed by this declaration, whether such liabilities are in the name of either or both of the undersigned, shall be borne by the two trusts which thus own such properties as tenants in common in the same proportions as they own such properties.

This declaration of exclusive trust ownership and waiver of interest is intended to be and shall be binding upon the undersigned's heirs, administrators, executors, and assigns and shall be revocable only by written instrument executed by one or more of the then Trustee(s) of either of said trusts (with or without indicating such fiduciary capacity) with all of the same formalities as accompanied the execution of this instrument.

This declaration is intended to revoke all prior declarations of ownership, if any, with respect to any and all properties governed by this declaration, whether executed by either or both of the undersigned.

Dated March 11, 1995.

_____

John Doe, Trustee

_____

Jane Doe, Trustee

Witnesses as to both:

_____

, Witness

_____

, Witness

STATE OF ANYWHERE	)
	) ss.
COUNTY OF JUNCTION	)

On March 11, 1995, before me, the undersigned Notary Public in and for said County and State, personally appeared JOHN DOE and JANE DOE, as Trustees, personally known to me (or presented _____ as identification) to be the persons who executed the foregoing Affidavit of Trust, and acknowledged executing the same for purposes herein contained.

WITNESS my hand and official seal.

_____

, Notary Public

My commission expires:

The advantages of Magic Wand title holding include:

- Joint property is converted to trust property without changing the record title to assets (except to place them in joint tenancy, if necessary).
- Joint property is legally converted to trust property without disclosing the existence of the trust.
- Joint ownership and its disadvantages are eliminated.
- Trust property is owned in a form of title that is familiar and comfortable for a husband and wife.
- Ownership of trust property can be in whatever proportion is appropriate, depending on the estate planning needs of the spouses.
- Upon the death of one of the joint tenants, the survivor holds record title even though the property is beneficially owned in trust; probate or disclosure of trust ownership is unnecessary.

Care must be taken when using the Magic Wand technique. For example, most transactions by joint owners require the signature of both of them. If it is necessary for one joint owner to carry out certain transactions unilaterally, a Joint Property Durable Power of Attorney that authorizes each joint owner to sign all joint property documents in his or her behalf in connection with all joint property transactions can be used. Form 1204 in the Appendix is an example of this kind of power of attorney.

It is very important that your lawyer makes sure that the joint tenancy wording is correct for real property held by you and your spouse in other states. Some states do not have joint and survivor ownership—for example, Louisiana; other states require special wording or recording of documentation disclosing the survivorship interest. Also, the trust itself *must* authorize the trustee to hold title to trust property without disclosing his or her fiduciary capacity.

After both joint tenants are deceased, the declaration itself is recorded to establish trust ownership and avoid probate. There are no income tax reporting requirements for the Magic Wand title-holding concept. The Internal Revenue Service recognizes and accepts this form of trust ownership. When the joint tenants are the co-trustees and co-trust makers, all income, deductions, and credits are reported on the couple's joint Form 1040 tax return, the same as if the trust held title directly. We must emphasize that this technique is new. You should be very careful in its use.

Payable-on-Death Accounts and Postmortem Assignments

In some states, a living trust can control some types of property upon your death even though the property was not owned by your trust while you were living. This is accomplished with a Payable-on-Death (POD) Account designation for financial assets, and with a Postmortem Assignment for other types of assets. A trust can control a very wide variety of property through Payable-on-Death Account designations where authorized by law.

Payable-on-Death Accounts

In at least half of the states, financial institution accounts such as checking, savings and share accounts, and certificates of deposit can designate a payee on death. If a living trust is named the POD beneficiary, when the owner dies the account proceeds pass automatically to the trust, bypassing the probate process. A POD designation is a simple method of transferring accounts to a trust at death. Generally speaking, a notation is made directly on the signature card or account agreement that states that the account is payable on death to a named beneficiary. An example of the language on the account is "Payable on death to John and Jane Doe, Trustees, U/A dated March 11, 1995." A serious drawback of a POD designation is that it does not provide for management of property during your disability. If POD designations are used to fund a trust, it is imperative that a Durable Special Power of Attorney is prepared to control the trust maker's property upon disability. We explain the Durable Special Power of Attorney later in this chapter.

Postmortem Assignments

Postmortem Assignments are sometimes used in lieu of POD designations, especially in those states that do not recognize PODs. They are used so that the title to certain types of property, including some types of financial accounts, contract rights to receive money, or benefits such as bonds, mortgages, promissory notes, retirement plans, insurance policies, and other third-party beneficiary contracts can be retained in the name of the trust maker during life, with the title or ownership documents providing for the property to be transferred directly into the trust upon his or her death. A Postmortem Assignment is viewed by some attorneys as a more convenient method for transferring these assets to a revocable living trust.

This method of transfer also has its drawbacks. The assignment might be contested, the form might be lost, or the individual in charge of the assignment might fail to act on instructions. Additionally, some institutions may not recognize Postmortem Assignments; an example is the New York Stock Exchange. Just like the POD designation, the Postmortem Assignment is not effective upon the maker's disability. A Durable Special Power of Attorney must be used in conjunction with a Postmortem Assignment. Form 1205 is an example of a Postmortem Assignment.

Transfer on Death of Securities

In a few states, statutes authorize registration of securities with a transfer-on-death designation. The Uniform Transfer on Death Security Registration Act (TOD Security Act) has been adopted by at least two states, Colorado and Wisconsin.

Some companies allow transfer-on-death registration of their stock without the necessity of probate. For example, Southwestern Bell Corporation has a transfer-on-death registration in which the company contracts with the stockholder to transfer the shares to named beneficiaries upon the death of the stockholder. The TOD registration contract selects Missouri Law to apply and accepts TOD directives from residents of Alaska, Arizona, California, Colorado, Idaho, Indiana, Kentucky, Maine, Missouri, Montana, Nebraska, New Mexico, North Dakota, South Carolina, Texas, Utah, Washington, and other states that have certain statutes that allow Postmortem Assignments.

If you are considering the use of TOD securities registration, ask your lawyer if it is an option available to you either under your state law, or directly through the companies in which you are a stockholder.

"Fail-Safe" Techniques

The unfortunate truth is that, in some instances, a trust is not fully funded when the trust maker becomes disabled or dies. We must recognize this fact of life and attempt to use planning that takes into account that people act like people and do not always do the correct thing. There are some so-called "fail-safe" planning techniques that ought to be a part of every living trust–centered plan.

Durable Special Powers of Attorney for Funding

A Durable Special Power of Attorney for Funding is a deviation from a standard Durable Power of Attorney. A standard Durable Power of Attorney usually has very broad powers that allow its agent to act on your behalf under almost all circumstances. In contrast, a Durable Special Power of Attorney for Funding restricts your agent's authority to those powers necessary to fund your living trust. Why? Because all of your instructions are in your trust where they belong. The agent cannot use your property in any manner your agent sees fit. Only your trustee can use your property, and then only subject to your trust instructions.

The Durable Special Power of Attorney for Funding is a fail-safe device in that, upon your disability, any property that has not already been transferred into your trust can then be transferred into your trust by your agent. All states allow Durable Power of Attorney to remain valid even after the incapacity of the principal.

An example of a Durable Special Power of Attorney for Funding is found in Form 1206. **Your lawyer must determine that the Durable Special Power of Attorney for Funding complies with your particular state law requirements for Durable Power of Attorney.**

Simplified Probate for Small Estates

Some states offer a special type of probate procedure called an informal or simplified probate. Informal probate has been suggested as an available fail-safe mechanism upon the death of the trust maker for small amounts of property that have been inadvertently left out of his or her trust. Some attorneys believe that informal probate procedures may be used to easily transfer property to a trust or directly to beneficiaries.

This is not an option in every state. It is not uncommon for a state to allow informal probate procedures only when the total value of all the decedent's assets, both nonprobate and probate, is under the statutory limit. Ask your lawyer whether your state law has a small estates procedures act, and, if so, whether it will be available to remedy omissions in funding.

As you can see, there are a lot of different funding methods available. Which method is best for you is based on how you now hold title to assets, what kinds of assets you own, your level of comfort, your family situation, the state in which you live, and the states in which you own property.

In the chapters that follow, we discuss virtually every type of asset and property. We then explain to you who is qualified to transfer this property to your trust, and what funding methods are commonly used for funding this type of asset. This information will allow you, along with your professional team, to determine who is going to take responsibility for funding each asset and which funding method is best for titling the asset in the name of your trust.

·13·

Bank Accounts and Certificates of Deposit

Establishing or changing a bank or other cash account to a trust account is accomplished in much the same way as opening a new account. For an existing account, a new signature card is required in the name of the trust, with the trustees as the authorized signers. A new account can be opened in the name of the trust by filling out an account agreement and a new signature card. The trustees of the living trust are named as the authorized signers.

Checking and Savings Accounts

It is generally advisable to transfer all checking and savings accounts into the name of your living trust. If you are married and you have joint accounts, some lawyers advise that you keep one account in joint tenancy. This joint account should not hold any more than a few thousand dollars at the most. It can be used as a convenient operating account. If possible, we recommend that you change all of your accounts to trust accounts. The drawback of having even one joint account is that under certain circumstances where both joint tenants are incapacitated, one joint tenant is incapacitated, or both joint tenants die, the account may be subject to a financial guardianship, probate, or both.

If you have a joint trust, then there is no question that all accounts should be in the trust's name. If you and your spouse have separate trusts, then each of you should have separate trust accounts. If this is not convenient, then you should open up one account as an operating account in the name of one of the trusts, but give each of you authority to withdraw funds as a trustee. Sometimes it is difficult to determine how to split up accounts to make each spouse comfortable. Your lawyer can recommend how this can be done. If splitting the accounts is difficult, you may want to open an account that shows each of your trusts as a tenant-in-common owner of one-half of the account. In this way, each trust owns half the account and either one of you, as trustee, can make withdrawals.

Title to your checking and savings accounts can be transferred to the name of your trust in person or by mail. The only materials that you need are signature cards and, depending on the institution you are dealing with, maybe a new account agreement. These can be mailed to you; then you can sign them and send them back.

We have provided form letters that you can use in requesting your bank or other financial institution to change your account to the name of your trust. To change a joint account between you and your spouse to a Joint Trust account, use Form 1301 in the Appendix. Use Form 1302 to transfer your joint account to a tenancy-in-common account owned by your trust and your spouse's trust. To transfer your individual account to your living trust, use Form 1303.

Checks for your trust accounts can list your trust's name or they can show the names of the people who have signature authority, usually the original trustees. If you are single, only your name would be on the check. If you are married, typically your name and your spouse's name would appear on the check, most probably in the same manner as they appear now.

Most people prefer not showing the trust's name on their checks for purposes of privacy and convenience. Frankly, it doesn't make much sense to put your trust's name on your checks, as it seems to just pique other people's curiosity. In fact, you may find that on occasion, someone may even be reluctant to take your check.

When you open accounts in the name of your trust, you will be faced with a decision. Some financial institutions may insist that you open a new account in the name of your trust and close your existing account. Others will be more than happy to change your existing account to a trust account by simply changing the information on the original signature card account number. If possible, try to keep your existing account. It provides continuity and does not require new checks or a new account number. The drawback of opening a new account is that you have to have new checks. And you must be careful that you don't close your old account before all of the outstanding checks clear. One problem that we have seen innumerable times is that even though the bank has instructions that outstanding old checks drawn on the old account are to be honored, they often aren't. It's embarrassing and very inconvenient to have to explain those bounced checks!

A sample of institution account agreements and how they should be completed by the institution are contained in Figure 13-1 for an individual trust and Figure 13-2 for a joint trust.

Credit unions are generally much more difficult to deal with than other institutions when it comes to opening up new accounts or changing existing accounts to the name of a trust. This difficulty does not arise because credit unions want to avoid trust accounts; sometimes, by law or their own charters, they simply cannot have trust accounts. Many times, credit unions are only allowed to have accounts for natural persons or certain entities like partnerships. If you have credit union accounts, you may wish to use a Nominee Partnership as the account owner. This form of ownership will probably be accepted by your credit union and will result in your trust controlling the account and avoiding probate. See Chapter Eleven, "The Different Types of Revocable Living Trusts," for more on the Nominee Partnership.

If you are married, you can also use the Magic Wand technique of holding title to a credit union account. This method is very effective for use with credit unions because the account—for purposes of the credit union's bookkeeping and reporting purposes—is held in joint tenancy between the trustees.

Money Market Accounts

Money market accounts are changed to trust ownership in exactly the same manner as a checking account. For most purposes, the two are treated in the same manner.

Certificates of Deposit

Prior to transferring your certificates of deposit to your living trust, you must determine whether to wait until the account matures before transferring it to the name of the trust in order to avoid possible interest penalties for early withdrawal. You should check with a bank officer about regulations concerning your account to determine whether a transfer of your certificate of deposit to the name of your trust is an event that causes withdrawal penalties. If there are no penalties, then a change of ownership is generally accomplished in the same manner as with a checking or savings account.

If it is necessary to wait for the certificate to mature before titling it in the name of the trust, then the certificate's title should be transferred into the trust.

Figure 13-1

CONSUMER ACCOUNT AGREEMENT

ENTERPRISE NATIONAL BANK
OF SARASOTA

OWNERSHIP OF ACCOUNT	
☐ INDIVIDUAL	DATE OF BIRTH __00/00/94__
☐ JOINT - WITH SURVIVORSHIP (and not as tenants in common)	HOME PHONE __813/000-0000__
☐ JOINT - NO SURVIVORSHIP (as tenants in common)	DATE OPENED __00/00/95__
☐ _____	OPENED BY _____
☒ TRUST - SEPARATE AGREEMENT:	INITIAL DEPOSIT $ __0000__
☐ REVOCABLE TRUST DESIGNATION AS DEFINED IN THIS AGREEMENT. Name and Address of Beneficiaries:	FORM: ☐ CASH ☒ __CHECK__
	PREVIOUS BANK __BARNETT__
	EMPLOYER _____
	ADDRESS _____
	TEL # __813/000-0000__
	LENGTH OF EMPLOYMENT _____

Form of Identification: _____ **DLN** _____

Name and address of someone who will always know your location. _____

All New Accounts will be verified through: _____

ADDITIONAL INFORMATION:

TYPE OF ACCOUNT	☒ NEW ☐ EXISTING	☒ CHECKING ☐ SAVINGS ☐	☐ MONEY MARKET	☐ TIME DEPOSIT	☐ NOW

ACCOUNT NAME: _____ **THE CLUB ACCOUNT** _____

(continued on following page)

ACCOUNT OWNER NAME & ADDRESS
JOHN DOE, TTEE
JANE DOE, TTEE
OR THEIR SUCCESSORS IN TRUST, UNDER
THE JOHN DOE LIVING TR., DATED 3/11/95
111 MAIN STREET
YOUR CITY, ANYWHERE 00001

ACCOUNT NUMBER   1234567

NUMBER OF SIGNATURES
REQUIRED FOR WITHDRAWAL ___1___

☐ This is a Temporary account agreement.

SIGNATURE(S) - THE UNDERSIGNED AGREE(S) TO THE TERMS STATED ON PAGES 1 AND 2 OF THIS AGREEMENT, AND ACKNOWLEDGE(S) RECEIPT OF A COMPLETED COPY ON TODAY'S DATE. THE UNDERSIGNED ALSO ACKNOWLEDGE(S) RECEIPT OF A COPY OF AND AGREE(S) TO THE TERMS OF THE FOLLOWING DISCLOSURE(S):

☒ Funds Availability Disclosure   ☐ _____

☒ Electronic Funds Transfer Disclosure   ☒ Truth in Savings Disclosure

(1): x ✓
_____
      JOHN DOE, TTEE

(2): x ✓
_____
      JANE DOE, TTEE

(3): x
_____

(4):
_____
        Signature(s)   **Identifying Info.**

☐ CONVENIENCE ACCOUNT (agent) _____
Individual Accounts Only

      x
_____

BACKUP WITHHOLDING CERTIFICATIONS

TIN: ___123–45–6789___

☒ **TAXPAYER I.D. NUMBER -** The Taxpayer Identification Number shown above (TIN) is my correct taxpayer identification number.

☒ **BACKUP WITHHOLDING -** I am not subject to backup withholding either because I have not been notified that I am subject to backup withholding as a result of a failure to report all interest or dividends, or the Internal Revenue Service has notified me that I am no longer subject to backup withholding.

☐ **EXEMPT RECIPIENTS -** I am an exempt recipient under the Internal Revenue Service Regulations.

☐ **NONRESIDENT ALIENS -** I am not a United States person, or if I am an individual, I am neither a citizen nor a resident of the United States.

SIGNATURE - I certify under penalties of perjury the statements checked in this section.

x ✓ _____

(page 1 of 2)

Figure 13-2

BUSINESS ACCOUNT AGREEMENT

≡

ENTERPRISE NATIONAL BANK
OF SARASOTA

OWNERSHIP OF ACCOUNT

☐ SOLE PROPRIETORSHIP   ☐ CORPORATION - NOT FOR PROFIT   ☐ CORPORATION - FOR PROFIT

☐ PARTNERSHIP   ☐ LIMITED LIABILITY CO.   ☒ **TRUST—SEPARATE AGREEMENT**

DATE OPENED __**00/00/00**__   INITIAL DEPOSIT $ __**00000**__

OPENED BY _____   FORM: ☐ CASH ☒ **CHECK**

AUTHORIZATION DATED _____   PREVIOUS BANK _____

BUSINESS _____
COUNTY AND STATE
OF ORGANIZATION _____

TELEPHONE NO.'S: __**813/000—0000**__

ALL NEW ACCOUNTS WILL BE VERIFIED THROUGH: _____

ADDITIONAL INFORMATION:

| **TYPE OF ACCOUNT** | ☒ NEW | ☒ CHECKING | ☐ MONEY MARKET | ☐ TIME DEPOSIT |
| | ☐ EXISTING | ☐ SAVINGS | ☐ _____ | |

ACCOUNT NAME: __**SELECT CHECKING**__

(continued on following page)

ACCOUNT OWNER NAME & ADDRESS
JOHN DOE AND JANE DOE, TRUSTEES, OR
THEIR SUCCESSORS IN TRUST, UNDER THE
DOE FAMILY LIVING TRUST DATED 3/11/95
AND ANY AMENDMENTS THERETO
111 MAIN STREET
ANYWHERE, USA 00001

ACCOUNT NUMBER 1234567

NUMBER OF SIGNATURES REQUIRED FOR WITHDRAWAL __2__

☐ This is a Temporary account agreement.

SIGNATURE(S) - THE UNDERSIGNED AGREE(S) TO THE TERMS STATED ON PAGES 1 AND 2 OF THIS AGREEMENT, AND ACKNOWLEDGE(S) RECEIPT OF A COMPLETED COPY ON TODAY'S DATE. THE UNDERSIGNED ALSO ACKNOWLEDGE(S) RECEIPT OF A COPY OF AND AGREE(S) TO THE TERMS OF THE FOLLOWING DISCLOSURE(S):

☒ Funds Availability Disclosure   ☐ _____

Signature(s)   **Identifying Info.**

(1): x ✓
JOHN DOE, TTEE

(2): x ✗
JANE DOE, TTEE

(3): x

(4): x

☐ FACSIMILE SIGNATURE

x _____

BACKUP WITHHOLDING CERTIFICATIONS

TIN: __012-34-5678__

☒ **TAXPAYER I.D. NUMBER -** The Taxpayer Identification Number shown above (TIN) is my correct taxpayer identification number.

☒ **BACKUP WITHHOLDING -** I am not subject to backup withholding either because I have not been notified that I am subject to backup withholding as a result of a failure to report all interest or dividends, or the Internal Revenue Service has notified me that I am no longer subject to backup withholding.

☐ **EXEMPT RECIPIENTS -** I am an exempt recipient under the Internal Revenue Service Regulations.

☐ **NONRESIDENT ALIENS -** I am not a United States person, or if I am an individual, I am neither a citizen nor a resident of the United States.

SIGNATURE - I certify under penalties of perjury the statements checked in this section.

x ✓ _____

© 1983, 1992 Bankers Systems, Inc., St. Cloud, MN (1-800-397-2341) Form AA-B-RA 2/19/93 ♻ Recycled   *(page 1 of 2)*

Form 1304 in the Appendix is a sample letter you can use to request a change in the certificate's title. Form 1305 is an Assignment of Certificates of Deposit. If you become disabled or die before the certificate has matured, then the Assignment of Certificates of Deposit can be used to transfer a certificate into your trust without the necessity of a court proceeding. Later, when the account matures, it can be renewed by executing a new account agreement in the name of your trust.

There should *not be a withdrawal penalty* for transferring your certificate of deposit to your living trust, since your taxpayer identification number on the account will remain the same. However, some institutions view a name change as a transaction that necessitates cancellation of the old certificate and reissuance of a new one, which could create a penalty for withdrawal and result in a lower interest rate. Be sure that you make it manifestly clear to your banker that you have no desire to pay such a penalty for a transaction that only accomplishes your estate planning objective of avoiding probate.

In summary, at the appropriate time, either upon creation of your trust or at the maturity of your certificate, depending on the bank policy on name changes, you should take an Affidavit of Trust (Form 1201) to the bank with a customized form letter for changing the name on a certificate of deposit. See Form 1304.

Coverage Under the FDIC

Federal law governs deposit insurance for federally chartered banks and savings and loans. The myriad of rules dealing with Federal Deposit Insurance Corporation (FDIC) insurance makes it very confusing to determine how your trust accounts are covered by deposit insurance. It is important for your lawyer or your banker to explain these rules to you so that your trust accounts can be structured to achieve the maximum insurance coverage.

An individual's funds in a federally chartered institution are insured up to $100,000 by the FDIC. The $100,000 limit applies whether the individual has one account or several accounts in the institution. For example, all an individual's savings, checking, money market, and certificates of deposit are aggregated for purposes of determining the $100,000 insured amount. The FDIC rules for insurance coverage provide that additional insurance above the $100,000 limit for each institution is available when an individual has joint ownership accounts or testamentary accounts in addition to an individual account.

One thing that is confusing about the FDIC rules is that it calls a testamentary account a "revocable trust" account. This type of account should not be confused with an account titled in the name of a living trust. The term *revocable trust* account when used by the FDIC refers to an account in which the funds are paid to a beneficiary upon the death of the account owner. These accounts must contain "In Trust for," "As Trustee for," or "Payable-on-Death" in the title of the account.

When you set up an account or accounts for your revocable living trust, it is possible to increase the FDIC coverage. For example, if John Doe has a living trust in which his wife and three children each have a "vested interest," then the maximum FDIC insurance coverage on a trust bank account is computed as follows:

> Number of trust makers then living (in our example, there is one, John) multiplied by the number of "qualifying" beneficiaries then living (John's wife and three children, four) multiplied by $100,000 = $400,000.

Before you get too excited about the fact that you can understand this government formula, please note this is the easy part and that there is more to come.

The FDIC defines "qualifying beneficiaries" as the trust maker's spouse, children, and grandchildren. So far, so good, except these beneficiaries must have a "vested interest." Determining a vested interest is much more difficult and depends on the particular provisions of the living trust. Your lawyer may be able to advise you on how many qualifying beneficiaries your trust has, but don't count on it. This is one area in which even estate planning lawyers are not totally familiar.

Your best bet is for you or your lawyer to get a copy of an FDIC memorandum dated November 30, 1990, titled "FDIC Legal Staff's Interpretive Guidelines on the Insurance of Revocable Trust Accounts (including Living Trust Accounts)." Because this is not a best-seller, you cannot buy it at your local bookstore. You can get it from your bank or directly from the FDIC Legal Division, Washington D.C. 20429.

If you have substantial accounts in a financial institution that is insured by the FDIC, it is important that you structure your accounts to maximize the FDIC coverage. Spend time with your lawyer and your banker to creatively title your trust accounts to take advantage of the FDIC rules regarding coverage. It may even be wise to open up several accounts in several banks to both diversify your holdings and increase your FDIC coverage.

· 14 ·

Publicly Traded Stocks, Bonds, and Other Securities

Atransfer agent, investment company, or government agency will be involved in transactions transferring publicly traded assets into your trust. We strongly recommend that you enlist the help of your nonlawyer advisors to assist you with transferring these assets into your trust.

Transferring Stocks, Bonds, and Other Publicly Traded Securities to a Living Trust

Publicly traded securities, such as stocks and bonds that are traded on a stock exchange, that you own in your own name or in joint tenancy, tenancy by the entirety, or tenancy in common are generally retitled in the name of your living trust by a stock transfer agent.

Stock

The name of the transfer agent is on the back of your stock certificates. You must send a request to the agent to transfer your stock ownership to the name of the trust. The transfer agent requires a properly completed and signed Stock Power.

Most stock certificates have a Stock Power on their reverse side. You can fill in this Stock Power, naming the trustees of your trust as the transferee. Your signature must be "guaranteed" to make the Stock Power acceptable to the transfer agent. This means that officers of banks, trust companies, financial advisors, and stockbrokers must witness your signature and then "guarantee" that it is your signature.

In 1992, the Securities and Exchange Commission instituted a procedure called the Medallion Guarantee Program. Most transfer agents will only accept guarantees from members of this program, so ask the person who is guaranteeing your signature if he or she is a member of this program. Figure 14-1 is a properly filled-in Stock Power found on the back of a stock certificate.

If you have several stock certificates for the same corporation or if your certificate does not have a Stock Power on its reverse side, then you can sign a separate Stock Power. The separate Stock Power serves exactly the same function as a Stock Power found on the reverse side of your stock certificate. See Form 1401 in the Appendix for an example of a Stock or Bond Power, which can be used for both stocks and bonds. Your signature must also be guaranteed on the separate Stock Power.

The stock certificate or certificates, a copy of your Affidavit of Trust (Form 1201), the separate Stock Power, if any, and a cover letter should be sent to the stock transfer agent. You should send this package by registered mail. See Forms 1402, 1403, and 1404 for sample letters to transfer agents. After processing your request, either the transfer agent or the company will send a new stock certificate registered in the name of your trust.

Another method for conveniently changing the title of stocks and bonds that you hold in your name into the name of your trust is to open up an account with a brokerage firm in the name of your trust; this is often referred to as a Street Name Account. You can then give your certificates to your broker. Your broker will provide you with the proper Stock Powers and signature guarantees to transfer the stock.

It is extremely important that you get a detailed receipt signed by your broker stating that he or she has taken your stocks, bonds, or other securities for the purposes of opening an account in your trust's name. If you do not take this step and your certificates are lost, destroyed, or misplaced, then you will have a difficult time getting the brokerage firm to replace those certificates.

For some people, this method of transferring title to their securities to their trust is uncomfortable. If you have a brokerage account, the brokerage firm holds the stock certificates themselves. Your evidence that you own the securities is the account statement that you receive listing the securities and what they are worth.

If you want to hold the securities themselves, most brokerage firms will accommodate your wishes. Ask your broker if he or she would transfer your securities into your trust and then return the securities to you. Usually your broker will be more than happy to accommodate you. He or she may charge a fee, but

Figure 14-1

For Value Received, I *hereby sell, assign and transfer unto* JOHN DOE and JANE DOE, Trustees, or their successors in trust, under the JOHN DOE LIVING TRUST dated March 11, 1995, and any amendments thereto *Shares represented by the within Certificate, and do hereby irrevocably constitute and appoint* Mr. Corporate Secretary *Attorney to transfer the said Shares on the books of the within named Corporation with full power of substitution in the premises.*

Dated ____________________ *19* __________

In presence of

____________________________ ____________________________

JOHN DOE

NOTICE: THE SIGNATURE TO THIS ASSIGNMENT MUST CORRESPOND WITH THE NAME AS WRITTEN UPON THE FACE OF THE CERTIFICATE IN EVERY PARTICULAR, WITHOUT ALTERATION OR ENLARGEMENT, OR ANY CHANGE WHATEVER.

that depends on the policy of the brokerage firm. You might find this course of action easier than doing it yourself. Once again, you must get a signed receipt from your broker listing any and all securities that you leave with him or her.

Brokerage Accounts

If you have an existing account with a stockbrokerage firm, you should contact your broker about changing the account into the name of your trust. Either a new account will be opened in the name of your trust or the name of your current account will be changed to your living trust. In either case, it might be necessary for you to provide an Affidavit of Trust and sign new signature cards; brokerage firms vary as to what they require. There is absolutely no need for the brokerage firm to review or copy your entire trust for their files. The information in your Affidavit of Trust is legally sufficient to demonstrate that the trust is valid, is currently in existence, and that the trustee has the power to open the account. When you open an account, you will also have to sign a Form W-9, which is required by the Internal Revenue Service.

Forms 1405 and 1406 in the Appendix are sample letters that you can use to request the brokerage house to transfer an account to your living trust.

"Lettered" Stock

You may own stock that is considered to be a security for purposes of federal securities law. This stock is restricted as to its transfer generally because it is "insider" stock. If you invested early in a corporation that plans to go public in the future or if you received special stock when a company went public, you may have received this type of stock.

Insider stock is called "lettered" stock because there is a brief statement on the face of the stock that says, in effect, that the transfer of the stock is restricted because of certain provisions of federal securities law. If you have this kind of stock, you must find out from the corporation's secretary about the proper procedure for transferring the stock to your trust.

Bonds

When you have bond certificates in your possession, transferring title is done the same way as for stocks. A Stock or Bond Power, such as the one shown in Form 1401 in the Appendix, can be used for purposes of transferring a publicly traded bond to your trust.

Bearer bonds are easy to transfer since they are not registered. Bearer bonds are treated like cash in that whoever holds the bond can buy, sell, or otherwise negotiate the bonds. Ownership of bearer bonds by your trust should be evidenced by an Assignment of Bearer Bonds form. Form 1407 in the Appendix is an assignment that provides you with complete instructions. Remember, however, that as long as your bearer bonds remain in bearer form, even if you have assigned them into your trust, if they are lost or stolen, the person who has possession can assert ownership. Because anyone who has the possession of bearer bonds can assert ownership, your bonds and their assignment into your trust should be kept in a safe-deposit box or another secure place. Be sure that you leave instructions as to where you have left them so if something happens to you, then your spouse or another person whom you trust has access to your bonds.

U.S. Treasury Bonds, Bills, Notes, and Direct Accounts

Investment in U.S. Treasury issues can take a number of forms. The government sells Treasury bills, notes, and Savings Bonds (Series EE and HH). Investment can be made through a U.S. Treasury Direct account as well. Transferring title of a Treasury Direct account to your living trust is accomplished by contacting the office where your Treasury Direct account is located and obtaining a Form PD F 5178, "Treasury Direct Transaction Request," form. The change-of-ownership section needs to be completed showing your trust as the new owner. Figure 14-2 is a copy of this form.

The federal government requires the use of Form PD 1851 for transferring U.S. savings bonds and notes. Most commonly, this form is used for Series E and EE bonds and Series H and HH bonds. On the back of this form are complete instructions. We have included this form as Figure 14-3.

After this form has been completed, your signature must be guaranteed, just as in the case of publicly held securities. The completed form and the bonds themselves are then sent to any Federal Reserve bank or branch, or they can be mailed to:

The Bureau of the Public Debt
200 Third Street
Parkersburg, West Virginia 26101

Figure 14-2

FORM PD F 5178
(February 1990)

TREASURY DIRECT ®

OMB No. 1535-0069
Expires: 09-30-92

TRANSACTION REQUEST

ACCOUNT IDENTIFICATION

FOR DEPARTMENT USE

ACCOUNT NUMBER   0000 - 111 - 2222

ACCOUNT NAME

JOHN DOE

DOCUMENT AUTHORITY

APPROVED BY

DATE APPROVED

TRANSACTIONS REQUESTED   CHECK THE BOX NEXT TO EACH TRANSACTION REQUESTED AND PRINT THE INFORMATION AS IT SHOULD APPEAR IN YOUR ACCOUNT.

[X]   NAME CHANGE (Certification may be required)

JOHN DOE and JANE DOE, Trustees, or their successors in trust,

under the JOHN DOE LIVING TRUST dated March 11, 1995,

and any amendments thereto.

[ ]   ADDRESS CHANGE

CITY   STATE   ZIP CODE

[ ]   TAXPAYER IDENTIFICATION NUMBER CHANGE

1ST NAMED
OWNER   __ __ - __ __ - __ __ __ __   **OR**   __ __ - __ __ __ __ __ __ __
         SOCIAL SECURITY NUMBER   EMPLOYER IDENTIFICATION NUMBER

[ ]   TELEPHONE NUMBER CHANGE

(___) ___ - ____   (___) ___ - ____
        WORK   HOME

[ ]   DIRECT DEPOSIT INFORMATION CHANGE (Certification Required)

ROUTING NUMBER _____

FINANCIAL INSTITUTION NAME _____

ACCOUNT NUMBER _____   ACCOUNT TYPE   [ ] CHECKING
                                         (Check One)
ACCOUNT NAME _____   [ ] SAVINGS

[ ]   CONSOLIDATION

_____   _____ - ____ - _____
CLOSING ACCOUNT NUMBER(S)   SURVIVING ACCOUNT NUMBER

SEE INSTRUCTIONS FOR PRIVACY ACT AND PAPERWORK REDUCTION ACT NOTICE

Figure 14-3

PD F 1851
Department of the Treasury
Bureau of the Public Debt
(Revised August 1993)

**REQUEST FOR REISSUE OF UNITED STATES SAVINGS BONDS/NOTES
IN NAME OF TRUSTEE OF PERSONAL TRUST ESTATE**

OMB No. 1535-0009
Expires 12/31/94

> **IMPORTANT: Follow instructions in filling out this form. You should be aware that the making of any false, fictitious or fraudulent claim to the United States is a crime punishable by imprisonment of not more than five years or a fine up to $250,000, or both, under 18 U.S.C. 287 and 18 U.S.C. 3571. Additionally, 31 U.S.C. 3729 provides for civil penalties for the maker of a false or fraudulent claim to the United States of an amount not less than $5,000 and not more than $10,000, plus treble the amount of the Government's damages as an additional sanction.**
> **PRINT IN INK OR TYPE ALL INFORMATION**

TO: Federal Reserve Bank

BEFORE FILLING OUT THIS FORM, READ TAX LIABILITY NOTICE ON PAGE 3
(The applicable statement(s) below MUST be completed; see instructions.)

1. I (we) hereby request reissue of the bonds described on the reverse hereof in the form set out in item 5 below to the extent of
$ __10,000__ (face amount).

2. In support of this request, I (we severally) certify that the trust estate described in item 5 below is a personal trust estate as defined in item 1 of the instructions on page 3 of this form, and
   a. [X] was created by __John Doe__
   (Name(s) of owner or both coowners creating trust)

   b. [ ] was created by one coowner, _____
   (Name of coowner creating trust)

   c. [ ] was created by some other person and
   (i) [ ] I am (one of us is) a beneficiary of the trust.
   [ ][ ] – [ ][ ] – [ ][ ][ ][ ]

   (ii) [ ] _____, a beneficiary of the trust, is related
   (Name)

   to _____ as _____
   (Name of owner or coowner)   *(Give exact relationship)*

3. You must check box a. or b. (SEE "TAX LIABILITY" SECTION OF INSTRUCTIONS):

   a. [X] I (we) certify that, for federal income tax purposes, I (we) will be treated as owner(s) of the portion of the trust represented by any tax-deferred accumulated interest on the surrendered bonds.

   b. [ ] I (we) certify that, for federal income tax purposes, I (we) will not be treated as owner(s) of the portion of the trust represented by any tax-deferred accumulated interest on the surrendered bonds, and therefore, I (we) will include the tax-deferred accumulated interest in gross income for the taxable year in which the bonds are reissued to the trust. I (we) am aware that a 1099 INT will be issued and the interest will be reported to the Internal Revenue Service by the agent that processes the transaction. The interest which will be reported includes deferred interest on H/HH bonds as well as interest earned on E/EE bonds from the issue date until the date of reissue.

4. _____ is the principal coowner of any bonds registered in coownership
   (Name of coowner)

   form submitted herewith. (A principal coowner is a coowner who (1) purchased the bonds with his or her own funds or (2) received them as a gift, inheritance or legacy, or as a result of judicial proceedings, and has them reissued in coownership form, provided he or she has received no contribution in money or money's worth for designating the other coowner on the bonds.) The above-named principal coowner is responsible for any tax liability arising from the reissue transaction requested hereon and his/her Social Security Account Number is:

   [ ][ ][ ] – [ ][ ] – [ ][ ][ ][ ]
   (Failure to furnish this information could cause rejection of the transaction.)

5. Form in which bonds are to be reissued. John Doe and Jane Doe Trustees, or their successors in trust under the John Doe Living Trust dated March 11, 1995 and any amendments thereto.
   (Inscription: include name(s) of trustee(s); name(s) of creator(s) or trustor(s) and date of trust's creation.)

   111 Main Street, Your City, Anywhere 00001
   (Address)

(Taxpayer Identifying
Number Assigned to
Trust)

[ ][ ] [ ][ ][ ][ ][ ][ ][ ]
(Employer Identification Number)

[0][1][2] – [3][4] – [5][6][7][8]
(Social Security Account Number)

If the new bonds are not to be
delivered to address shown
thereon deliver them to:

_____
(Name)

_____
(Street Address)

_____   _____   _____
(City or town)   *(State)*   *(Zip Code)*

OWNER AND OTHER REGISTRANTS MUST SIGN AND HAVE THEIR SIGNATURES CERTIFIED ON PAGE 2

SEE INSTRUCTIONS FOR PRIVACY ACT AND PAPERWORK REDUCTION ACT NOTICE

Under penalty of perjury, I, the undersigned grantor (creator) of the trust, certify that the above taxpayer identification number assigned to the trust is correct; and that I am not subject to backup withholding either (i) because I have not been notified that I am subject to backup withholding (as a result of a failure to report all interest or dividends), or (ii) because I have been notified by the Internal Revenue Service that I am no longer subject to backup withholding. I further certify that the trust estate is not subject to backup withholding for one of the aforesaid reasons. (See Item 3 of the instructions on page 3.) (If an employer identification number, i.e., 12-3456789, has been assigned to the trust estate, then the trustee must furnish an I.R.S. Form W-9.)

John Doe	
(Signature of Owner or coowner)	(Signature of coowner or beneficiary)
111 Main Street, Your City, Anywhere 00001	
(Home Address)	(Home Address)
012-34-5678	
(Social Security Account Number)	(Social Security Account Number)

Telephone No. _____   Telephone No. _____

I CERTIFY that _____ John Doe _____, whose   I CERTIFY that _____, whose
identify is well-known or proved to me, personally appeared before   identity is well-known or proved to me, personally appeared before

me this __11th__ day of __March__, 19 __95__   me this _____ day of _____, 19 _____

at __Your City, Anywhere__,   at _____,
(City or State)   (City or State)

and signed the above request, acknowledging the same to be a free   and signed the above request, acknowledging the same to be a free
act and deed.   act and deed.

(OFFICIAL STAMP   _____   *(OFFICIAL STAMP*   _____
OR SEAL)   (Signature and title of certifying officer)   *OR SEAL)*   (Signature and title of certifying)

_____   _____
(Address)   (Address)

RESERVED FOR IDENTIFICATION NOTATIONS

☐ Customer Account Number and Date Established: ☐ Document(s) - Description:_____

☐ Identified by (Signature and Address): _____

FOR OFFICIAL USE ONLY

☐ This transaction was a taxable event
  $_____ was reported under _____ for _____.
                                        (Social Security Account Number)   (Year)

☐ This transaction was not a taxable event. No interest was reported.

DESCRIPTION OF UNITED STATES SAVINGS BONDS PRESENTED AND SURRENDERED

ISSUE DATE	DENOMINATION (FACE AMOUNT)	SERIAL NUMBER	INSCRIPTION (Please type or print names, including middle names or initials, social security account number, if any, and addresses as inscribed on the bonds.)

(If space is insufficient, use sheet on page 4, sign it and refer to it above - or use PD F 3500 for this purpose.)

(2)

INSTRUCTION
"BONDS" AS REFERRED TO BELOW ALSO INCLUDES SAVINGS NOTES WHEN APPROPRIATE

1. This form is to be used to request reissue of United States Savings Bonds in the name(s) of the trustee(s) of a personal trust estate created by:

    a. The owner or both coowners.

    b. Either of the coowners.

    c. Some other person, provided (i) the owner is a beneficiary of the trust, or a beneficiary of the trust is related to the owner by blood (including legal adoption), or marriage, or (ii) either coowner is a beneficiary of the trust or a beneficiary of the trust is related to either coowner by blood (including legal adoption), or marriage.

    "Personal trust estate" as used herein is a trust estate established by natural persons in their own right for the benefit of themselves or other natural persons in whole or in part, and common trust funds comprised in whole or in part of such estates. A bank, trust company or other financial institution, appointed as trustee of a personal trust estate, should submit Form PD 1455 with this form if the bonds are to be reissued in its name as trustee of its common trust fund.

2. After the form has been completed, it should be signed by the owner or by both coowners. If a beneficiary is named on the securities and they are Series E or H bonds or savings notes, the beneficiary must also sign the request. The home address and social security account number of the owner or both coowners must be furnished. The form may not be executed by a person under any legal disability, except for a minor of sufficient competency to sign the request and to understand the nature of the transaction. If any person whose signature is required is deceased, submit proof of death.

3. If a grantor (creator) of the trust who signs this form has been notified by the Internal Revenue Service that he or she is subject to backup withholding or if the Internal Revenue Service has notified appropriate persons that the trust estate is subject to backup withholding, the applicable statements immediately above the signature line to the effect that the owner, principal coowner, or trust is not subject to backup withholding should be crossed out. (If box 2.c. was checked on page 1 of this form to indicate that the trust was created by some other person, that person should obtain an I.R.S. Form W-9 from a financial institution or I.R.S. office, complete the form, and sign it. That form should be submitted with this form.) (If an employer identification number, i.e., 12-3456789, has been assigned to the trust estate, the trustee must furnish an I.R.S. Form W-9.)

4. Any person who is to execute the form must appear before and establish identification to the satisfaction of an authorized certifying officer, and in the presence of the officer sign the request. The certifying officer must then complete the certification. Authorized certifying officers are available at banking institutions in the United States. For a complete list of such officers, see Department of the Treasury Circular No. 530, current revision, or Public Debt Series No. 3-80.

5. Send the duly completed form and the bonds to any Federal Reserve Bank or Branch.

TAX LIABILITY

Upon the reissuance of savings bonds and/or notes to a trust, you must include in your gross income any accumulated interest on the bonds, including any tax-deferred increment noted on Series H/HH bonds, if you have not already reported it, unless, under the grantor trust provisions of the Internal Revenue Code, you are treated as the owner of the portion of the trust represented by any tax-deferred accumulated interest on the reissued bonds. If you are treated as the owner of that portion, the accumulated interest continues to be your income rather than that of the trust, and therefore, you may continue to defer reporting the interest earned each year. You must include the total accumulated interest in your gross income when the bonds are disposed of or finally mature, whichever is earlier. These rules apply when bonds being reissued are Series E or EE bonds, savings notes, or Series H or HH bonds that you have received in exchange for Series E or EE bonds or savings notes if you are the owner of the portion of the trust represented by the tax-deferred accumulated interest.

Generally, you will be treated as the owner of a trust that you have created to the extent that you retain certain powers over or interests in the trust. For example, you will be treated as the owner of the portion of the trust represented by any tax-deferred accumulated interest on the reissued bonds under the following circumstances:

(1) You will be treated as the owner of a trust to the extent that you have an unconditional power to revest in yourself title to the trust assets. Thus, if you can, at your discretion, revoke all or part of the trust so that the bonds will be returned to you, you will be treated as the owner of the portion of the trust represented by any accumulated interest on the bonds.

(2) If the trust instrument provides that the reissued bonds or the proceeds from the redemption or disposition of those bonds must be distributed to you or your spouse, or held or accumulated for future distribution to you or your spouse, you will be treated as the owner of the portion of the trust represented by any accumulated interest on the bonds. You will be treated as the owner in this circumstance irrespective of the term of the trust.

(3) You will be treated as the owner of a trust to the extent that you retain a power to control the beneficial enjoyment of property transferred to a trust. Thus, if you retain, under the terms of the trust instrument, an immediately exercisable power to determine, in your sole discretion, who will receive the bonds or the proceeds from the redemption or disposition of the bonds, then you will be treated as the owner of the portion of the trust represented by any accumulated interest.

The examples outlined above are illustrative only and they are not intended to cover all possible situations in which you could be treated as the owner of a trust or a portion of a trust. Furthermore, events can occur, such as the renunciation of a retained power or interest, which would cause you to cease being treated as the owner of a trust. If you are not sure whether you will be treated as the owner of a trust, you may request a letter ruling from the Internal Revenue Service. A request for a letter ruling should be sent to:

Internal Revenue Service
Associate Chief Counsel (Technical)
Attention CC:IND:S:3:3
Room 6545
1111 Constitution Avenue, N.W.
Washington, D.C. 20224

If you have any questions concerning the information to be submitted in connection with a letter ruling request, you may call (202) 566-3297 and speak to a representative of the Financial Institutions and Products Division.

NOTICE UNDER THE PRIVACY AND PAPERWORK REDUCTION ACTS

The collection of the information you are requested to provide on this form is authorized by 31 U.S.C. Ch. 31 relating to the public debt of the United States. The furnishing of a social security number, if requested, is also required by Section 6109 of the Internal Revenue Code (26 U.S.C. 6109).

The purpose for requesting the information is to enable the Bureau of the Public Debt and its agents to issue securities, process transactions, make payments, identify owners and their accounts, and provide reports to the Internal Revenue Service. Furnishing the information is voluntary; however, without the information Public Debt may be unable to process transactions.

Information concerning securities holdings and transactions is considered confidential under Treasury regulations (31 CFR, Part 323) and the Privacy Act. This information may be disclosed to a law enforcement agency for investigation purposes; courts and counsel for litigation purposes; others entitled to distribution or payment; agents and contractors to administer the public debt; agencies or entities for debt collection or to obtain current addresses for payment; agencies through approved computer matches; Congressional offices in response to an inquiry by the individual to whom the record pertains; as otherwise authorized by law or regulation.

We estimate that it will take you about 15 minutes to complete this form. This includes the time it will take to read the instructions, gather the necessary facts and fill out the form. If you have comments or suggestions regarding the above estimate or ways to simplify this form, forward correspondence to Bureau of the Public Debt, Forms Management Officer, Parkersburg, WV 26106-1328 and the Office of Management and Budget, Paperwork Reduction Project 1535-0009, Washington, DC 20503. **DO NOT SEND completed form to either of the above addresses; instead, send to the correct address shown in the Instructions on this form.**

DESCRIPTION OF UNITED STATES SAVINGS BONDS PRESENTED AND SURRENDERED
(Continuation)

ISSUE DATE	DENOMINATION (FACE AMOUNT)	SERIAL NUMBER	INSCRIPTION (Please type or print names, including middle names or initials, social security account number, if any, and addresses as inscribed on the bonds.)

Income Tax Consequences

Transferring Series EE bonds to a revocable trust results in no adverse income tax ramifications. The IRS has ruled that Series E and EE bonds held in a revocable living trust are treated the same as if they were owned by the trust maker as an individual. Transfer of the bonds to a living trust does not cause the accrued interest to be currently taxable. The same is true for Series H and HH bonds as well.

Flower Bonds

Certain Treasury notes issued prior to March 4, 1971, known as "Flower Bonds," are redeemable at their face value, plus accrued interest, if they are used to pay federal estate tax. The face value of these bonds is included in the gross estate of the decedent, even though they were purchased at a discount.

In instances where an individual is terminally ill, it may be advantageous to purchase these bonds for purposes of paying federal estate tax. The net result of using a Flower Bond is that federal estate tax is paid at a discount because the full value of the discounted bond is used to pay the federal estate tax.

To be eligible for redemption, these bonds must be owned by the decedent at the time of his or her death and be included in the decedent's gross estate. They can be purchased in the name of a revocable living trust.

Flower Bonds held in a living trust only qualify for redemption if the trustee is required to pay the decedent's federal estate taxes pursuant to the terms of the trust. Every well-drafted living trust should refer to these bonds and grant the trustee the power to redeem them.

Mutual Fund Accounts

The process of titling a mutual fund account that has been set up directly with the mutual fund into the name of a living trust varies somewhat depending on the particular fund involved. For the most part, the transfer will involve the assignment of your existing account into your living trust or opening a new account in the name of your living trust.

Either method will probably require showing your Affidavit of Trust (Form 1201 in the Appendix) to the agent of the mutual fund, and your signature will probably have to be guaranteed. Look in the paperwork that you received from the fund when you purchased it. Somewhere in the literature, there will be instructions as to how to transfer title to the account. If you cannot find this information, call the fund directly; someone there will send you what you need.

If you purchased the mutual fund account through a broker, contact the broker for information about how the account can be transferred. It is likely that the broker can handle this for you. In the event you are working with a financial advisor in funding your trust, your advisor will probably be well versed in making this type of transfer.

Investment Limited Partnerships

Transfer to your trust of investment limited partnerships that were purchased through a broker is usually accomplished by an Assignment of Limited Partnership with Consent, Form 1408 in the Appendix. This form includes a Consent to Assignment to be signed by the general partner. It is almost a certainty that the limited partnership agreement will provide that approval of the general partner is required. If approval is required, you must write the general partner for permission to make the transfer. A sample letter is provided in Form 1409 in the Appendix to inform the general partner that you wish to transfer ownership of your partnership interest to your living trust.

Employee Incentive Stock Options

Under the Internal Revenue Code, an employee who receives an incentive stock option (ISO) from a qualified stock option plan does not have to take the value of the stock option into income when he or she receives it; gain is only recognized upon the later sale or exercise of the option.

Because of the complex rules governing the exercise of options and the disposition of stock and stock options, a qualified stock option *should not* be transferred to your revocable living trust; also, for a period of two years after acquisition of stock, stock acquired through a qualified option should not be transferred to your revocable living trust. Under current rules found in the Internal Revenue Code, only you as the employee, your estate, or a person who inherits the option from you can exercise the option. Living trusts are not specifically mentioned.

For stock that is acquired by exercise of an ISO, if you sell it or give it away within two years of exercising the option or within one year of receiving the stock, it will result in recognition of gain, even if the disposition is a nontaxable gift to a trust.

It is not clear whether transfer of either a stock option or stock acquired through an option to a living trust will violate the holding period rules that qualify the stock for the special treatment. Currently, the definition of disposition by the Treasury regulations includes a change of title that is merely from an owner to the trustee of his or her trust. The result of these regulations is somewhat inconsistent with the established general principle that a living trust is not a separate entity for tax purposes.

The IRS could determine that transfer to a trust is not a disposition that ends the holding period, for certain purposes. However, until the IRS rules on this or until Congress changes the law, do not transfer an ISO to your trust and do not transfer stock to your trust during the subsequent holding period. Only after the holding period should you transfer the stock to your trust. Even then, check with your attorney first to make sure that there are no problems.

· 15 ·

Personal Effects and Other Tangible Personal Property

In funding a trust, clients, lawyers, and other professional advisors often overlook personal property: personal effects such as jewelry, furniture, golf clubs, china, and the myriad of other types of property that have sentimental as well as real worth. Yet this property needs to be controlled by a living trust to avoid a financial guardianship and probate.

In this chapter, we show you how to get your personal effects into your trust and how to control them for planning purposes. You can have your lawyer transfer your personal effects into your trust or your attorney can provide forms and instructions to you so that you or your other advisors can transfer property with registered title to your trust.

Tangible Personal Property in General

Tangible personal property includes property that is not used for business or investment. Such property is tangible in that, unlike a stock or a bond, you actually possess and use the property. This kind of personal property can be divided into two general categories: property without title registration and property with title registration.

Property without registered title is usually transferred to a trust by a bill of sale or an assignment. There are no significant differences between a bill of sale and an assignment. Legally, they serve virtually the same function and have the same ability to convey personal property of almost all types. Usually, the decision as to whether to use a bill of sale or an assignment is more a matter of personal choice or local usage. We recommend that you ask your lawyer which type is more appropriate for the state or locale in which you live. For purposes of this workbook, we will use bill of sale and assignment interchangeably.

For property with registered title, you can register title in the name of your living trust, or in any other manner your lawyer recommends.

Property Without Registered Title

Many forms of tangible personal property do not require title registration with the state. Some examples are:

- Personal effects
- Household furniture and furnishings
- China
- Jewelry
- Artwork
- Collectibles
- Some small watercraft

While your lawyer can furnish you with a bill of sale or an assignment, we have included some samples of these documents in Forms 1501, 1502, 1503, and 1504 in the Appendix.

For individual assets of significant value, such as expensive jewelry, artwork, or other collectibles, we recommend that you transfer these assets using a separate assignment or bill of sale that specifies the particular items transferred. The same is true for small watercraft that do not have any form of title registration.

For all other tangible personal property that you own at the time of signing your living trust, a general bill of sale or a general assignment are sufficient. A general bill of sale or a general assignment do not transfer specific assets; they refer to categories of assets. By referring to general categories, the general bill of sale and the general assignment avoid the need for you to inventory each and every personal effect that you own.

The general bill of sale or assignment that you may have signed when you first funded your trust with personal property may not be adequate to transfer personal property into your trust that was acquired after you signed the bill of sale or assignment. It is a good idea to sign a general bill of sale or general assignment each year on a particular day so that all personal property acquired in the prior year is in your trust. Using a significant day will help you remember to transfer your "after-acquired" personal property. For example, you might want to sign one on April 15 of each year, because that is a significant financial date! See Forms 1505 and 1506 in the Appendix for examples of a general bill of sale and Forms 1507 and 1508 for general assignments.

It would be wise to notify your property and casualty insurance agent of the creation of your living trust–centered plan. He or she can then change your policy or policies to reflect the change in ownership. Form 1509 is a sample letter to your property and casualty agent notifying him or her of your trust.

Property with Registered Title

Under state law some types of personal property must be registered with the state or local authorities. Examples of personal property requiring registration are:

- Automobiles
- Boats (depending on boat size and locality)
- Motorcycles
- Airplanes

Sometimes problems arise in transferring registered property to a living trust. These include:

- A state title registry's lack of familiarity with the trust form of ownership
- Insurance agencies and state registries confusing the trust with a business and attempting to charge commercial business fees for transfers to the trust
- Possible attempt by the state to impose impact or other transfer fees on the transfer to your trust

Here are some practical ideas that will help you transfer particular assets to your trust with the least amount of resistance, time, energy, and expense.

Automobiles

Automobiles in every state have registered title. Generally speaking, to transfer the title of your car to your trust, you need to look at the title to your automobile. Odds are that it will have a section on it that you must complete in order to transfer title to your vehicle. Once this is done, you can mail or take the title to the appropriate government office.

We suggest that you personally deliver the change of title to avoid any confusion. Also, you may have to sign some type of waiver so that you are not charged the same fee as someone who has sold the car to a third party. Most states exempt from any taxes the transfer of vehicles to living trusts. There may, however, be a small title registration fee.

In some states, you can use a bill of sale to transfer an automobile to your trust. Form 1510 in the Appendix is a bill of sale that may be used for automobiles, mobile homes that are not considered to be real property, trailers, recreational vehicles, and small boats that can be transferred under state law.

Sometimes it may not be necessary to transfer title of an automobile to a living trust. In Florida, for example, state law exempts from probate all automobiles titled in the decedent's name and regularly used by the decedent or his or her family for personal use. Check with your lawyer to find out the law in your state.

Some lawyers tell their clients to leave their automobiles out of the trust and let the heirs rely on the state Small Estates Act to transfer property to the trust without probate. This may be a mistake. For example, a state's Small Estates Act may provide that no probate is required when the value of the decedent's estate is less than $25,000. In many states, Small Estates Act procedures are not available unless the entire estate, including probate *and* nonprobate assets, is under the property value ceiling. For example, some lawyers believe that if a client leaves $20,000 worth of property outside of a trust that has assets of $800,000, the $20,000 can be transferred taking advantage of the Small Estates Act. This may not be true; Small Estates Act procedures may only apply if all property of the decedent, including property in trust, is less than the ceiling amount.

Other lawyers suggest it may be sufficient to hold personal-use vehicles in joint tenancy between you and your spouse. However, joint ownership of an automobile may subject both spouses' assets to exposure to a judgment if the automobile is involved in an accident. It makes more sense to title the automobile in the trust of the person who uses it most.

If problems arise with the local Department of Motor Vehicles in transferring automobiles to your trust, you may wish to wait until you acquire a new vehicle and take title directly in the name of your trust. Often this is the most practical solution to funding your trust with an automobile.

Airplanes

Pursuant to federal statute, all civil aircraft located in America must be registered with the Federal Aviation Administration. Since Congress has provided for a federal system for registration and recording transfers of ownership, state law is not involved.

When you acquire an aircraft, you are issued a certificate of registration. To transfer the aircraft to your living trust, you can sign an assignment to your trust and forward the certificate of registration along with the signed assignment to the Federal Aviation Administration for issuance of a new certificate of registration in the name of your living trust. You can use the assignment found in Form 1511 in the Appendix to make the transfer. In Form 1512, we have included a sample letter that you can use.

Boats

Small, so-called pleasure craft are typically registered with a state agency. Ownership transfer to your trust can be achieved through completion of a transfer form obtained from the state agency. As in automobile registrations, there may be a section on your registration certificate that you must complete to make a transfer. Look at your current registration certificate to ascertain what paperwork needs to be accomplished. There may or may not be a fee, depending on the state, but in any event it should be minimal for a transfer to your living trust.

Large vessels are required to be registered with the U.S. Coast Guard and have a Certificate of Documentation that is issued by the U.S. Coast Guard. If you own a vessel with a Certificate of Documentation, a number of documents are required to transfer your vessel to your trust. All the required documents are provided by the U.S. Coast Guard and you may obtain the forms by calling 800-821-2464 or writing to: Commanding Officer, United States Coast Guard Documentation Department, Claude Pepper Federal Building, 5th Floor, 51 S.W. First Avenue, Miami, FL 33130. The U.S. Coast Guard will provide you with the following documents:

- Original Certificate of Documentation
- An original and one copy of a notarized bill of sale transferring your boat to your trust

- Declaration of Citizenship
- Certificate of Marking
- Application for Documentation or for Surrender, Replacement, or Redocumentation
- Trust Information Sheet

Additionally, if there is an outstanding lien on your vessel, a Consent of Mortgagee form will be required.

When you receive the forms from the U.S. Coast Guard, you will fill them in showing transfer of your vessel to your living trust. Then you need to send the completed forms to the U.S. Coast Guard along with their processing fee. Form 1513 in the Appendix is a sample letter you can use to send with these documents. Upon receipt of these documents, the U.S. Coast Guard will issue a new Certificate of Documentation showing your trust as the owner of your vessel.

Manufactured or Mobile Homes

Whether or not manufactured or mobile homes are registered and the manner of registration, if any, varies widely from state to state. Check with your lawyer or your appropriate state agency to find out how your state handles title changes to manufactured or mobile homes. You will find the name of this agency in the documents of sale that you received when you purchased the mobile home.

In California, for example, a mobile home is not considered to be either a vehicle or real estate, and a special agency handles transfers of ownership interests in mobile homes. In Florida, however, a mobile home is treated differently based on whether it is permanently affixed to real property or it is indeed mobile. If the mobile home is not affixed, title is transferred to the trust by completing the transfer information contained on the certificate of title and sending it to the Department of Motor Vehicles along with the necessary transfer fee. A new certificate of title in the name of the trust will then be issued. If the mobile home is permanently affixed to real property, it is transferred via deed, as with other real property.

Memorandum of Personal Property

A Memorandum of Personal Property is a separate piece of paper that gives specific items of tangible personal property to specific people. For example, if you want your collection of dolls to go to your niece, then you can write that on the memorandum. If you want your fly rods to go to your brother, that gift would be written on a memorandum. The advantage of using a Memorandum of Personal Property is that it can be changed without the inconvenience and expense of making a change to your planning documents. If you decide you are mad at your niece and want those dolls to go to your cousin, you merely tear up your old memorandum and do another.

For purposes of a living trust–centered plan, a Memorandum of Personal Property may not be as effective as other methods for giving your personal property away at your death. A Memorandum of Personal Property is usually allowed in conjunction with a will rather than a trust. Those states that have adopted the appropriate parts of a law called the Uniform Probate Code can use a Memorandum of Personal Property as part of their will planning. A Memorandum of Personal Property can be used with a trust, but it may not be as effective as when used with a will. The reason for this disparity is that the statutes that created the Memorandum of Personal Property are unclear as to whether a memorandum is enforceable when used in a trust. Your trustee would follow your Memorandum of Personal Property not because the trustee is necessarily bound to, but because the trustee is attempting to follow your written instructions.

In the unlikely event that the memorandum was ever challenged by disappointed heirs, a court might hold that the memorandum has no statutory basis and is not operative. This means that your personal property would be distributed by the terms of your trust agreement. We use a Memorandum of Personal Property as part of a living trust–centered plan in those instances where we believe there will be little or no controversy about how the personal property will pass. As long as the items listed on the memorandum are not of major value, there is little harm and a lot of convenience in using the memorandum to dispose of minor amounts of personal property. Form 1514 in the Appendix is a Memorandum of Personal Property.

Because a Memorandum of Personal Property may not be as effective when used with a trust as it is with a will, some lawyers suggest that you do not transfer to your trust those items of personal property that you wish to pass by memorandum. These items would be subject to the will, and the memorandum would be valid. It is likely that if these were the only assets to pass through the will, there would be minimal probate expense. However, if you are concerned that your personal property will not pass to exactly those people to whom you want it to go, the better course of action is to put special instructions in your trust as to who should get this personal property. Then you should transfer the title of this personal property into your trust by any of the methods we have noted earlier.

If your trust is written correctly and has been prepared by a competent estate planning lawyer, your trust will be much harder for disgruntled heirs to attack than a will. For more information about how a trust is harder to attack than wills, see Chapter 7 of *The Living Trust Revolution.*

We suggest if you believe that your family members will respect your wishes after you have passed away, that you use the Memorandum of Personal Property even if your personal property is in your trust. In this way, it is extremely likely your wishes will be met.

Trust Amendment

Another alternative to a Memorandum of Personal Property for distributing items of tangible personal property to specific beneficiaries from a living trust is by a trust amendment. Your lawyer would draft the equivalent of a Memorandum of Personal Property in the form of a trust amendment. Each time you decide to change how your personal property is to be distributed, you would sign a trust amendment that would change or modify what you have done previously in your trust concerning those specific personal effects.

The trust amendment method of passing tangible personal property ensures that the property will be distributed pursuant to your instructions as a valid part of your living trust agreement. Trust amendments are easy to prepare and sign. Form 1515 in the Appendix is an example of a Memorandum of Personal Property in the form of a trust amendment.

For distributing items of personal property that have a significant value, a Memorandum of Personal Property and a trust amendment should not be used. This property should be titled in the trust's name like any other tangible personal property and should be treated as a special gift under the provisions of your living trust or as an asset that passes exclusively by the terms of your trust.

Personal effects and other tangible personal property can be valuable in terms of actual worth or for strictly sentimental reasons. In either case, they should be specifically addressed in your living trust–centered plan. You should take care to insure that your personal property passes to your loved ones the way you want with the least amount of legal red tape. We suggest that you consult with your lawyer as to the best way for you to transfer your tangible personal property into your trust, and then decide the best way to distribute it to your loved ones after you have passed away.

·16·

Insurance and Retirement Plans

aming your living trust as the beneficiary of your insurance and retirement plan proceeds allows your trust, and the instructions in it, to control those proceeds. However, there are a few legal and tax issues for you to analyze and understand before you name your living trust as the beneficiary of these types of assets. Because of these issues, it is imperative for you to talk with your lawyer, financial advisor, and accountant to verify that your living trust should be the beneficiary of insurance and retirement proceeds in your particular situation.

Life Insurance Policies

Your living trust should be named as the primary beneficiary of all of the life insurance that you own on your life. To name your trust as the primary beneficiary, you need to fill in and sign a Change of Beneficiary Designation for each policy that you own on your life.

The beneficiary designations of life insurance policies can be changed to the name of your trust either by you or your life insurance advisor. We highly recommend that you use your life insurance advisor to make the changes if you can. If you do not choose to use your advisor, Form 1601 in the Appendix is a letter that can be used to request a change of beneficiary.

Most insurance companies only accept a limited number of change-of-beneficiary forms. Although there are various forms available for changing beneficiary designations, as a practical matter, it is usually best to obtain a change of beneficiary form directly from the insurance company. Form 1602 is a universal form that is printed by the American Bar Association. It has been approved by many, but not all, companies. This type of form can be used as an interim measure until such time as you can obtain and complete a company's approved form. Remember, this is a temporary measure that should not be relied upon in the long term. You can obtain this form from your lawyer or directly from the American Bar Association.

Here are some practical tips for completing change-of-beneficiary forms:

- Forms that are completed by your agent or the insurance company should be reviewed by you or your lawyer to assure there have been no mistakes made or any misunderstandings.
- If the insurance company requests a copy of your trust, provide the Affidavit of Trust.
- It is not necessary to send the insurance policy to the company unless it is specifically requested.

If you have a life insurance policy that has cash value, it is a good idea to change the ownership of the policy and its beneficiary designation to your trust. The reason that the ownership of the policy is changed to the name of your trust is that if you become disabled, your trustee can exercise rights under the policy. Without transferring ownership of the insurance policy to your trust, only a court-appointed guardian could access the cash value upon your disability.

For those people whose estates are subject to federal estate tax, it makes federal estate tax planning sense to consider an Irrevocable Life Insurance Trust. An Irrevocable Life Insurance Trust can be used to keep all life insurance proceeds totally free from federal estate tax. If you have life insurance and your estate is in excess of $600,000, you should ask your lawyer and your life insurance agent about an Irrevocable Life Insurance Trust. For more information about this excellent estate planning technique, read our books *Loving Trust* and *Protect Your Estate.*

Group Insurance

If you have group life insurance, you should make sure that your trust is the primary beneficiary. Talk to the person in your company's benefits department who handles this insurance and ask for a change-of-beneficiary form. Name your trust as the primary beneficiary of your group life insurance.

Disability Income Insurance

Most disability insurance companies do not permit the owner of disability insurance to name the trust as the direct beneficiary of any disability payments. This makes no sense when you consider that, if payments are made to someone who is totally incompetent, the proceeds may have to be subject to a court-ordered incompetency proceeding. These proceeds should be payable to the living trust in order to avoid the courts and so that the trustee can control the proceeds under the instructions contained in the trust agreement.

We suggest that you contact your agent to inquire into whether or not there is a beneficiary designation for your disability policy. If there is, get one and fill it out. If there is not, write the company, with a copy to your agent. Form 1603 in the Appendix is a letter that you can use.

Some employers offer group disability insurance to their employees. If you are one of these lucky employees, seek out the person in your company who routinely handles these benefits and ask for a beneficiary designation. The odds are good that you will need to write the disability insurance company. Notify them that if payments are made from the policy, you want the checks payable to your trust. You can use the same letter as shown in Form 1603.

If, for any reason, your benefits cannot be made payable to your trust, a Durable Special Power of Attorney form can be used for these proceeds. Do not control these proceeds with a general Durable Power of Attorney, however. A general power does not have any instructions in it; assets controlled by the general power of attorney are not subject to the control of your trust and they might not be used in the manner that you wish. If for some reason you cannot change the beneficiary of your disability insurance to your trust, use the Durable Special Power of Attorney for Funding found in Form 1206 in the Appendix. The person who holds the Power of Attorney can then place the disability policy proceeds that are paid directly to you into your trust so that your trust will control them.

Commercial Annuities

A commercial annuity is a contract between the owner and an insurance company that provides that, in exchange for single or multiple payments by the owner to the insurance company, the insurance company will pay a periodic income to the owner.

There are many types of annuities. However, they fall into two general categories: an immediate annuity and a deferred annuity. An immediate annuity commences periodic payments from the time it is initially acquired. A deferred annuity commences payment to the annuity owner at some future date.

Annuities are given preferential treatment under the Internal Revenue Code. Income earned on the annuity while sums are held by the insurance company is not taxed until distributed to the owner. Thus, the inside cash buildup of an annuity is allowed to grow tax-free.

Like disability policies, the beneficiary of the annuity while you are alive is you. In many cases, the company that has issued the annuity may not want to name your trust as the lifetime beneficiary, especially if it is a joint and survivor annuity. A joint and survivor annuity is an annuity that pays out over the lives of two or more people. Many times, a husband and a wife have a joint and survivor annuity that pays out until both of them have passed away.

The best method for getting annuity payments paid to your trust is for you to work through the agent who sold it to you or through your current financial advisor. He or she will know the intricacies of accomplishing this task. If you are one of the unfortunate people who do not have an advisor to work with, then you should contact the insurance company and inquire about their suggested method for paying annuity proceeds to a living trust. Form 1604 in the Appendix is a letter that serves that purpose.

It may be that there is no acceptable method, at least to the insurance company. In that event, as was the case with disability insurance, it is especially important to have a Durable Special Power of Attorney for Funding, as found in Form 1206.

An annuity contract can provide for the designation of a death beneficiary similar to a life insurance contract. An annuity is not a probate asset unless the death beneficiary is the owner's estate or there is no death beneficiary named and payment is made to the owner's estate. It is probably not advisable, or necessary, to transfer ownership of the annuity to your living trust. The annuity is not a probate asset, and therefore it is not necessary for your living trust to own the annuity to avoid probate. In any event, transfer of ownership of the annuity to a living trust *could* cause the annuity to lose its preferential income tax treatment, so you must seek expert advice before you make any changes.

The living trust can also be named as the death beneficiary of the annuity so that after your death the annuity payments will be managed by your successor trustee and distributed under the terms of your trust. Again, there are income tax ramifications, so you should seek out the advice of your tax advisor before making any changes. See Form 1605 in the Appendix for a sample letter directing the insurance company to change the death beneficiary designation to your trust.

Private Annuities

A private annuity is similar to a commercial annuity. The primary difference between the two is that a private annuity is issued by a private party rather than a company that sells annuities.

For the most part, private annuities are used as an estate planning technique when one family member purchases property from another. Payments are made only as long as the recipient of the payments is living. An annuity is a gamble; if the recipient dies prematurely, the person who is paying the annuity has made a great bargain because the payments cease at that time. However, if the recipient lives longer than expected, the person making the payments will pay in excess of the value of the asset. On the death of the recipient of the annuity, the payments cease and the value of the annuity is not included in his or her estate. This offers some attractive planning possibilities. For more information about using private annuities for planning, see our book *Protect Your Estate*.

Transferring a private annuity to a trust is quite simple. You can assign your interest into your trust by an assignment. You should notify the person paying the annuity that checks should be made payable to the trust rather than to you. Form 1606 in the Appendix is an Assignment of Private Annuity. Form 1607 is a letter notifying the person making the payments that future payments should be made to your trust.

Qualified Retirement Plans

Qualified retirement plans include company pension and profit-sharing plans, employee stock ownership plans (ESOPs), individual retirement plans (IRAs), and simplified employee pension plans (SEPs).

There is no change in ownership required for retirement plans or accounts. During your lifetime, you will remain the owner and beneficiary of these accounts. To make sure the proceeds are protected if you become disabled, you should have a Durable Special Power of Attorney for Funding (Form 1206) as part of your living trust–centered plan. The person whom you name in the

Durable Special Power of Attorney can then make sure these proceeds get into your trust. If you are already taking benefits from a qualified plan, the best way we have found to get your proceeds into your revocable living trust is to contact the administrator of your qualified retirement plan and ask that the benefits be deposited directly into a checking account that is in the name of your living trust. If you become disabled, the direct deposits will continue without having to make any other changes. This arrangement will keep your benefits from being tied up in the courts.

It is often appropriate for a living trust to be named as the primary beneficiary of retirement plans upon the death of the owner. However, if a living trust or anyone other than the spouse is designated as a beneficiary, then the spouse is required to waive his or her rights in writing. Form 1608 in the Appendix is a type of Spousal Waiver. This form may or may not be appropriate for your plan. You should contact the plan administrator and ask for the form that is required in your plan.

Selecting a Designated Beneficiary

A designated beneficiary is generally defined as an individual who is named as the beneficiary under the terms of a qualified retirement plan. The designated beneficiary is selected by the participant or, if the participant fails to select the beneficiary, or the selected beneficiary has died with no successor selected, the retirement plan determines the designated beneficiary, such as the spouse, children, or the participant's estate. The designated beneficiary is important for calculating the payments that must be taken from the plan during the lifetime of the participant and after the participant has died.

Generally, if, at the death of the participant, the beneficiary is a qualified designated beneficiary, the benefits may be paid out over the life expectancy of the beneficiary. If the designated beneficiary is not "qualified," the accrued retirement benefits must usually be paid out within five years of the death of the participant.

In planning for distributions from qualified retirement plans to either the participant or a designated beneficiary upon the death of the participant, most financial advisors view deferral of income taxation as the only planning goal. Maximum deferral is achieved by having the plan assets remain in the plan for the longest possible period and, when benefits must be withdrawn, taking out the absolute minimum amount over the longest period of time possible.

To achieve this goal, many advisors tell plan participants to name their spouse as the designated beneficiary to allow for the greatest deferral during lifetime and at the participant's death. This planning does not necessarily adequately address the particular estate planning needs of the participant, which may in fact be contrary to such narrow-vision income tax planning strategies.

Living Trust as Designated Beneficiary

A living trust is an excellent choice as the designated beneficiary of a retirement plan. A living trust will satisfy the statutory requirements for a designated beneficiary as long as it meets the following specific requirements:

- The trust must be valid under state law.
- The trust must be irrevocable at the "required beginning date"; a term that will be explained presently.
- The beneficiaries of the trust must be identifiable from the trust instrument.
- A copy of the trust instrument must be provided to the plan administrator.

If a living trust is a designated beneficiary, the distributions from the retirement plan to the trust can be deferred, offering certain income tax benefits.

A living trust cannot be a designated beneficiary if the participant has reached the "required beginning date" prior to his or her death. The required beginning date is defined in the Internal Revenue Code and the Treasury Regulations as April 1 of the year following the year that the participant reaches age seventy and one-half. For example, if you reach the age of seventy and one-half on June 19, 1998, then your required beginning date is April 1, 1999. At this time, you *must* begin taking distributions from your qualified retirement plan. The reason that a living trust cannot be the designated beneficiary is that the trust will not be irrevocable as of the required beginning date. A living trust is only irrevocable on the death of its maker. It is revocable until then.

If the living trust is named as the beneficiary of a qualified retirement plan after the required beginning date, then the trust can only take out income over a maximum of five years after the participant dies. This can be an income tax disadvantage in some cases, especially if long-term income tax deferral is important.

So what do you do? Your first step is talk to a financial advisor who is well versed in retirement planning and income tax planning. Usually, the financial advisor member of your estate planning team can help you here. In some instances, your lawyer or accountant may have expertise in this area. Get advice about what course of action is best for you. You should also read the discussion of the designated beneficiary that is found in our book *The Living Trust Revolution*. It goes into more detail as to the rules about naming a living trust as the beneficiary of one of these plans.

If you decide to name the living trust as the beneficiary of your retirement plan, then you must get a proper beneficiary designation form. The plan administrator of your plan will provide you with one. Next, have your financial advisor or lawyer complete the appropriate company form. Don't try to do it yourself. This is an area where you should defer to your professional advisors.

If there is any doubt about how your beneficiary designation should read and you are not taking benefits from your retirement plan, we suggest that you name your living trust as the primary beneficiary. Your living trust will then control the proceeds of the plan. This method may not give you maximum income tax benefits, but it will give you maximum control over your assets. If we look to the definition of estate planning, this, for most people, is the number one concern.

The contingent beneficiary should be your spouse if you are married. If you are not married, then name those beneficiaries whom you would like to have these benefits if your trust is not in existence. This contingent beneficiary becomes important if your trust is not in existence.

If you have reached your required beginning date or if income tax considerations are of paramount concern, name your spouse as the primary beneficiary of your retirement plan. If you are not married, name the person or persons whom you want to receive the proceeds. Then name your living trust as the contingent beneficiary so that if the primary beneficiary does not want the proceeds or determines that the living trust should receive the proceeds, then the trust will be available.

If you have reached your required beginning date but are more concerned that your instructions in your trust control the plan proceeds than income tax issues, name the trust as the primary beneficiary and your spouse or someone else as contingent beneficiary.

When you change the beneficiary of a retirement plan to a living trust, you must notify the plan administrator in writing. See Form 1609 in the Appendix for a sample notification letter.

These suggestions will apply in a vast majority of situations if you have a qualified retirement plan. There are more variations, but they are better left to your professional advisors, who are intimately familiar with your objectives and your financial situation. We remind you once again that you should *always* seek the advice of experts in this area before making any change to the beneficiary designation of a qualified plan or IRA.

Nonqualified Deferred Compensation Plans

It is not uncommon for corporations to offer nonqualified compensation plans to certain employees. A nonqualified plan is one that does not meet the rules for retirement plans found in the Internal Revenue Code. These plans are extra benefits that do not offer all of the income tax benefits of a qualified plan.

As you can imagine, the terms of these plans vary widely. The benefits derived from these plans should be assigned to your living trust. If your company does not provide a form, use the assignments in Forms 1503 or 1504 in the Appendix, depending on whether you have a separate trust or a joint trust, to transfer these benefits into your trust. The assignment should describe the benefits in as much detail as possible. The description should include the name of the plan, the date it was effective, and a brief summary of the plan's benefits.

Review the plan to see if it can be assigned. If it can, then you only need to notify the company to make sure that any benefits paid are payable to your trust rather than to you directly. If the plan requires permission, then you must get the permission in writing from the company. In some plans, there may be insurance or there may be some benefits that are controlled by a beneficiary designation. Make sure that you name your trust as the beneficiary. Use the company's form for this purpose.

° 17 °

Mortgages, Notes, and Other Receivables

When you are owed money, whether for some property you sold over a period of time or for a loan, it is important that the obligation to receive payments is transferred into your living trust. If you do not transfer the obligation into your trust, then the payments made during incapacity or after death may be caught up in the probate process.

These types of receivables can be readily transferred into your trust if you work with your lawyer and other estate planning advisors. If you have the correct forms, most of the work can be done by you or your nonlawyer advisors. It is important, however, to have your lawyer review the documents. You do not want to create a potential problem in the future by having documentation that does not adequately protect you and your family.

Mortgages

The most common type of mortgage is a legal document that shows that real property is being used as security for a debt. The debt can arise from the sale of the real property or from a loan where the real property is the security for the loan. When property is subject to a mortgage, the person who lent the money to purchase the property has a security interest in the property and must be paid before the property is subsequently transferred. Sometimes a person who lends money to another will insist on having real estate as collateral for the loan. A mortgage is generally recorded as part of the public record.

If you have a mortgage on property, you can assign that mortgage to your living trust by using an assignment similar to that found in Figure 17-1. The assignment should include the original recording information for the mortgage.

A mortgage will have a promissory note which also should be transferred to the living trust. An Assignment of a Promissory Note and Letter of Notification of Assignment can be found in Forms 1701 and 1702 in the Appendix, which are discussed later in this chapter.

If a mortgage is not transferred to the trust during the mortgage holder's lifetime, a Postmortem Assignment (Form 1205) can be used to transfer the mortgage to the trust upon death in those states that have adopted the Uniform Probate Code or a similar statute. Your lawyer can advise you about what method of funding is best for you; we recommend that you assign the mortgage directly to your living trust.

Deeds of Trust

A Deed of Trust is used in lieu of a mortgage in many states. It is a legal instrument that is given as security for a promissory note on the sale of real property. Legal title to the real property is placed in the name of an independent trustee until the underlying promissory note is paid in full, at which time the ownership of the property passes to the buyer. The Deed of Trust can be assigned to your living trust using an Assignment of Deed of Trust as shown in Figure 17-2.

The Assignment of Deed of Trust should include the full legal description of the property and the essential information about the original recording of the Deed of Trust. Additionally, the promissory note that shows the actual amount owed and the payment terms should be assigned to your trust. The person who owes the money to you should be notified to make all future payments directly to your living trust. See Form 1702, discussed later in this chapter.

As an alternative to directly funding your trust, the rights under the Deed of Trust along with the promissory note can be transferred to your living trust in most UPC states with a Postmortem Assignment (Form 1205).

Installment Sale Contracts

It is not uncommon for people to sell land or other assets over time. This results in an installment sale contract, which is the contract that describes the terms of the sale, the money owed, and how it is to be paid.

Figure 17-1

ASSIGNMENT OF MORTGAGE

RECORDING REQUESTED BY:

_____

When Recorded Mail To:

_____

_____

_____

Mail Tax Statements to Above Address

For no consideration, JOHN DOE and JANE DOE, Grantors, [Husband and Wife as joint tenants] do hereby transfer and assign, all right, title and interest which they now have in that certain Mortgage dated March 11, 1990, executed by JOHN DOE and JANE DOE as Mortgagors, to JUNCTION BANK AND TRUST, Mortgagee, and recorded as Instrument #1234567, on March 12, 1990, in Book 300, at File/Page #1257 of Official Records in the Office of the County Recorder, County of Junction, State of Anywhere, describing land therein as:

(Legal Description)

[together with the Note or Notes therein described or referred to, the money due and to become due thereon with interest, and all rights accrued or to accrue under said mortgage]
to: JOHN DOE and JANE DOE, Trustees, or their successors in trust, under the DOE FAMILY LIVING TRUST, dated March 11, 1995, and any amendments thereto.

Dated: March 11, 1990.

Witnesses as to both:

_____   _____

John Doe, Grantor   , Witness

_____   _____

Jane Doe, Grantor   , Witness

(continued on following page)

STATE OF ANYWHERE   )
) ss.
COUNTY OF JUNCTION   )

On March 11, 1995, before me, the undersigned Notary Public in and for said County and State, personally appeared JOHN DOE and JANE DOE, personally known to me (or presented _____ as identification) to be the persons who executed the foregoing instrument, and acknowledged executing the same for the purposes herein contained.

WITNESS my hand and official seal.

_____
                              , Notary Public

My commission expires:

Figure 17-2

ASSIGNMENT OF DEED OF TRUST

Recording Requested By:

_____

When Recorded Mail To:

_____

_____

Mail Tax Statements to Above Address

For good and valuable consideration, receipt of which is hereby acknowledged, JOHN DOE and JANE DOE, Grantors, do hereby transfer and assign, to JOHN DOE and JANE DOE, Trustees, or their successors in trust, under the DOE FAMILY LIVING TRUST, dated March 11, 1995, and any amendments thereto: all beneficial interest under that certain **Deed of Trust** dated March 11, 1990, executed by JOHN DOE and JANE DOE, as Trustors, to JOHN DOE and JANE DOE, as Trustees, and recorded as Instrument #1234567, on March 12, 1990, in Book 300, at File/Page #1257 of Official Records in the Office of the County Recorder, County of Junction, State of Anywhere, describing land therein as:

(Legal Description)

Together with the Note or Notes therein described or referred to, the money due and to become due thereon with interest, and all rights accrued or to accrue under said mortgage.

Dated: March 11, 1995.

Witnesses as to both:

_____   _____
John Doe, Grantor   , Witness

_____   _____
Jane Doe, Grantor   , Witness

(continued on following page)

STATE OF ANYWHERE   )
) ss.

COUNTY OF JUNCTION   )

On March 11, 1995, before me, the undersigned Notary Public, in and for said County and State, personally appeared JOHN DOE and JANE DOE, personally known to me (or presented _____ as identification) to be the persons who executed the foregoing instrument, and acknowledged executing the same for the purposes herein contained.

WITNESS my hand and official seal.

_____

                 , Notary Public

My commission expires:

Figure 17-3

ASSIGNMENT TO LIVING TRUST
OF
INSTALLMENT SALE CONTRACT

For good and valuable consideration, the receipt and sufficiency of which are hereby acknowledged, JOHN DOE and JANE DOE, husband and wife, of 111 Main Street, the City of Yours, State of Anywhere, 00001, GRANTORS, do hereby sell, assign, convey and transfer, all of their right, title and interest in that certain Installment Sale Contract dated March 11, 1990, executed by and between JOHN DOE and JANE DOE, husband and wife, as Seller, and JOHN SMITH and MARY SMITH, husband and wife, as Buyer, a copy of which is attached hereto, to JOHN DOE and JANE DOE, Trustees, or their successors in trust, under the DOE LIVING TRUST dated March 11, 1995, and any amendments thereto.

Legal Description of Property:

Dated: March 11, 1995.

Witnesses as to both:

_____   _____
John Doe, Grantor   , Witness

_____   _____
Jane Doe, Grantor   , Witness

STATE OF ANYWHERE   )
)   ss.
COUNTY OF JUNCTION   )

On March 11, 1995, before me, the undersigned Notary Public, in and for said County and State, personally appeared JOHN DOE and JANE DOE, personally known to me (or presented _____ as identification) to be the persons who executed the foregoing Assignment of Installment Sale Contract, and acknowledged executing the same for the purposes herein contained.

WITNESS my hand and official seal.

_____
, Notary Public

My commission expires:

Generally, the right to receive payments under an installment sale contract are freely assignable unless the contract specifically prohibits assignment, which is rare. Assignment of the contract to your living trust can be accomplished by using Figure 17-3.

An installment sale can be evidenced by a land contract (which is described in the next section), a mortgage, or a deed of trust. You must determine which type of instrument you have before making an assignment to your trust. If you have any doubt whatsoever, have your lawyer help you determine how best to assign your installment sale contract.

In addition to the installment sale contract, there will be a promissory note that must also be transferred to your trust. See Form 1701 in the Appendix for the assignment and Form 1702 for the letter of notification of the assignment.

Income Tax Ramifications of Transferring an Installment Sale Contract

When you sell property pursuant to an installment sale contract, the odds are that you are reporting the taxable income, for federal income tax purposes, when you receive it. This is a benefit to you, since you would not want, under ordinary circumstances, to pay taxes on income that you have not yet received.

The transfer of an installment sale contract to a third party results in an acceleration of income for federal income tax purposes. This is obviously not very good tax planning—income taxes payable on income not yet received! The good news is that this income recognition is not accelerated when you transfer an installment sale contract to your revocable trust. Nor does your death result in acceleration of the gain, even though the obligation is held in your trust.

Land Sale Contracts

Under a land sale contract, the seller continues to hold title to the property subject to the contract until all payments have been made by the buyer. Unless the contract provides otherwise, the interest of both the buyer and the seller in the contract can be transferred to a living trust by an assignment, such as the assignment shown in Figure 17-4. The assignment should include a full legal description of the property as it appears on the deed, and a copy of the land sale contract should be attached to the assignment.

If you are the seller, you may also have a promissory note that the buyer has signed. This too must be assigned to the trust. See Form 1701 in the Appendix.

Figure 17-4

ASSIGNMENT TO LIVING TRUST
OF
LAND SALE CONTRACT

For good and valuable consideration, the receipt and sufficiency of which are hereby acknowledged, JOHN DOE and JANE DOE, husband and wife, of 111 Main Street, the City of Yours, State of Anywhere, 00001, GRANTORS, do hereby sell, assign, convey and transfer, all of their right, title and interest in that certain Land Sale Contract dated March 11, 1990, executed by and between JOHN DOE and JANE DOE, husband and wife, as Seller, and WILLIAM SMITH and SUSAN SMITH, husband and wife, as Buyer, a copy of which is attached hereto, to JOHN DOE and JANE DOE, Trustees, or their successors in trust, under the DOE LIVING TRUST, dated March 11, 1995, and any amendments thereto.

Legal Description of Property:

Dated: March 11, 1995.

Witnesses as to both:

_____   _____
John Doe, Grantor   , Witness

_____   _____
Jane Doe, Grantor   , Witness

STATE OF ANYWHERE   )
) ss.
COUNTY OF JUNCTION   )

On March 11, 1995, before me, the undersigned Notary Public, in and for said County and State, personally appeared JOHN DOE and JANE DOE, personally known to me (or presented _____ as identification) to be the persons who executed the foregoing instrument, and acknowledged executing the same for the purposes herein contained.

WITNESS my hand and official seal.

_____
                  , Notary Public

My commission expires:

For federal income tax purposes, a land sale contract may be treated as an installment sale, so its transfer to a living trust will not accelerate the income tax due.

Promissory Notes

Unless prohibited by its terms, a promissory note can be assigned to a living trust by using a form such as that found in Form 1701 in the Appendix. If you assign a promissory note to your living trust, you should contact the person or persons who owe the money—in writing—and advise them to make all future checks payable to your trust, not to you individually. See sample letter, Form 1702. Otherwise, the checks you receive may be subject to probate if you die prior to depositing the checks in your trust account. Furthermore, all checks paid following your death will go through probate until the promissory note is transferred from the probate estate to your living trust.

Security Interests in Accounts Receivable

You may have a security interest in the accounts receivable of a company or an individual to whom you have loaned money. Security interests in accounts receivable are governed by Article Nine of the Uniform Commercial Code (UCC), a variation of which has been adopted in every state.

To obtain a valid security interest in accounts receivable, you must file a document called a UCC One Financing Statement in the state that has jurisdiction over the accounts receivable. Figure 17-5 is an example of a completed UCC One Financing Statement. The purpose of this filing is to provide notice to all other potential creditors that you have a security interest in those accounts receivable that is evidenced by a promissory note.

When you assign the promissory note to your trust, you should also assign your security interest in the accounts receivable. You should then notify the company or person who owes you the money of the assignment and you should file notice with the state where the original UCC One was filed. This is generally done on a UCC Three, which is shown in Figure 17-6.

Figure 17-5

STATE OF FLORIDA
UNIFORM COMMERCIAL CODE — FINANCING STATEMENT — FORM UCC-1 REV. 1981

THIS FINANCING STATEMENT is presented to a filing officer for filing pursuant to the Uniform Commercial Code:

ONLY ONE NAME PER BOX

DEBTOR (Last Name First if a Person)

1A NAME Debtor, Mark

MAILING ADDRESS 100 First Street

CITY Fields STATE Idaho 00112

1B MULTIPLE DEBTOR (IF ANY) (Last Name First if a Person)

NAME

MAILING ADDRESS

CITY STATE

1C MULTIPLE DEBTOR (IF ANY) (Last Name First if a Person)

NAME

MAILING ADDRESS

CITY STATE

2A SECURED PARTY (Last Name First if a Person)

NAME John Doe and Jane Doe, Trustees, or their successors in trust, under the John Doe Living Trust dated March 11, 1995 and any amendments thereto

MAILING ADDRESS

CITY STATE

2B MULTIPLE SECURED PARTY (IF ANY) (Last Name First if a Person)

NAME

MAILING ADDRESS

CITY STATE

3 ASSIGNEE OF SECURED PARTY (IF ANY) (Last Name First if a Person)

NAME

MAILING ADDRESS

CITY STATE

THIS SPACE FOR USE OF FILING OFFICER
Date, Time, Number & Filing Office

AUDIT UPDATE

VALIDATION INFORMATION

---

4. This FINANCING STATEMENT covers the following types or items of property (*include description of real property on which located and owner of record when required*). If more space is required, attach additional sheets 8½" x 11".

[Description of Property]

5. Proceeds of collateral are covered as provided in Sections 679.203 and 679.306, F.S.

6. Filed with: Secretary of State

7. No. of additional Sheets presented:

8. (Check ☐) ☐ All documentary stamp taxes due and payable or to become due and payable pursuant to Section 201.22, F.S., have been paid.

☐ Florida Documentary Stamp Tax is not required.

9. This statement is filed without the debtor's signature to perfect a security interest in collateral (Check ☐ if so)

☐ already subject to a security interest in another jurisdiction when it was brought into this state or debtor's location changed to this state.

☐ which is proceeds of the original collateral described above in which a security interest was perfected.

☐ as to which the filing has lapsed.

☐ acquired after a change of name, identity, or corporate structure of the
☐ debtor or ☐ secured party.

10. (Check ☐ if so)

☐ Debtor is a transmitting utility

☐ Products of collateral are covered

11. SIGNATURE(S) OF DEBTOR(S)

Mark Debtor

12. SIGNATURE(S) OF SECURED PARTY(IES) OR ASSIGNEE

John Doe and Jane Doe, Trustees

13. Return copy to:

NAME John Doe and Jane Doe, Trustees
ADDRESS 111 Main Street
CITY Your City
STATE Anywhere ZIP CODE 00001

NAME AND ADDRESS OF PREPARER

FILING OFFICER COPY STANDARD FORM — FORM UCC-1 Approved by Secretary of State, State of Florida

Figure 17-6

STATE OF FLORIDA
UNIFORM COMMERCIAL CODE — STATEMENT OF CHANGE — FORM UCC-3 REV. 1981
THIS FINANCING STATEMENT is presented to a filing officer for filing pursuant to the Uniform Commercial Code:

<table>
<tr><td colspan="2">Information in items 1 and 2 must agree exactly with the original filing information or as previously amended.</td><td>THIS SPACE FOR USE OF FILING OFFICER
Date, Time, Number & Filing Office</td></tr>
<tr><td rowspan="8" style="writing-mode: vertical;">ONLY ONE NAME PER BOX</td><td>DEBTOR (Last Name First if a Person)
NAME

1A   Debtor, Mark
MAILING ADDRESS
   100 First Street
CITY Fields   STATE Idaho   00112</td><td></td></tr>
<tr><td>MULTIPLE DEBTOR   (IF ANY)   (Last Name First if a Person)
NAME

1B
MAILING ADDRESS

CITY   STATE</td><td></td></tr>
<tr><td>MULTIPLE DEBTOR   (IF ANY)   (Last Name First if a Person)
NAME

1C
MAILING ADDRESS

CITY   STATE</td><td></td></tr>
<tr><td>SECURED PARTY (Last Name First if a Person)
NAME

2A   Doe, John
MAILING ADDRESS
   111 Main Street
CITY Your City   STATE Anywhere   00001</td><td>UPDATE

AUDIT</td></tr>
<tr><td>MULTIPLE SECURED PARTY   (IF ANY)   (Last Name First if a Person)
NAME

2B
MAILING ADDRESS

CITY   STATE</td><td>VALIDATION INFORMATION</td></tr>
</table>

3. This statement refers to original Financing Statement bearing File Number _____ and filed with

Secretary of State   The original was filed on ____ 19__

4. ☐ Continuation.   The original financing statement between the foregoing Debtor(s) and Secured Party(ies) bearing file number shown above, is still effective.

5. ☐ Termination.   Secured party no longer claims a security interest under the financing statement bearing file number shown above.

6. ☐ Partial   Some of Secured party's rights under the Financing Statement have been assigned to the assignee whose name and address are set forth in
     Assignment   Item 11. A description of the collateral subject to the assignment is also set forth in Item 11.

7. ☐ Full   All of Secured Party's rights under the Financing Statement have been assigned to the assignee whose name and address are set forth
     Assignment   in Item 11.

8. ☐ Amendment.   Financing Statement bearing file number shown above is amended as set forth in Item 11. Signature of Debtor(s) required at Item 14 pursuant to
     Section 679.402(4), Florida Statutes.

9. ☐ Release.   Secured party releases only the collateral described in Item 11 from the financing statement bearing file number shown above.

10. ☐ Check if true.   All documentary stamp taxes due and payable or to become due and payable pursuant to Chapter 201.22, F.S. have been paid.

11. If more space is required, attach additional sheets 8½ x 11.

John Doe and Jane Doe, Trustees, or their successors in trust, under the
John Doe Living Trust dated March 11, 1995 and any amendments thereto

<table>
<tr><td></td><td>**12.** No. of Additional Sheets presented:</td><td>**14.** SIGNATURE(S) OF DEBTOR(S) Necessary Only For Amendment. See Item 8.</td></tr>
<tr><td>**13.**   Return Copy to:
NAME   John Doe and Jane Doe, Trustees
ADDRESS   111 Main Street
CITY   Your City
STATE   Anywhere   ZIP CODE 00001</td><td></td><td>**15.** SIGNATURE(S) OF SECURED PARTY(IES) OR ASSIGNEE

John Doe</td></tr>
</table>

STANDARD FORM — FORM UCC-3   Approved by Secretary of State, State of Florida

·18·

Business and Professional Interests

Business and professional interests are usually held in one of the traditional business entities: sole proprietorships, partnerships, or corporations. Transfers of partnership interests and shares of stock into your living trust can be relatively simple. However, care must be exercised when transferring any business interest because of sophisticated tax and transfer issues. You should always consult with a lawyer for any but the most rudimentary assets so that you fully understand the ramifications of the transfers.

Sole Proprietorships

A sole proprietorship is not a formal business entity. Rather, it is an amalgamation of assets and liabilities that, when taken together, constitute a trade or business. Therefore, a single blanket assignment of "the entire business" should not be used. The proper way to transfer the personal property used in a sole proprietorship into a living trust is with an assignment. All items of tangible personal property should be named either individually or by category in the assignment.

The assignment shown in Form 1801 in the Appendix lists general categories of sole proprietorship assets to be transferred into a living trust. For the assignment to be more tailored, a sole proprietorship's depreciation schedule and balance sheet should be examined so that specific assets can be referred to. A sole proprietor's accountant should be involved in the funding process because the accountant, more than any other professional, will have a good grasp of the property used in the proprietorship.

If your sole proprietorship has any accounts receivable, they should be specifically assigned to your trust. If you have pledged the accounts receivable or given anyone a security interest in your accounts receivable or in any of the sole proprietorship's assets, you must notify the person or entity who holds the security interest to communicate your intentions and obtain their permission to make the transfer. A new Uniform Commercial Code Financing Statement (Figure 17-5) should then be filed that shows the change in the ownership of the accounts receivable and/or other assets subject to the security interest.

Assets acquired by the business after the initial transfer of assets to your living trust can be transferred into the name of the trust by assignment as they are purchased or they can be purchased directly in the name of the trust.

When all of a sole proprietorship's assets are held in the name of a living trust, the sole proprietorship must do business in the name of the trust. There is no legal reason that a trust cannot do business in its own name. However, there may be practical limitations to this course of action.

It is likely that third parties doing business with the trust and its trustees will continually want evidence that the trustees have the powers to transact business. Vendors and other companies with which business is transacted are probably not familiar with dealing with trusts and trustees, so they may be reluctant to extend credit or enter into contracts. For these very practical reasons, it may be better for a trust to do business in another way.

Use of a Fictitious Name

In most states, a living trust can carry on a business under a trade name or fictitious name. When a trust—or an individual, for that matter—does business under a trade name or a fictitious name, an affidavit of some type must be filed with your state's Secretary of State or in the county where the business is to be transacted. Some states require that the name be published in a newspaper for a period of time; others have different requirements. Because of the variety of methods that are used in the various states, you should consult with your lawyer with regard to registering a trade or fictitious name for your trust.

Creation of a Nominee Partnership

A Nominee Partnership can be created to hold title to trust assets. The business can then do business as a Nominee Partnership. See the discussion of Nominee Partnership in Chapter Twelve, "Methods of Funding."

Income Tax Note

Under certain circumstances, a living trust that carries on a trade or business could be taxable as a corporation for federal income tax purposes. However, this characterization can be avoided if the primary purpose of the living trust is to protect or conserve property for estate planning purposes. If you choose to carry on the business in trust, your lawyer should create documentation that makes it clear that the primary reason for holding the sole proprietorship in trust is to protect and conserve the property for purposes of estate planning.

It is also a good idea to consult with your lawyer and other advisors about the possibility of changing the sole proprietorship to another form of business, such as a partnership or a corporation.

Privately Owned Corporations

The transfer of stock in a corporation that is not publicly traded to a trust can be done easily. The shareholder must only complete the Stock Power that is usually found on the reverse side of the stock certificate. See Figure 14-1 for an example of this type of Stock Power. The shareholder must then deliver the stock certificate to the secretary of the company, who will reissue a new stock certificate in the name of the trust.

A Stock Power can be used in lieu of signing the power found on the reverse of the stock certificate. Form 1401 in the Appendix is a sample power that can be used to transfer stocks or bonds. This Stock Power, along with the certificate or certificates that are to be transferred, is then delivered to the corporation's secretary, who will then issue a new stock certificate in the name of the living trust.

Restrictions on the Transfer of Stock

Before you transfer your stock into your trust, you and your lawyer should find out if there are any restrictions on the transfer of the stock. Sometimes these restrictions are found on the stock certificate, in the corporation's articles of incorporation, or in its bylaws. If there is more than one shareholder, a shareholders' agreement or buy-sell agreement may be in force. This inquiry should be accomplished prior to making any transfer of closely held stock into your trust.

If there is a prohibition against transfers of the stock, it will be necessary

Figure 18-1

TRANSFER TO LIVING TRUST—
SHAREHOLDERS OR BUY-SELL AGREEMENT

ARTICLE I
GENERAL RESTRICTIONS ON TRANSFER OF STOCK

Section 1.1   Restrictions. While this Agreement is in force, no Shareholder shall, directly or indirectly, transfer, sell, encumber or otherwise deal with or dispose of all or any part of the Shares now owned or hereafter acquired by him without first obtaining the written consent of the Corporation and the other Shareholder, or without complying with the terms and conditions of this Agreement.

Section 1.2   Exceptions. Notwithstanding the foregoing, a Shareholder may at any time transfer his Shares to a Revocable Living Trust or its nominee established by such Shareholder making the transfer, provided that the Shareholder shall be designated as and shall in good faith act as Trustee or one of the Trustees of the Revocable Living Trust to which the Shares are transferred.

The Trustees and their successors in trust shall be subject to all of the provisions of this Agreement. If Shares are assigned by the Trustees in any manner other than to the Shareholder creating the Trust, the assignment shall be effective only upon the consent of the Corporation and the other Shareholder.

to obtain written permission from the other shareholders in order to make the transfer. Any shareholders' agreement or buy-sell agreement should be modified to provide for ownership by a living trust. See a sample provision that can be added to a buy-sell or shareholders' agreement in Figure 18-1.

Section 1244 Stock

Under most circumstances, when a person sells stock for a loss, that person can only use the loss in two ways. First, the loss can be offset against any capital gains. Then any losses that are left can be taken against all other income, but the deduction cannot exceed $3,000.

The Internal Revenue Code offers a special tax benefit to the owners of some closely held corporation stock. This benefit is called Section 1244 stock. Any losses that are taken on Section 1244 stock because it is sold at a loss or because it becomes worthless can be fully deducted against the owner's other taxable income. This type of loss is called an "ordinary loss." Without Section 1244 treatment, the stock's owner would have the choice of delaying these losses or offsetting them against capital gain income.

Here is an example of the benefits of Section 1244 stock:

Margaret Johnson owned a corporation called Extravagances of the Night, Inc., which sold top-of-the-line formal wear for women. Margaret invested $50,000 in her corporation, which had to go into bankruptcy. Luckily, Margaret had a full-time job as a buyer for a department store. She made $75,000. Because Margaret's stock qualified for Section 1244 benefits, she was able to deduct her $50,000 investment from her $75,000 salary for income tax purposes.

Contrast that example with what would happen without Section 1244 stock:

Margaret Johnson's stock did not qualify for Section 1244 benefits. She was only able to deduct $3,000 of her $50,000 investment from her $75,000 salary for income tax purposes. She can use $3,000 per year of the remaining $47,000 loss to offset her salary income, but it will take her sixteen years to use it up.

Margaret could use up her loss faster if she sells some assets that create capital gain income. Capital gain income is generated when someone sells an asset for more than he or she bought it for. If Margaret sells publicly traded stock, land, or other assets and has a gain, she can offset her loss on her investment against these gains.

If Section 1244 stock is held by or transferred to a living trust, the income tax benefits of Section 1244 will not be available. Accordingly, Section 1244 stock should not be transferred to your living trust without conferring with your lawyer and accountant; they will take into account the effects of the loss of Section 1244 status and advise you accordingly.

The importance of Section 1244 treatment must be weighed against the benefits of placing ownership of the stock in your trust. In some situations, Section 1244 status is not required if:

- The corporation is highly profitable and there is little chance of a loss occurring
- The corporate owners have capital gains that can offset a capital loss of stock
- The corporation is an S corporation; this is explained later in this chapter

However, if it is possible that you will sell your Section 1244 stock at a loss, then you should not transfer it into your living trust. The sale of Section 1244 stock at a loss creates an ordinary loss. If it is held in the name of your trust, it will create a capital loss.

It is imperative that you ask your lawyer whether any of your stock qualifies for Section 1244 treatment. If it does, then a full discussion of the ramifications of its transfer to your trust must be held between you, your accountant, and your lawyer.

S Corporations

In our experience, a great number of our entrepreneurial clients own stock in S corporations. S corporations are a special type of corporation that are taxed much like partnerships. A regular corporation, called a C corporation, has its own income tax bracket. That means that all of its income is taxed to the corporation at its then-current bracket. If a stockholder wants to take out money as a dividend, the stockholder must pay income tax on that dividend. That means that the dividend has really been taxed twice: once at the corporation's tax bracket and then again at the stockholder's tax bracket.

Also, if a C corporation has losses, those losses stay in the corporation. The stockholders cannot take the losses against their individual income. In order to report a loss on their income tax returns, the stockholders have to sell the stock at a loss or declare the stock as worthless. When this loss is reported, it is a capital loss unless the stock qualifies for Section 1244 treatment as discussed earlier.

An S corporation "passes through" its taxable income and losses to its stockholders. The corporation does not have its own income tax bracket, so any taxable income or loss is divided up among the stockholders based on their percentage ownership. Only one tax is paid on dividends: the tax that the stockholders pay. If there are losses, then the stockholders can take them up to the amount of investment they have made in the S corporation. These losses can be offset against all losses. They are just like having a Section 1244 loss without having to qualify for Section 1244 treatment.

Because there is only one tax on dividends paid out of an S corporation, it is not unusual for clients to prefer them to C corporations. And because losses in an S corporation can be taken immediately rather than waiting until the stock is sold at a loss or becomes worthless, clients prefer S corporations in situations where there is a chance of losing money. This ability to take losses against all income immediately means that an S corporation can be transferred into a revocable living trust without worrying too much about Section 1244 treatment. In fact, you may freely transfer S corporation stock into your trust. Living trust ownership does not end the S corporation election or its income tax benefits.

A revocable living trust is specifically allowed to be an S corporation stockholder since it is a "grantor" trust. A husband and wife who file a joint income tax return where neither of them is a nonresident alien can transfer their stock in an S corporation to a joint trust in which they have the joint right to revoke the trust, and the trust will nevertheless be an eligible S corporation stockholder.

After the death of a trust maker, however, there are important restrictions on trust ownership of S corporation stock. As long as the value of the trust is included in the estate of the trust maker for federal estate tax purposes, any revocable living trust is permitted to hold subchapter S stock for a period of two years after the trust maker's death. After this time, the terms of the trust must satisfy additional requirements in order for the corporation to retain its S status. If you expect your trust to hold S corporation stock for more than two years after your death, you must have your lawyer put special provisions in your trust to preserve your corporation's S status.

Professional Corporations

Every state requires that certain professionals, such as doctors, lawyers, CPAs, and engineers, cannot incorporate their practices unless those professionals control the corporation. Control usually means that only professionals can be shareholders and directors of the corporation. These professional corporation laws protect the public by making sure that a nonlicensed professional cannot usurp the decision-making authority granted to professionals.

Because most state laws that authorize professional corporations require shareholders and directors to be licensed professionals, there is a question as to whether or not professional corporation stock can be transferred into a revocable living trust. Whether the stock of a professional corporation can technically be transferred to a trust depends on applicable state laws.

Unfortunately, only one state that we know of—Michigan—specifically authorizes the ownership of professional corporation stock by a living trust. No other state specifically authorizes, *or prohibits*, trust ownership. Since there are currently no laws that specifically prohibit the transfer of a professional corporation to a living trust, you may wish to do so, subject to the advice of your lawyer. Transfer to a professional's living trust does not thwart any of the results sought by these types of laws, which are on the books to assure the public that laypersons are not involved in making decisions that should be made only by licensed professionals. Funding your trust with your professional corporation stock allows you to do proper estate planning—no more, no less.

In states that allow postmortem assignments (primarily UPC states), professional corporation stock can be transferred through a Postmortem Assignment. See Form 1802 in the Appendix. However, as we have pointed out before, a Postmortem Assignment cannot help if the maker becomes incapacitated. If a Postmortem Assignment is used for professional corporation stock, it is imperative that a Durable Special Power of Attorney for Funding be used so that the professional corporation stock can be controlled upon the professional's incapacity. See Form 1206.

One way to accomplish funding without too much risk is to sign a blank Stock Power or properly sign the reverse side of the professional corporation stock certificate. This certificate can be held in a safe-deposit box or other secure place until your death or disability, at which time it can be used to make a proper transfer to your living trust.

The only danger to this approach, and it is not great, is that the stock is "negotiable" once it is signed. That means that whoever possesses the certificate can claim ownership. As a practical matter, because a professional corporation is so personal in nature, it is highly unlikely that someone is going to try to make this kind of claim even if they end up with the stock.

Partnership Interests

There are two different types of partnerships: a general partnership and a limited partnership. In a general partnership, all of the partners are involved in the management of the partnership and can contractually bind the partnership without the approval of the other general partners. Thus the general partners are individually liable for all of the partnership liabilities. In a limited partnership, there are both general and limited partners. The general partners manage the partnership, can bind it contractually, and are individually liable. The limited partners cannot be involved in the management of the partnership, cannot contractually bind the partnership, and are only liable to the extent of their investment in the partnership. Limited partners are passive investors.

A revocable living trust can own a general or limited partnership interest, unless specifically prohibited by state statute or case law, which is rare. When a partnership interest is transferred into a living trust, the trust maker continues to be treated as the partner for federal income tax purposes.

The first order of business in transferring a partnership interest to a trust is to review the partnership agreement to make sure that there are no restrictions on transferring the interest to a living trust. If there are restrictions, you and your lawyer will have to comply with the provisions of the agreement in making the transfer. Just as in corporations, it is relatively easy to comply; since ownership by your living trust is much like outright ownership by you, the ownership of your partnership interest by your trust does not adversely affect the partnership or any of the other partners.

General Partnership Interests

If there are no restrictions in your general partnership agreement, your interest in the general partnership is transferred through an Assignment of Partnership Interest. The example shown in Form 1803 in the Appendix is a commonly used Assignment of General Partnership Interest.

Limited Partnership Interests

Transfer of an interest in a limited partnership is accomplished in the same way as the transfer of a general partnership interest. You can assign the limited partnership interest to the trust using a form such as the Assignment of Limited

Partnership, Form 1408 in the Appendix. This form includes a Consent to Assignment, which must be signed by the general partner.

Partnership Postmortem Assignments

In some states, mostly those that have adopted some version of the Uniform Probate Code, a partnership interest may be transferred at the death of a limited partner by a Postmortem Assignment. If one of these is used, it should be a special type of Postmortem Assignment that is more like a fully revocable beneficiary designation. The beneficiary should agree to be subject to the terms of the partnership agreement and should receive the partnership interest subject to any applicable purchase option or buy-sell agreement. See Form 1804 in the Appendix.

Successor in Interest

Some states allow partnership agreements to provide that a partner may designate a ''successor in interest'' on the partner's death or incapacity. Such a provision may even allow the conversion of a general partnership interest to a limited partnership interest. This provision can be used to automatically fund your living trust on your death or incapacity.

Since a designation of successor in interest is such a specialized provision, you should have your lawyer draft the appropriate document.

Professional Partnerships

For those states that prohibit nonprofessional partners in a professional partnership, a Postmortem Assignment and a designation of successor in interest are ideal for purposes of funding a revocable living trust. However, if you live in a state that does not allow either of these alternatives, you should use an assignment. Professional partnerships are invariably general partnerships, so Form 1803 in the Appendix could be used.

It is highly likely that a professional partnership will have some sort of transfer restriction or buy-sell agreement. If that is the case, you are going to have to meet with your other partners to work out a method so that you—and your partners—can transfer partnership interests to your respective trusts.

Keep in mind that it is to all of the partners' advantage to have their partnership interests held in living trusts. This will expedite a buyout at the death or disability of a partner and will eliminate the expense and delay of a financial guardianship or probate.

Limited Liability Companies

A number of states have followed the lead of Wyoming and created laws that allow Limited Liability Companies. A Limited Liability Company combines the most favorable aspects of corporations and partnerships.

The stockholders of a Limited Liability Company receive protection from creditors of the company just as if it were a regular corporation. However, for federal income tax purposes, a Limited Liability Company is treated as a partnership. Thus, in a Limited Liability Company there is no federal income tax liability at the corporate level and therefore double taxation is avoided. Limited Liability Company stock can be freely transferred to a living trust in the same manner as corporation stock.

Special Business or Income-Producing Property

Many types of business property are owned outside of corporations, partnerships, and Limited Liability Companies. Some of them are held in sole proprietorships, and others are held for investment. Because of their special nature, sometimes it is difficult to know exactly how these interests should be transferred into a revocable living trust. The rule of thumb is: When in doubt, use an assignment. Following are some special types of business property and how they are transferred into a trust.

Livestock

Many types of livestock carry a brand, which is the evidence of ownership of the livestock. In order to fund your living trust with branded livestock, the brand must be transferred to the trust. See Form 1805 in the Appendix for one type of brand assignment. Because states often regulate brands, this form may not be acceptable in your state. Check with your state for the forms that are acceptable there.

Sometimes an individual animal, such as a racehorse or other valuable animal, is not branded but is valuable because of its husbandry or other unique trait. For such livestock, the registration must be transferred to the name of your trust. The form of registration varies from animal to animal and from breed to breed. While Form 1805 may work, you should contact that organization that registers the particular type and breed of animal so that you can obtain its form. The form generally contains instructions as to how the registration can be transferred.

In some cases, an animal will not be branded and will not have a registration. See Form 1806 in the Appendix for an Unregistered Livestock Bill of Sale.

Farm Equipment

Equipment without registered title can be transferred by a bill of sale or assignment. Most farm equipment, except for motor vehicles, does not have a formal document of title. For vehicles with registered title, the title registration must be changed to your living trust. This can generally be done by you after consultation with your lawyer. See Chapter Fifteen, ''Personal Effects and Other Tangible Personal Property.''

Royalty Interests, Copyrights, Trademarks, Licenses

Intangible personal property, such as royalty interests, copyrights, trademarks, and licenses, is transferred to your living trust by assignment. Notice of the transfer of registration should be filed with the state and federal authorities in which the interest is originally registered. Typically, only a nominal filing fee should be charged.

We have included several forms for your use. Form 1807 in the Appendix is an Assignment of Royalty Interest, Form 1808 is an Assignment of Copyright, Form 1809 is an Assignment of Trademark, and Form 1810 is an Assignment of Liquor License.

Special Tax Rules for Business Property

Business property is often subject to special tax benefits. Installment payments of federal estate tax, special use valuation, and waiver of attribution rules are three of the more important of those benefits. For the most part, none of those benefits is lost when the property is transferred to a revocable living trust.

Installment Payment of Federal Estate Tax

The transfer of a business interest, including a farm, ranch, or closely held business, to a living trust does not adversely affect the availability of an election to defer payments of federal estate tax. *Business interest* is an all-encompassing term used in the Internal Revenue Code that means all or some of the stock in a business corporation, a general or limited partnership interest, a sole proprietorship, or any other ownership in a business.

If the value of an interest in the business is more than 35 percent of the value of the adjusted gross estate of the deceased owner, an election can be made to defer payments of federal estate tax attributable to the business interest. Under this election, the federal estate tax can be paid in ten equal installments beginning five years after the tax would otherwise have been due. Only interest is due for the first five years. A special 4 percent interest rate is applied for the federal estate tax attributed to the first $1 million in value of the business interest; for any federal estate tax attributed to value in excess of $1 million, the normal government interest rate then in effect must be paid.

Waiver of Attribution Rules for a Family-Owned Corporation

"Attribution rules" prevent certain closely related family members from selling stock back to their corporation in order to avoid having the proceeds taxed as a dividend rather than a capital gain. The Internal Revenue Code provides that the shareholders of a corporation that buys back the stock of a family member must sign certain documents waiving these rules and promising that the sale is not a way to cheat on taxes.

Even if a family member owns his or her stock in a living trust, the Trustees may waive the family attribution rules in the redemption of stock of a family member. For more information, see *The Living Trust Revolution* (pp. 175 and 176).

Special Use Valuation Property

Property used in a farm, ranch, or other qualified business that is part of an estate can be valued based on methods that determine the value of the ongoing business, rather than the highest and best use. This method of valuation is called special use valuation. Transferring such property to a living trust does not adversely affect special use valuation.

Property acquired by a beneficiary from a living trust is eligible for special use valuation to the extent that the property is included in the decedent's gross estate. An heir who receives special use property from a decedent may also transfer the property to his or her revocable living trust as long as the heir retains full control over the trustee and maintains his or her right to revoke the trust.

There is a great variety of business and professional interests. These interests often are worth a substantial amount, so care must be taken when they are transferred into a revocable living trust. The rule for transferring these interests into your living trust is that if you or your nonlawyer advisors have any question whatsoever about how a transfer is to be accomplished, or there is concern about the ramifications of such a transfer, your lawyer should be consulted.

· 19 ·

Real Property Interests

Y ou should never attempt to transfer real estate into your living trust without the help of a lawyer licensed to practice in the state of the location of the property. The transfer of real estate is not merely the preparation of a deed. Many potential problems arise if the wrong deed is used or the deed is improperly completed or filed. Certain types of real property are subject to various title standards and rules and regulations. In addition, if the property is subject to any type of debt, lien, or mortgage, a transfer may inadvertently cause the debt to come due or force you to renegotiate the interest rate to a higher level.

We cannot emphasize enough the importance of getting help in this area. However, because we feel strongly that education will make you more likely to understand the need for a lawyer's assistance, the purpose of this chapter is to discuss a number of different types of interests in real estate and how they should be treated for purposes of funding a trust. The examples that we give here are not meant to be forms; they are merely illustrations of what the documents of transfer look like.

Transferring Real Property to a Living Trust

There are a number of issues that need to be considered when transferring real property to trust ownership. These include the kind of deed that you use, transfer taxes, liabilities, and property and title insurance.

Types of Deeds

Deeds that transfer interests in real property come in several varieties. The type of deed that is used to transfer real property into a trust varies depending on the state in which the property is located and the type of property that is being transferred.

Warranty Deed vs. Quitclaim Deed

A Quitclaim Deed is generally sufficient to transfer real property to a living trust. A Quitclaim Deed transfers your entire interest in the property to your trust, but does not "warrant" that the new owner is receiving good title to the property. Quitclaim Deeds are often used when a transfer is taking place between related parties, such as a trust maker and a trust, or when an owner of property is not sure how good his or her title is to the property. Figure 19-1 shows a sample Quitclaim Deed.

A Quitclaim Deed warrants nothing. It only promises that the current owner transfers whatever interest in the property he or she has. There is no warranty that the title is good for any purpose.

A Warranty Deed may be required to preserve the chain of warranties for purposes of maintaining title insurance coverage. Figure 19-2 is a form of Warranty Deed. A "warranty" in a Warranty Deed simply means that the owner who is transferring the property guarantees to the new owner that the new owner is receiving clear title to the property except those exceptions that are disclosed on the public record. Exceptions include easements, mortgages, and liens.

When you transfer title from yourself to your trust, it often doesn't really matter if you make a warranty of title or not. After all, you are only transferring property that you already own to a trust that you fully control; this is much like transferring your own property to yourself. Generally, warranties of title are not important in this case. However, if the trust later sells the property, the buyer may wonder why a transfer was made that did not warrant title. Sometimes a title company may not issue a title policy if there is a conveyance that does not warrant title.

The area of real estate conveyances is controlled in many geographic regions by title companies. In some locations, transfers to living trusts using a Quitclaim Deed rather than a Warranty Deed may cause the title insurance coverage to lapse. You must check with your lawyer and your title insurance company before a transfer is made in order to ensure that your title insurance coverage will be maintained.

Figure 19-1

QUITCLAIM DEED

KNOW ALL MEN BY THESE PRESENTS that JOHN DOE and JANE DOE, husband and wife, Grantors, for and in consideration of Ten Dollars ($10.00) and other good and valuable consideration in hand paid, receipt of which is hereby acknowledged, remise, release and forever quitclaim unto JOHN DOE and JANE DOE, Trustees, or their successors in trust, under the DOE LIVING TRUST, dated March 11, 1995, and any amendments thereto, GRANTEES, all right, title, interest, claim and demand that the Trust Makers have or ought to have, whether now owned or hereafter acquired, in and to all of the following real property situated in the County of Junction, State of Anywhere, to wit:

Legal Description of Property:

SUBJECT TO current taxes, assessments, reservations in patents and all easements, rights of way, encumbrances, liens, covenants, conditions and restrictions as may appear of record.

IN WITNESS WHEREOF this instrument has been duly executed and delivered on March 11, 1995.

Witnesses as to both:

_____   _____
John Doe   Witness

_____   _____
Jane Doe   Witness

STATE OF ANYWHERE   )
) ss.
COUNTY OF JUNCTION   )

On March 11, 1995, before me personally appeared JOHN DOE and JANE DOE, as Grantors. WITNESS my hand and official seal.

_____
Notary Public

My commission expires:

Figure 19-2

WARRANTY DEED

JOHN DOE and JANE DOE, husband and wife as tenants by the entireties, Grantors, of Junction County, State of Anywhere, for and in consideration of TEN DOLLARS ($10.00) and other good and valuable consideration, in hand paid, receipt of which is hereby acknowledged, CONVEY AND WARRANT to JOHN DOE and JANE DOE, husband and wife as tenants in common, GRANTEES, whose address is 111 Main Street, Your City, Anywhere, 00001, the following described real estate, situated in the County of Junction, State of Anywhere, hereby waiving and releasing all rights under and by virtue of the homestead exemption laws of the State of Anywhere, to wit:

Legal Description of Property:

WITNESS our hands on March 11, 1995.

Witnesses as to both:

_____   _____
John Doe   Witness

_____   _____
Jane Doe   Witness

STATE OF ANYWHERE   )
)   ss.
COUNTY OF JUNCTION   )

On March 11, 1995, before me personally appeared JOHN DOE and JANE DOE, as Grantors. WITNESS my hand and official seal.

_____

Notary Public

My commission expires:

Trustee's Deed or Fiduciary Deed

Some states require special language in a deed when real property is conveyed to a trustee. For example, in Florida a Warranty Deed made to a trust needs to contain the following language:

> Trustees are hereby conferred with the power and authority to protect, conserve, sell, lease, encumber, and otherwise to manage and dispose of the above property as Trustees under the provisions of Section 689.071 Florida Statutes, and the interest of any beneficiary under the Trust shall be personal property only.

Your lawyer will know what special language, if any, your state requires in a deed that conveys real property to a trustee.

Unrecorded Deeds

This method of trust funding keeps title to real property in your name during your lifetime, but avoids the need for the probate process to transfer the property to the trust on your death or incapacity. There are several commonplace situations in which unrecorded deeds are used. An unrecorded deed is used to prevent disclosure of trust terms in jurisdictions that require recording the trust document when real property is titled in the name of the trust. It is also used when special state law advantages, such as homestead status, may not be available to property held in trust. Unrecorded deeds are also convenient in funding a married couple's separate trusts with joint property. Additionally, the unrecorded deed offers convenience and the avoidance of immediate recording fees, even though these fees are almost always nominal.

The unrecorded deed method of funding for real estate is relatively simple. You sign a deed that transfers your real estate to your trust. The deed is not recorded until your incapacity or death. For the transfer of real property using an unrecorded deed to be effective, there must be "delivery" to the trustee. This means that after you sign the deed, there must be some evidence that the trustee, probably you, saw and accepted the deed after it was signed. Therefore, it is wise for the trustee to sign a receipt stating that the Trustee has received the unrecorded deed. In the event that the transfer is later questioned, there is written evidence of delivery. See Form 1901 in the Appendix for a sample receipt.

If you wish to dispose of the property during your lifetime, the trustee returns the deed to you and you can destroy it. Otherwise, the deed is recorded upon your death or disability and the property does not pass through the probate process since it is titled in the name of your trust.

This technique can be used only in states in which unrecorded deeds are recognized as valid. In some states, because of title standards, case law, or statute, unrecorded deeds are not valid. You must check with your lawyer to see if this technique works in your state.

A drawback to the use of unrecorded deeds is that the property will not be controlled by the trust upon your disability or death unless the deeds are recorded as planned. Good records must be kept, and of course the deeds must be kept in a safe place.

Transfer Taxes

The state transfer taxes, usually called documentary taxes, that typically apply to real estate transfers do not generally apply to transfers of your real estate to your revocable trust. There are several reasons why no documentary tax is imposed on trust funding. The most common reason for no tax is that the amount of the tax due on real estate transfers is computed as a percentage of the amount paid. Since no money passes hands on a transfer to a living trust, no tax is due. Another reason that no tax may be due is that in some states the legislature has given a specific exemption for transfers of real property to living trusts.

A limited number of states require that specific deeds have to be used when transferring assets to a living trust to avoid payment of a transfer tax on funding a revocable trust. Your lawyer will advise you if there are any special procedures in your state that must be followed to transfer real property to your trust without incurring transfer taxes.

Property and Title Insurance

You or your lawyer should contact your local agent for your homeowner's insurance company so that you can comply with any requirements to continue liability and property coverage on property titled in your living trust. As mentioned earlier, you or your lawyer should also contact your title insurance company to make sure that they are aware of the transfer and to ensure continuing coverage of your title insurance.

Whenever you acquire new property after you have a living trust, the property should be purchased directly by the trust in the title form that your lawyer deems advisable. When property is purchased directly by the living trust, none of the title insurance problems discussed earlier will apply, since the title insurance will be in the trust's name from the outset.

Issues That Commonly Arise
When Title to Real Property Is Held in Trust

Funding your trust with real property routinely generates a number of financial and legal issues that need to be addressed. If you are aware of these issues, the operation of your trust is much simpler.

Mortgage Refinancing

Lenders occasionally are reluctant to refinance property held in trust. There is no good reason for this reluctance. The original mortgagors continue to be personally liable on the mortgage after it is transferred to their living trust. Additionally, the property continues to be encumbered by the mortgage. Any refinancing gives the lender the same recourse as the original financing.

There are several approaches to take whenever you are dealing with a lender who is unwilling to agree to refinance trust property. You could offer to sign the refinancing documents both as trustee and as an individual. Or, as a last resort, you could transfer the property out of the trust, finalize the loan documents, record them, and then transfer the property back to the trust by unrecorded deed or even by recording the deed.

Care must be taken if you record the deed in the name of the trust after you refinance it. There may be a "due on sale clause" that would cause the mortgage to become due if you transfer the property to your trust. If this is of concern to you, see the section later in this chapter titled "Property Subject to Indebtedness: Mortgages and Land Sale Contracts" for more information.

Successor Trustee

One of the benefits of a fully funded living trust is that upon your death or disability, property can be subsequently transferred out of your trust without a court proceeding. However, unless there is a clear continuity of trustees that will be accepted by the county recorder's office, title companies, and a future buyer's lawyer, some problems can arise that may delay the transfer.

One of the most common problems that arises after a trustee resigns, becomes incapacitated, dies, or is no longer acting as a trustee for any other reason is that the real estate is held in the name of the original trustees. If you remember, title to real estate owned in a trust is generally taken in the following manner:

> *JOHN DOE and JANE DOE, Trustees, or their successors in trust, under the JOHN DOE LIVING TRUST, dated March 11, 1995, and any amendments thereto.*

If either John Doe or Jane Doe is not serving as trustee, there is a problem if a third party, such as a title company, requires that both trustees sign off on a transaction.

One method to cure this problem, especially upon the death of a trustee, is to record an Affidavit of Successor Trustee along with the original trustee's death certificate. The affidavit, an example of which is shown as Form 1902 in the Appendix, refers to the trust provisions that name a successor trustee. It also includes a legal description of the property to establish a link from the previous trustee to the successor. This concept is similar to the typical process used to clear title to jointly owned property on the death of the first joint tenant.

For a trustee who is disabled or resigns, a similar affidavit can be filed, substituting a letter of resignation or a physician's certificate of incapacity for the death certificate. Forms 1903 and 1904, respectively, in the Appendix are examples of these two additional affidavits.

Specific Types of Real Property

Specific types of real property have specific funding problems and tax consequences. Following is a discussion of most of these types of real property.

Residences

A primary residence is perhaps the single most valuable asset for many Americans. Because of its importance, special care must be taken when transferring residences into a trust, especially in light of issues dealing with real estate taxation and income tax issues. As part of the process of placing your residence into your living trust, you should notify your property and casualty agent of the transfer of ownership. The agent will instruct your insurance company to change the name of the insured to your living trust. A sample notification letter is provided in Form 1509.

Homestead Exemptions

Many states have a homestead exemption for purposes of excluding personal residences from property taxes, the claims of creditors, or both. Homestead provisions are personal to the owners of the homestead, and in a number of states it is uncertain whether a residence that is transferred to a trust will retain its homestead status because the owner is a trust rather than a person or persons. You must check with your attorney to determine whether your homestead should be transferred to your trust. In our experience, there are few, if any, jurisdictions that take away your homestead just because you decide to accomplish proper estate planning. If you decide not to transfer homestead property to a living trust because of the potential loss of homestead status, state law sometimes provides that this property will not pass through probate in any event.

In some states, a transfer of a homestead to a trust will not adversely affect the homestead status of the property. In Oklahoma, for example, it is pretty clear that transferring the homestead to a living trust will not affect the homestead exemption for property taxes. In Florida, homestead property can be titled in the name of a living trust; however, because of Florida's unique homestead law, transferring a homestead to a trust is not necessary in many cases.

In Texas, there is some question as to whether or not a living trust is entitled to a homestead exemption. To be assured that the homestead will be preserved, Texas attorneys often create a life tenancy in the name of the trust maker or makers, with the remainder passing into the revocable living trust after the death of the trust maker or makers. This legal sleight of hand retains the homestead exemption and the property passes into the living trust probate-free.

Income Tax Effects of Transferring Your Residence to Your Trust

The Internal Revenue Code gives special tax treatment to homeowners when they sell their houses. These benefits include the one-time exclusion for the gain on the sale of a principal residence by a person who is age fifty-five or older and the nonrecognition of gain on the sale of a principal residence when the gain is used to purchase a new residence within two years. Residences that are transferred to a revocable living trust retain these important income tax advantages.

Vacation Homes

Property used exclusively by you as a vacation home can be transferred to your living trust in the same fashion as other real property. There are no unique issues that apply exclusively to vacation homes.

Cooperative Apartments

Approval of the cooperative's board of directors is generally required for transfers of your cooperative stock, including funding your living trust. The board might object to the transfer of the shares in the cooperative to a living trust if the board's policy is to allow only individual ownership. A board will not usually deny trust ownership when it is explained that the living trust is the alter ego of the trust maker.

A cooperative is denied favorable income tax treatment when less than 80 percent of its units are not owned by "tenant-stockholders," a term that is found in the Internal Revenue Code. This income tax provision is worrisome to cooperative boards, so they are often reluctant to grant approval to new owners. However, living trusts are considered to be "tenant-stockholders," so any fear that a trust's owning cooperative stock will have adverse income tax consequences to the cooperative is unfounded.

To begin the process of transferring your cooperative stock to your trust, you generally must ask the board of directors for permission to make the transfer. Form 1905 in the Appendix is a sample letter to the board of a cooperative requesting such a transfer. Your cooperative directors will then furnish you and your attorney with the proper agreements to transfer your cooperative stock to your trust.

Condominiums

Generally, condominium associations also require the approval of the board of directors prior to any transfer of title of a condominium unit. Standard condominium bylaws often prohibit ownership by entities other than individuals, who often are required to reside in the unit. Usually, an exception is available when the owner wishes to transfer title of the unit to the owner's revocable living trust. Your lawyer should review the condominium bylaws and take the necessary steps to obtain approval of the condominium association to the transfer of your unit to your living trust.

Form 1906 in the Appendix is a letter asking the board of directors of a condominium association for permission to transfer a condominium unit to a living trust. Your condominium association will provide you and your attorney with the proper agreements to transfer your condominium to your trust.

Time-shares

A time-share is a unit of ownership in a resort or vacation property. The vacation property is divided into specific time periods during which the unit owner has the exclusive right to occupy the property. The time periods of occupancy usually are for the same one or two weeks each year.

Legal ownership of a time-share unit is usually created in one of three ways. In a "vacation license," the owner has the right to occupy an unspecified unit at a certain vacation resort during specific days for a determined number of years. This "vacation license" form of time-share may or may not be an interest in real property, depending on state law. If it is not an interest in real estate, it is considered to be a contract with the developer/owner.

A second type of ownership in a time-share unit is called appropriately "time-share ownership." This form of ownership gives the owner an ownership interest in the unit and the exclusive right to occupy it during specified time periods. The final form of ownership is known as the "vacation lease." In this type of time-share ownership, the owner has the right to occupy a specific unit during specific time periods for a specific number of years. These last two types of time-share ownership are interests in real property.

Ownership of your time-share should be transferred to your living trust by deed, contract, or lease, depending on how the ownership interest was originally obtained. If the evidence of ownership is a deed, transfer of the time-share should be by a Warranty or Quitclaim Deed in the same manner as a residence is transferred. See Figure 19-3.

If the evidence of ownership is a lease or contract, the interest in the time-share should be assigned to the trust. Figure 19-4 is an example of this kind of assignment. A photocopy of the original time-share lease or contract should be attached to the assignment.

Rental Real Estate

Property such as apartments, duplexes, condominium units, warehouses, farms, office buildings, and the like that you own and lease to third parties is typically transferred to your revocable living trust in the same manner as other real estate. It is important that your attorney review the lease agreement to make

Figure 19-3

DEED OF CONVEYANCE

This Indenture, Made this 11th of March, 1995, between JOHN DOE, GRANTOR, whose address is 111 Main Street, Your City, Anywhere, and JOHN DOE, sole trustee, or his successors in trust under the JOHN DOE LIVING TRUST, dated March 11, 1995, and any amendments thereto, GRANTEE, whose address is 111 Main Street, Your City, Anywhere.

Witnesseth, nthat the Grantor, for and in consideration of Ten and no/100 Dollars ($10.00) and other good and valuable consideration to Grantors in hand paid by Grantee, the receipt and sufficiency of which is hereby acknowledged, has granted, bargained, and sold to the said Grantee and Grantee's successors and assigns forever, the following described property from 12:00 noon of the first day until 12:00 noon on the last day assigned to said Grantees during the below described unit weeks numbers as said unit weeks are numbered and defined in the Declaration of Condominium recorded in the public records of Junction County, Anywhere, in the Book and at the Page Numbers hereinafter described below, which estate is to be succeeded forthwith by a succession of other estates in consecutive and chronological order, revolving among the other unit weeks described in the aforesaid Declaration of Condominium, in order annually, it being the intent of this instrument that each unit week shall be considered a separate estate held separately and independently by the respective owners thereof for and during the period of time assigned to each in said Declaration of Condominium, each said estate being succeeded by the next in unending succession governed by said Declaration of Condominium until 12:00 noon on the first Saturday in the year _____ at which date said estate shall terminate:

Together with a remainder over in fee simple absolute, as tenant in common with the other owners of all the unit weeks in the hereafter described condominium parcel in that percentage interest determined and established by Exhibit Number __ (Titled Percentage of Ownership) to the aforesaid Declaration of Condominium for the following described real estate located in the County of _____ and State of _____, as follows:

Trustee is hereby conferred with the power and authority to protect, conserve, sell, lease, encumber, and otherwise to manage and dispose of the above property as Trustees under the provisions of Section _____, _____ Statutes, and the interest of any beneficiary under the Trust shall be personal property only.

(continued on following page)

IN WITNESS WHEREOF, the Grantor has hereunto set her hand and seal on the day and year first above written.

_____   _____
Witness   Grantor

_____
Witness

STATE OF ANYWHERE   )
) ss.
COUNTY OF JUNCTION   )

On March 11, 1995, before me, the undersigned Notary Public, in and for said County and State, personally appeared JOHN DOE, Grantor, who is personally known to me (or produced _____ as identification) to be the person who executed the foregoing instrument, and acknowledged executing the same for the purposes herein contained.

_____
Notary Public   This document prepared by:

My commission expires:

Figure 19-4

ASSIGNMENT TO LIVING TRUST OF TIME-SHARE

JOHN DOE and JANE DOE, Husband and Wife, do hereby transfer and assign, without consideration and in order to change formal title only, all right, title and interest which they now have in that certain Timeshare, a copy of which is attached hereto, to JOHN DOE and JANE DOE, Trustees, or their Successors in Trust, under the DOE FAMILY TRUST, dated March 11, 1995, and any amendments thereto.

Dated: March 11, 1995.

Witnesses as to both:

_____   _____
John Doe   Witness

_____   _____
Jane Doe   Witness

STATE OF ANYWHERE   )
) ss.
COUNTY OF JUNCTION   )

On March 11, 1995, before me, the undersigned, a Notary Public and for said County and State, personally appeared JOHN DOE and JANE DOE, known to me to be the persons whose names are subscribed to the within instrument and acknowledged that they executed the same.

WITNESS my hand and official seal.

_____
Notary Public

My commission expires:

sure that the lease itself can be transferred to your living trust. This is important because you want your tenants to make rent checks payable to your trust, not to you individually.

Assignment of Lease

If payments are being made directly to you because the lease has not been assigned to your trust, then upon your incapacity or death, the rent is subject to either a financial guardianship in the case of disability or a probate in the case of death. This is true even if the real estate itself has been transferred into your trust. Thus it is imperative that your lease or leases with your tenants be in your trust. Figure 19-5 is an example of an Assignment of a Lease.

Income Tax Consequences of Transferring Rental Real Estate into a Living Trust

A unique income tax issue can arise when you own rental real estate that you want to transfer into your trust. Rental real estate activities are subject to the complex "passive activity" rules under the Internal Revenue Code. These rules were passed by Congress in an attempt to close many of the tax shelter loopholes that proliferated in the 1970s and 1980s.

In general, when you own real estate as an investment, you are considered to be a passive investor. Any losses from the rental real estate can only be deducted to the extent that you have income earned from other passive activities. For example, let's say you have one rental property that makes income, but another that loses income. Generally, you can offset your losses on the one property against the taxable income on the other. Any losses in excess of the taxable income can be used in later years when passive income exceeds the losses.

There is, however, an exception to this general rule. You can offset up to $25,000 of passive losses incurred each year from rental real estate activities against your other taxable income. This $25,000 deductible amount is phased out when a taxpayer's adjusted gross income exceeds $100,000 and is totally eliminated when it reaches $150,000. So if your adjusted gross income is under $100,000, you can deduct up to $25,000 per year from passive rental real estate. This deduction is allowed even if you transfer your rental real estate to your trust during your life.

After you die, however, your living trust becomes irrevocable and cannot take these losses immediately because an irrevocable trust is not allowed to take these deductions. These losses are added to the cost basis of the property, so they are not lost and will benefit the trust when the property is sold. A probated estate *can* take these losses for two years after the death of the property owner. Therefore, before transferring rental real estate to your living trust, you should discuss with your lawyer and accountant the relative merits of making the transfer based

Figure 19-5

ASSIGNMENT TO DOE LIVING TRUST
OF LEASE

JOHN DOE and JANE DOE, Grantors and Lessors, do hereby transfer and assign, without consideration and in order to change formal title only, all right, title and interest which they now have in that certain Lease made by and between JOHN DOE and JANE DOE (Lessors) and _____ (Lessee), on _____; a copy of the Lease Agreement is attached hereto and by this reference made a part hereof, unto:

JOHN DOE and JANE DOE, Trustees, or their successors in trust, under the DOE LIVING TRUST, dated March 11, 1995, and any amendments thereto,

Dated: _____   Witnesses as to both:

_____   _____
John Doe   Witness

_____   _____
Jane Doe   Witness

STATE OF ANYWHERE   )
) ss.
COUNTY OF JUNCTION   )

On March 11, 1995, before me personally appeared JOHN DOE and JANE DOE known to me to be the persons described in and who executed the foregoing Assignment, and acknowledged that they executed the same as their free act and deed.

WITNESS my hand and official seal.

_____

Notary Public

My commission expires:

on income tax considerations as opposed to the advantages of having your property owned in your living trust.

Out-of-State Real Property

If you own real property that is located in another state, probate proceedings will also be required in that state upon your death. Multiple probates are needlessly expensive and time-consuming, and can be eliminated when your real property is transferred to your living trust.

Title to your out-of-state real property should be transferred by a deed prepared by a lawyer in the state in which the property is located. Real property owned by your revocable trust avoids any probate proceedings in the state where the real property is situated and in your home state. This is a major benefit of a living trust over wills and probate.

Property Subject to Indebtedness: Mortgages and Land Sale Contracts

A creditor does not lose any rights in your real property that is secured by a mortgage or land contract when that property is retitled in the name of your living trust. It is clear that debt on secured property follows the property, no matter to whom the property is transferred.

In spite of this definitive rule of law, problems arise because creditors do not understand living trusts and they fear that they may be losing or impairing their rights. Under most circumstances, when the transaction and the law are explained, the creditor usually withdraws any objection.

Due-on-Sale Clauses

Prior to any transfer of mortgaged property into your living trust, your lawyer should determine whether there is any clause that restricts your ability to transfer the property to your trust. In some mortgages, there is a due-on-sale clause. A due-on-sale clause states that if the owner of the property transfers the property, then the holder of the mortgage has the right to be paid off immediately. In some of these clauses, the lender can increase the interest rate to the current market rate if a transfer is made.

Lenders will frequently waive their rights under a due-on-sale clause for transfers to living trusts. We feel strongly that it is in their best interests to do so.

Lenders have an important stake in whether or not you have accomplished proper estate planning. In a financial guardianship or a probate, all creditors, even those who are secured by a mortgage, are often not paid for several months or more because of the legal red tape required in these proceedings. Secured creditors, by law, cannot foreclose or otherwise take any action, so they must wait, just like everyone else, to be paid.

Property in a living trust avoids this delay. Secured creditors continue to be paid without the expense and complications that arise in financial guardianships and probate. It is also our experience that people who have done proper estate planning using the Esperti Peterson Planning Process are more likely to have their affairs in order, for purposes of financial and estate planning. These are people who are better risks for any creditor because they have taken the time and energy to plan to preserve their wealth.

It is important that lenders are properly notified and that approval is obtained prior to transferring real property to a trust that is subject to indebtedness. To do this, you or your lawyer can use the sample letter provided in Form 1907 in the Appendix.

The Garn–St. Germain Act

When you transfer your residence to your living trust, a federal law called the Garn–St. Germain Depository Institutions Act of 1982 prohibits a number of federally chartered or insured banking institutions from exercising a due-on-sale clause. The due-on-sale clause cannot be triggered as long as these three conditions apply:

- The property is residential property of less than five dwelling units
- The borrower is the beneficiary of the trust
- The borrower *retains the right to occupy the residence*

Even if this law applies to you, the lender should be notified prior to transfer. According to the regulations that have been issued to supplement the Garn–St. Germain Act, the lender is authorized to require certain assurances from the trust maker, including a promise to provide notification if the property should be subsequently sold.

The purpose of the Garn–St. Germain Act was to establish uniform policies and administration for federally backed loans. The ability of a borrower to place his or her home in a living trust is obviously supported by this law. Form 1908 in the Appendix is a letter you or your attorney can use to notify a lender of your intent to transfer property subject to the Garn–St. Germain Act to your revocable living trust.

Real Property Subject to Land Sale Contracts

In a land sale contract, the deed to the real property being purchased is held by the seller until the buyer completes the payments. If you are buying property under a land sale contract, you can assign the land sale contract to your trust using an Assignment of Land Sale Contract. Figure 19-6 shows one type of assignment for this purpose. The assignment must contain a full legal description of the property. A copy of the land sale contract should be attached to the assignment. This land sale contract may prohibit assignment without the permission of the seller. Your lawyer should review the land sale contract before you transfer it into your trust.

If you have sold property under a land sale contract, refer to Chapter Fifteen, which explains how you transfer your interest in the property to your trust.

Oil, Gas, and Mineral Interests

The method of transferring interests in oil, minerals, and gas depends on whether the rights or interests are owned or leased. If these interests are owned, generally your lawyer will prepare and record a Quitclaim Deed. Of course, your lawyer may choose to use other methods of transfer under your circumstances.

If you are leasing oil, gas, or mineral interests, then your rights as a lessee under the lease should be assigned to your living trust. An Assignment of Lease for Oil, Gas, or Mineral Interests is shown in Figure 19-7. A photocopy of the lease agreement should be attached to the assignment.

If you are the owner of an oil, gas, or mineral interest that is leased out, then you or your attorney should forward to the lessee a copy of the recorded deed and an assignment of the lease to the trust, so the lessee can make the change on its books and commence paying royalties directly to your living trust.

The transfer of proven oil and gas reserves to a revocable living trust does not adversely affect the trust maker's right to percentage depletion. Similarly, a transfer back to the maker from the trust will not affect the maker's right to percentage depletion. After the death of the maker, the trust can take percentage depletion, and so can trust beneficiaries to whom the proven oil and gas reserves are transferred.

Figure 19-6

ASSIGNMENT TO LIVING TRUST
OF LAND SALE CONTRACT—BUYER

JOHN DOE and JANE DOE, Husband and Wife, do hereby transfer and assign, without consideration and in order to change formal title only, all of our right, title and interest in that certain Land Sale Contract, executed by JOHN SMITH, a copy of which is attached hereto, to JOHN DOE and JANE DOE, Trustees, or their Successors in Trust, under the DOE FAMILY TRUST, dated March 11, 1995, and any amendments thereto.

[Lot One (1) of Junction County Certified Survey Map No. 2035.
Lot Five (5) of Junction County Certified Survey Map No. 2035.]

Dated: March 11, 1995.

Witnesses as to both:

_____   _____
Grantor   Witness

_____   _____
Grantor   Witness

STATE OF ANYWHERE   )
) ss.
COUNTY OF JUNCTION   )

On March 11, 1995, before me, the undersigned, a Notary Public and for said County and State, personally appeared JOHN DOE and JANE DOE as Grantors, known to me to be the persons whose names are subscribed to the within instrument and acknowledged that they executed the same.

WITNESS my hand and official seal.

_____

Notary Public

My commission expires:

Figure 19-7

ASSIGNMENT OF LEASE FOR OIL, GAS, OR MINERAL INTERESTS

JOHN DOE, of 111 Main Street, Your City, Anywhere, 00001, herein referred to as "Assignor," for and in consideration of the sum of TEN DOLLARS ($10.00) and OTHER GOOD AND VALUABLE CONSIDERATION, in hand paid, the receipt and sufficiency of which is hereby acknowledged, does hereby assign, transfer and convey all right, title, and interest to JOHN DOE and JANE DOE, Trustees, or their successors in trust, under the DOE LIVING TRUST, dated March 11, 1995, and any amendments thereto, herein referred to as "Assignee" all overriding royalty, royalty interests and mineral interests.

A description of which is attached hereto marked Exhibit "A" and by this reference made a part hereof. Reference is made in this particular assignment of mineral interests from the Company's Transfer Order and Attachment with Lease Names, Lease Numbers, and Legal Descriptions, and is recorded in the County of Junction in Book _____, Pages _____ and _____.

Dated: March 11, 1995.

_____   _____
John Doe   Witness

                                        _____
                                        Witness

STATE OF ANYWHERE   )
) ss.
COUNTY OF JUNCTION   )

On March 11, 1995, before me personally appeared JOHN DOE as Assignor, known to me to be the person described in and who executed the foregoing Assignment, and acknowledged that he executed the same as his free act and deed.

WITNESS my hand and official seal.

_____
Notary Public

My commission expires:

Leases

If you are leasing property, you may want to transfer your lease into your trust. This is especially true if you have a long-term lease that has favorable terms. In many cases, such a lease is a valuable asset.

You may transfer your leasehold interest to your living trust by signing an assignment to your trust. Figure 19-8 is a typical example of this kind of assignment. Before assigning your lease, you and your lawyer must make sure that the lease agreement does not prohibit assignment. If it does, you will have to obtain the landlord's permission to make this transfer. The landlord's consent to the assignment must not be unreasonably withheld. In our experience, just like for secured creditors, it is very much in the landlord's interest to have the lease held by a living trust. Probate can be as hard on creditors as it can be on a family.

Figure 19-8

ASSIGNMENT TO DOE LIVING TRUST
OF LEASEHOLD

JOHN DOE and JANE DOE, Grantors and Lessees, do hereby transfer and assign, without consideration and in order to change formal title only, all right, title and interest which they now have in that certain Lease made by and between _____ (Lessor) and JOHN DOE and JANE DOE (Lessees) on _____; a copy of the Lease Agreement is attached hereto and by this reference made a part hereof, unto:

> JOHN DOE and JANE DOE, Trustees, or their successors in trust, under the DOE LIVING TRUST, dated March 11, 1995, and any amendments thereto,

Dated: March 11, 1995   Witnesses as to both:

_____   _____

John Doe   Witness

_____   _____

Jane Doe   Witness

STATE OF ANYWHERE   )
)   ss.
COUNTY OF JUNCTION   )

On March 11, 1995, before me personally appeared JOHN DOE and JANE DOE known to me to be the persons described in and who executed the foregoing Assignment, and acknowledged that they executed the same as their free act and deed.

WITNESS my hand and official seal.

_____

Notary Public

My commission expires:

·20·

Miscellaneous Property

There are several types of property that are somewhat unusual, but still must be considered when funding a living trust. These types of property have value and will be subject to a financial guardianship and probate if they are left out of the trust. Funding a living trust with these property interests is not particularly difficult in most instances, but as with all other assets, you should seek the help of your lawyer and other advisors if any complications arise or if you have any questions.

Safe-Deposit Boxes

Typically, the right to the use of a safe-deposit box is created in the form of a rental agreement between a financial institution and a customer. The financial institution may deny access to a safe-deposit box upon the death of the customer, especially in those states that have an estate or inheritance tax. The institution will generally only open the box after receiving a court order to do so. A problem with the delay associated with obtaining a court order is that the customer's original will may be in the safe-deposit box! If a will is the only estate planning document, no action can be taken by anyone until the original will is filed with the probate court.

A fully funded living trust–centered plan can avoid the problem of having access to a safe-deposit box denied upon the disability or death of the trust maker if the safe-deposit box is in the name of the trust rather than in an individual name. Transfer of a safe-deposit box to a living trust is accomplished by assigning the rights under the existing rental agreement to the living trust or by having the trust enter into a new rental agreement with the financial institution. The trustees of the trust then sign the rental agreement and a signature card.

It is a good idea to allow a successor trustee to have authority to get into the safe-deposit box. If the primary trustees are incapacitated or deceased, then the successor trustee can get into the box.

An Affidavit of Trust is sometimes effective when a successor trustee does not have signature authority over the box. Since the affidavit, Form 1201 in the Appendix, includes the names of successor trustees, if the safe-deposit box is in the name of the trust, the financial institution should not have any qualms about allowing a successor trustee access.

Cemetery Plots

Generally, ownership of a cemetery plot is evidenced by a contract with the entity owning the cemetery rather than through a deed to real property. You may transfer your cemetery plot to your living trust by assignment. We have provided two types of forms. Form 2001 in the Appendix is an Assignment of Certificate of Interment Rights and Form 2002 is an Assignment of Burial Plot/Mausoleum. The one that you will use depends on the contract you have. You will have to ask the company that sold you the cemetery plot which one is appropriate for you.

Memberships

A club membership is often a valuable asset that can be transferred upon the death of a member. If you own a club membership, your club membership agreement should state whether your membership rights are assignable. If the agreement is silent concerning assignment or does not generally permit assignment, then you should petition the board of directors to approve an assignment to your living trust. Form 2003 in the Appendix is an Assignment of Membership that can be used to get your club membership into your trust.

Judgments

A judgment is a court order that grants a party in a lawsuit certain rights against other parties. A judgment often has value because when it is executed, it results in the acquisition of cash or property. Because of its value, a judgment should be transferred into a living trust.

Any interest you have in a judgment is an interest in personal property and can be transferred to your living trust by an Assignment of Judgment. See Form 2004 in the Appendix. A copy of the original judgment should be attached to the assignment.

For most types of personal property, an assignment is sufficient to transfer the property to your trust. If ever you are in doubt, we suggest you use an assignment; however, be sure to have your lawyer review the assignment, especially if the personal property is of a type that is subject to an agreement or other documents that may have an impact as to whether or not the underlying asset can be assigned.

·21·

Other Important Elements of Your Living Trust–Centered Plan

Initiating, designing, creating, and funding your living trust–centered plan are critical steps in accomplishing your estate planning objectives. However, to be completely organized and prepared, a few last steps are important too.

In this chapter, we want to offer you several ideas about additional documentation that you should consider. These include a Location List for your important documents, a list of those people who should be contacted upon your incapacity or death, anatomical gifts, and burial and memorial instructions.

Location of Your Important Documents

You should have at least two duplicate original sets of almost all of your living trust–centered documents. The only exception to this rule is your Pour-Over Will. Because of the complex legal requirements that govern wills and their validity, *you should have one and only one signed, original will.*

One original set of your living trust–centered plan, including your Pour-Over Will, should be kept in a secure location. We do not recommend that you use a safe-deposit box because of the difficulties that sometimes arise in having access to the box. A fireproof box or a safe in your home or business is a good place to put these original documents. If you have named a bank or other corporate trustee in your plan, it is likely that you will be able to keep your documents in the corporate trustee's vault at no charge.

The other set of your duplicate originals, which should include a copy of your will, not the original, should be kept in your home. This home set should be readily accessible. The reason that you want to have one set of documents at home that is accessible is simple. If something happens to you—or to you or your spouse if you are married—then you want people whom you love or trust to know exactly where your estate planning documents are. If you have not notified others where your papers are, the process of finding them can create all kinds of delays and uncomfortable problems for your loved ones. Thus having a set of documents readily available is important.

You may even want other sets of your documents, depending on your situation. It is not uncommon for some people to ask their attorney to keep a duplicate set of documents. While this is not absolutely necessary, there is some comfort in knowing that the attorney who prepared the documents has a copy just in case any questions arise as to their whereabouts. In some instances, you may want your successor trustees to have a copy of the documents. If they are called to serve because of your incapacity or death, they are then fully prepared.

Any of these choices are based on your personal situation and your feelings about how important it is to you who has copies of your living trust–centered plan. The same is true about your other important papers that deal with estate planning. They should be able to be located if something happens to you. That is why you should keep a Location List to help others locate your important estate planning documents if you are not available. Your Location List should be kept in an easy-to-get-to spot. Several people should know exactly where this list is kept so that in an emergency, they can find it. It is a good idea, in fact, to make several copies and give them to your spouse, children, close relatives, successor trustees, friends, or advisors so they know where to look for your important papers.

People Who Should Be Contacted

Now that you have a professional team, you have key advisors. These advisors need to be contacted upon your death or disability. A list of these advisors should be part of your Location List. In that way, those advisors who are important to you can help as soon as they are notified of your death or incapacity.

In addition, you may have some close friends or relatives that you want to be contacted. A list of them should be part of your Location List. Add to your Location List those people whom you want to be contacted upon your incapacity or death.

Anatomical Gifts

Many people would like to make anatomical gifts after they have passed away. Anatomical gifts can save the lives of those who are in need of transplants or organs, or can allow them to live better, more healthy lives.

States differ as to the requirements for making anatomical gifts. In some states, forms for donating anatomical gifts can be filed as part of procuring a driver's license. In other states, anatomical gifts can be made by will or other document that is signed and witnessed. Because of the differing state requirements, you should consult with your attorney about how it is done in your state.

Form 2101 in the Appendix is an example of an Anatomical Gift Form that may be valid in your state. Have your attorney review this form to make certain it is valid in your state; if it is not, your attorney can furnish you one that is.

Burial and Memorial Instructions

In our experience, many of our clients want to leave instructions about how they wish to be buried and the type of memorial they would like. As in many areas of the law, the way in which this is legally accomplished varies from state to state.

Many states, either by case law or statute, require an executor or close relatives to follow any written burial and memorial instructions that are left by a decedent. These can be in the decedent's will or can be in a separate writing. Other states do not require that a decedent's wishes be followed. In these states, it is not uncommon for the spouse or other relatives to have the authority to deal with these matters despite any instructions to the contrary that are left by the decedent.

Here is another area where you must seek out the advice of your attorney. Since it is extremely likely that your spouse, relatives, friends, or advisors will honor your wishes, you should write down clearly what your burial and memorial instructions are. In Form 2102 in the Appendix we have included a Memorial Letter that allows you to express your feelings in these matters. Please remember, you must find out about your state's laws if you have strong feelings about how you are to be buried and the types of memorials that you want.

Location Lists

This section contains forms that pinpoint the location of your important documents and tell your loved ones and trustees who should be notified on your disability or death.

These location lists will be extraordinarily helpful to your loved ones and trustees and should be kept current.

DOCUMENT FINDER

Living Trust Portfolio   Location _____

Home address _____

Location 1 _____   Location 2 _____

Location 3 _____   Location 4 _____

Safe-deposit box   Box number _____

Bank _____   Key location _____

Advisor 1 _____   Address _____

Advisor 2 _____   Address _____

		Living Trust Portfolio	Home Location 1	Home Location 2	Home Location 3	Home Location 4	Safe-Deposit Box	Advisor 1	Advisor 2
Trusts	Living trust, husband	✓							
	Living trust, wife	✓							
Ancillary Estate Planning Documents	Original will, husband								
	Original will, wife								
	Copies of wills	✓							
	Living will	✓							
	Memorial instructions, husband	✓							
	Memorial instructions, wife	✓							
	Affidavit of trust	✓							
	Durable Special Power of Attorney for Health Care	✓							

		Living Trust Portfolio	Home Location 1	Home Location 2	Home Location 3	Home Location 4	Safe-Deposit Box	Advisor 1	Advisor 2
	Anatomical gift form	✓							
	Cemetery plot deed								
Business papers	Employment contracts								
	Partnership agreements								
	Corporation documents								
	Leases								
	Bills of sale								
Securities	Investment securities								
	Brokerage account								
	Stock certificates								
	Bonds								
	Annuity contracts								
	Stock-option plan								
Retirement plans	Pension plan								
	Profit sharing plan								
	H.R. 10								
	IRA								
Cash	Checkbook(s)								
	Savings passbook(s)								

		Living Trust Portfolio	Home Location 1	Home Location 2	Home Location 3	Home Location 4	Safe-Deposit Box	Advisor 1	Advisor 2
	Credit cards								
	CDs								
	Bank statements and canceled checks								
Tax records	Income tax returns								
	Gift tax returns								
Real estate	Deeds to real estate								
	Title insurance								
	Rental property records								
	Notes and loan agreements								
	Mortgages								
Personal effects and other assets	Distribution memorandum								
	Car titles								
	Boat/plane titles								
	Durable Special Power of Attorney for Funding	✓							
	Tenancy agreement or community agreement	✓							
	Nominee Partnership Agreement								
	Nominee agreement								
	List of insurance policies	✓							
	Marriage certificate								

	Living Trust Portfolio	Home Location 1	Home Location 2	Home Location 3	Home Location 4	Safe-Deposit Box	Advisor 1	Advisor 2
Divorce/separation papers								
Birth certificates								
Adoption papers								
Citizenship papers								
Military papers								
List of friends, relatives, and advisors	✓							
Other								

KEY ADVISORS TO BE CONTACTED

Accountant _____

Phone _____   Firm _____

Address _____

Attorney _____

Phone _____   Firm _____

Address _____

Auto insurance agent _____

Phone _____   Firm _____

Address _____

Banker _____

Phone _____   Firm _____

Address _____

Clergyman/rabbi _____

Phone _____   Church/Synagogue _____

Address _____

Doctor _____

Phone _____   Hospital _____

Address _____

Employer _____

Phone _____   Firm _____

Address _____

Financial advisor _____

Phone _____   Firm _____

Address _____

RELATIVES AND CLOSE FRIENDS TO BE CONTACTED

Name _____
Relationship _____   Phone _____
Address _____

Name _____
Relationship _____   Phone _____
Address _____

Name _____
Relationship _____   Phone _____
Address _____

Name _____
Relationship _____   Phone _____
Address _____

Name _____
Relationship _____   Phone _____
Address _____

Name _____
Relationship _____   Phone _____
Address _____

Name _____
Relationship _____   Phone _____
Address _____

Name _____
Relationship _____   Phone _____
Address _____

·22·

A Final Word

Estate planning is an act of love, not an act of death. It is a process that you can control and participate in, not as a victim who has to die to make it work, but as the focal point of the process. The Esperti Peterson Planning Process is by far the best way for you to establish and accomplish your estate planning objectives.

It is our sincere hope that you will follow the Esperti Peterson Planning Process whether you are just beginning your estate planning, you are in the midst of planning your estate, or you have finished your plan but are not totally comfortable with the result.

Thousands of people have successfully completed the Esperti Peterson Planning Process and have estate plans that control their property and care for them and their loved ones if they become incapacitated. Their plans allow them to give their money and property to whom they want, the way they want, and when they want at the least possible cost. Their living trust–centered plans meet the definition of estate planning.

This workbook is to help you participate in the planning process, not as a lone ranger, but as part of an estate planning team. We encourage you to seek out a member of the National Network of Estate Planning Attorneys or other competent estate planning attorney. We hope that you will also find other professional advisors who are interested in helping you and your family meet the definition of estate planning.

Our promise to you is that if you follow our planning process, you and your professional team will create a plan that reflects your planning objectives and that will give you the comfort and peace of mind that you have done meaningful planning for you and your loved ones.

APPENDIX

■

Forms

Form 401

Letter to Confirm Appointment with Your Attorney

Date:

Address:

_____

_____

_____

Dear

I look forward to meeting with you at your office on _____ at _____ . It is my understanding that there will be no charge for this meeting and that it will take between one and two hours.

The purpose of our first meeting is to discuss the design and preparation of my estate planning.

I am enclosing my completed "My Checklist for Designing My Plan" and "My Personal Information Checklist." My spouse will be attending our meeting.

If there are any changes, or if any of my statements are not consistent with your understanding, please contact me at your earliest convenience.

Sincerely yours,

Form 801

Letter to Confirm Your Fee and Second Meeting

Date:

Address:

_____

_____

_____

Dear

My spouse and I enjoyed meeting with you and look forward to working with you on our estate planning.

This letter is to confirm those agreements that we made in our meeting. For a total fee of _____, you are going to prepare our living trust–centered plan, based on the planning we discussed. On _____ , my spouse and I will meet with you in your office to review and sign our living trust–centered documents.

If this is not your understanding, please get back to me as soon as possible.

Sincerely yours,

Form 901

Letter About Changes in the Law

Date:
Address:

_____

_____

_____

Dear

I would like to thank you once again for preparing my living trust–centered plan. As you can imagine, I am vitally concerned that my planning is kept up to date with changes in the laws. While I recognize that I have a responsibility to apprise you of changes in my life that may affect my estate planning, I want to make sure that you will notify me whenever you believe a change in the law will affect my estate planning.

I will rely on you to keep me informed as to changes in the laws and with respect to your recommendations as well.

I understand that any changes I make in my planning will not be covered by my original fee and will be subject to a fee arrangement that we will agree on.

Sincerely yours,

Form 1001

The Income Tax Ramifications of My Living Trust

My revocable living trust is a Grantor Trust as described in Internal Revenue Code Section 671 and Regulations Section 1.671-4. Therefore, it is not required to file a separate Form 1041. All income and expense are reported on my Form 1040.

Under Internal Revenue Code Regulation Section 301.6109-1(a)(2), when a grantor or a grantor's spouse is acting as the trustee of a Grantor Trust, the Federal Identification Number for a Grantor Trust is the same as the grantor's Social Security number. Because I am serving as a trustee of my revocable living trust, the trust's Federal Identification Number is my Social Security number. My trust's name, my Social Security number, my name, address and phone number are provided below for your convenience.

The name of my Trust is:

My Social Security Number is:

My name, address and telephone number are:

_____

(Please sign your name here)

Form 1201

Affidavit of Trust

1. The following trust is the subject of this Affidavit:

    _____ and _____ , Trustees, or their successors in trust, under the _____ LIVING TRUST dated _____ , and any amendments thereto.

2. The names and addresses of the current Trustees of the trust agreement are as follows:

Name: **Name:**

_____

Address: **Address:**

_____

_____

3. The trust is currently in full force and effect.

4. Attached to this Affidavit and incorporated in it are selected provisions of the trust including the pages naming the initial trustees, creating the trust, trustees' powers, statement of revocability of the trust, the designation of successor trustees, and a copy of the signature pages.

5. The trust provisions which are not attached to this Affidavit are of a personal nature and set forth the distribution of trust property. They do not modify the powers of the Trustees.

6. The signatories of this Affidavit are currently the acting Trustees of the trust and declare that the foregoing statements and the attached trust provisions are true and correct, under penalty of perjury.

7. This Affidavit is dated _____ .

                                                          Witness as to both:

_____

              , Trustee   , Witness

_____

              , Trustee   , Witness

STATE OF   )

) ss.

COUNTY OF   )

The foregoing Affidavit of Trust was acknowledged before me on _____ , by _____ and _____ , as Trustees; _____ and _____ , as Witnesses, all of whom personally appeared before me, are personally known to me, or who presented _____ as identification.

Witness my hand and official seal.

_____

                    , Notary Public

My commission expires:

Form 1202

ATTORNEY'S CERTIFICATE

1. The following Trust is the subject of this Certificate:

   _____ and _____ , Trustees, or their successors in trust, under the _____ LIVING TRUST dated _____,
   and any amendments thereto.

2. The Trustees currently serving are:

   _____

   _____

3. The Trust is currently in full force and effect.

4. Attached to this Certificate and incorporated in it are selected provisions of the Trust including the pages naming the initial trustees, creating the trust, trustees' powers, statement of revocability of the trust, the designation of successor trustees, and a copy of the signature pages.

5. The Trust provisions which are not attached to this Certificate are of a personal nature and set forth the distribution of Trust property. They do not modify the powers of the Trustees.

6. The signatory of this Certificate is an attorney licensed to practice in the State of _____ and is an active member of the State Bar of _____, and he declares that the foregoing statements and the attached Trust provisions are true and correct, under penalty of perjury under the laws of the State of _____.

7. This Certificate was executed at _____ County, State of _____, on _____.

_____
, ATTORNEY

Form 1203

AFFIDAVIT OF SUCCESSOR TRUSTEE

1. The following Trust is the subject of this Affidavit:

   _____ and _____ , Trustees, or their successors in trust, under the _____ LIVING TRUST dated _____ ,
   and any amendments thereto.

2. Section _____ of Article _____ states that in the event of the resignation of an initial Trustee, _____ shall serve as a Successor Trustee.

3. One of the initial Trustees, _____ , resigned on _____ , 19____ .

4. The trust is currently in full force and effect.

5. Attached to this Affidavit and incorporated in it are selected provisions of the Trust including the pages naming the initial trustees, creating the trust, trustees' powers, statement of revocability of the trust, the designation of successor trustees, a copy of the signature pages, and resignations for _____ .

6. The Trust provisions which are not attached to this Affidavit are of a personal nature and set forth the distribution of Trust property. They do not modify the powers of the Trustees.

7. The signatory of this Affidavit is currently the acting Trustee of the Trust and she declares that the foregoing statements and the attached Trust provisions are true and correct, under penalty of perjury under the laws of the State of _____ .

8. This Affidavit was executed at _____ County, State of _____ , on _____ .

_____   _____
, Successor Trustee   , Successor Trustee

Form 1204

JOINT PROPERTY DURABLE SPECIAL POWER OF ATTORNEY

We, _____ and _____, of the City of _____, County of _____, State of _____, hereby each appoint the other to serve as such principal's attorney-in-fact ("Agent"), giving to the Agent the power to accomplish the following acts in said principal's name and for such principal's benefit, as follows:

1. Joint Property

Each Agent is hereby given the full power and authority to do everything necessary to carry out all transactions involving any and all property titled in the names of the principals as joint tenants with the right to survivorship or as tenancy by the entirety (these property interests are hereinafter collectively referred to as "joint property").

2. Enumeration of Specific Powers

In order for the Agents to fully deal with the joint property, the following powers are set forth to provide guidance as to some of the powers granted to each Agent:

To sell, exchange, or pledge any part of such joint property, real or personal, for such consideration and upon such terms as the Agent shall think fit, and to execute and deliver sufficient stock powers, deeds, or other instruments for the conveyance and transfer of the same, with such covenants or warranties or otherwise as the Agent shall see fit and to give good and effectual receipts for all and any part of the purchase price or other consideration.

To enter into oral or written agreements and to execute, acknowledge, and deliver any agreement, stock power, deed, instrument or other document for the accomplishment of or relating to any of the foregoing acts, giving and granting unto the Agent full power and authority to do and perform all, any and every act and thing whatsoever necessary to be done in and about the joint property as fully to all intents and purposes as the principal could do.

(continued on following page)

3. Transfer to Trust

The Agent shall have the full power and authority to do everything necessary to transfer, assign, convey, and deliver any interest in the joint property to:

_____ and _____ , Trustees, or their successors in trust, under the _____ LIVING TRUST dated _____ , and any amendments thereto.

4. Reliance upon Representations of My Agent

No person who acts in reliance on the representations of my Agent or the authority granted under this Durable Special Power of Attorney shall incur any liability to us, our heirs, or assigns as a result of permitting our Agent to exercise any power granted under this Durable Special Power of Attorney.

5. My Disability

This Durable Special Power of Attorney shall not be affected if one or either of us becomes disabled or incapacitated.

6. Property Held by Either of Us in a Fiduciary Capacity

Our Agent shall have no power under this Durable Special Power of Attorney with regard to any act, power, duty, right, or obligation that either of us may have relating to any person, matter, transaction, or property held by either of us or in my custody as a trustee, custodian, personal representative, or other fiduciary capacity.

Dated:

_____ , Principal _____ , Agent

_____ , Principal _____ , Agent

STATE OF)
) ss.
COUNTY OF)

The foregoing Durable Special Power of Attorney was acknowledged before me on _____ , by _____ and _____ , as both Principals and Agents, both of whom personally appeared before me, are personally known to me or presented _____ as identification.

WITNESS my hand and official seal.

_____ , Notary Public

My commission expires:

Form 1205

POSTMORTEM ASSIGNMENT

FOR VALUE RECEIVED, the undersigned does hereby assign to and designate:

_____ and _____ , Trustees, or their successors in trust, under the _____ LIVING TRUST dated _____, and any amendments thereto,

the beneficiary of all my right, title and interest in and to _____ and I direct that the same be delivered to said beneficiary at my death. Any party delivering the property assigned hereunder shall have no liability for making such delivery without a court order or without any authority other than this assignment. This assignment and designation of beneficiary is made pursuant to Section [_____] of the _____ [State] Probate Code.

Dated _____.

_____
, Trustmaker

_____
, Witness

_____
, Witness

STATE OF   )
) ss.
COUNTY OF   )

    On _____, before me, the undersigned Notary Public, in and for said County and State, personally appeared _____ , personally known to me (or produced _____ as identification) to be the person who executed the foregoing instrument, and acknowledged executing the same for the purposes herein contained.

WITNESS my hand and official seal.

_____
, Notary Public

My commission expires:

Form 1206

DURABLE SPECIAL POWER OF ATTORNEY FOR FUNDING

I, _____, of the City of _____, the County of
_____, State of _____, hereby appoint _____
to serve as my attorney-in-fact (my "Agent"), giving to my Agent the power to accomplish the
following acts in my name and for my benefit, as follows:

1. Transfer to Trust

I grant my Agent full power and authority to do everything necessary to transfer, assign, convey,
and deliver any interest I may have in property owned by me to:

      _____ and _____, Trustees, or their succes-
      sors in trust, under the _____ LIVING TRUST dated _____,
      and any amendments thereto.

2. Transfer to Partnership

My Agent may also transfer, assign, convey, and deliver my interest in and to my assets which I may
own now or in the future to _____, a partnership.

3. Enumeration of Specific Powers

In order for my Agent to transfer my property under this Durable Special Power of Attorney, the
following powers are set forth to provide guidance as to some of the powers granted by me to my
Agent:

    My Agent may convey real or personal property, whether tangible or intangible, or any
interest therein.

    My Agent may transfer, convey, and assign stocks, bonds, securities, accounts held with
securities firms, commodities, options, metals, and all other types of intangible property.

    My Agent may receive and endorse checks and drafts, deposits and withdraw funds, and
acquire and redeem certificates of deposit in banks, savings and loans, and all other financial institutions.

    My Agent may execute or release mortgages, deeds of trust, or other security agreements
as may be necessary to accomplish the purpose of this Durable Special Power of Attorney.

    My Agent may apply for, endorse, and transfer certificates of title for any motor vehicle.

(continued on following page)

My Agent may endorse, convey, and otherwise transfer all business interests that I may now own or hereafter acquire.

My Agent may have access to any safe deposit box rented by me and remove the contents of such safe deposit box, and any institution in which a safe deposit box is located shall be relieved of any liability to me, my heirs, or assigns as a result of my Agent's exercise of this power.

My Agent may prepare, sign, and file joint or separate income tax returns or declarations of estimated tax for any year; prepare, sign, and file gift tax returns with respect to gifts made by me for any year; and prepare, sign, and file any claims for refund of any tax.

My agent may also file income tax returns and all other forms of tax returns with respect to any business interest owned by me. My agent may compromise and settle tax disputes and execute any agreements regarding such disputes with any tax authority. My Agent may act in my behalf in all tax matters before all officers of the Internal Revenue Service and for any other taxing authority, including the receipt of confidential information.

4. Reliance upon Representations of My Agent
No person who acts in reliance on the representations of my Agent or the authority granted under this Durable Special Power of Attorney shall incur any liability to me, my heirs, or assigns as a result of permitting my Agent to exercise any power granted under this Durable Special Power of Attorney.

5. My Disability
This Durable Special Power of Attorney shall not be affected if I become disabled or incapacitated.

6. Life Insurance on the Life of My Agent
My Agent shall have no rights or powers with respect to any policy of insurance owned by me on the life of my Agent.

7. Property Held by Me in a Fiduciary Capacity
My Agent shall have no power under this Durable Special Power of Attorney with regard to any act, power, duty, right, or obligation that I may have relating to any person, matter, transaction, or

(continued on following page)

property held by me or in my custody as a trustee, custodian, personal representative, or other fiduciary capacity.

Dated _____

_____
                              , Principal

_____
                              , Agent

STATE OF   )
) ss.
COUNTY OF   )

On _____, before me, the undersigned Notary Public, in and for said County and State, personally appeared _____, principal, personally known to me (or produced _____ as identification) to be the person who executed the foregoing instrument, and acknowledged executing the same for the purposes herein contained.

WITNESS my hand and official seal.

_____
                              , Notary Public

My commission expires:

STATE OF   )
) ss.
COUNTY OF   )

On _____, before me, the undersigned Notary Public, in and for said County and State, personally appeared _____, Agent, personally known to me (or produced _____ as identification) to be the person who executed the foregoing instrument, and acknowledged executing the same for the purposes herein contained.

Witness my hand and official seal.

_____
                              , Notary Public

My commission expires:

Form 1301

Letter to Bank—Joint Trust

Date:
Address:

_____

_____

_____

Subject: _____

      Account Number:

Dear Sir or Madam:

Please change the above-referenced account to the name of our revocable living trust. The name of our trust is as follows:

_____ and _____ , Trustees, or their successors in trust, under the _____ LIVING TRUST dated _____, and any amendments thereto.

Both of us, as Trustees, will have authority to sign on the account. However, only the signature of one Trustee will be necessary to sign on behalf of the account. The checks are to remain the same as they are currently. Please use Social Security number ___-__-____ as the taxpayer identification number for this account.

We are providing an Affidavit of Trust* which evidences creation of our trust. Attached to the Affidavit and incorporated in it are selected provisions of the trust evidencing creation of the trust and the initial Trustees, statement of revocability of the trust, the designation of successor Trustees, powers of the Trustees, and signature pages from the trust agreement.

We are relying on you to make this change in account name accurately and as soon as possible, as we are doing personal planning for ourselves and our family.

Thank you for your assistance in this matter.

Sincerely,

_____

_____

Enclosure

* See Form 1201.

Form 1302

Letter to Bank—Separate Trusts/Tenants in Common

Date:

Address:

_____

_____

_____

Subject: _____

    Account Number:

Dear Sir or Madam:

Please change the above-referenced account to the name of our respective revocable trust agreements as tenants in common. The names and taxpayer identification numbers of our trusts are as follows:

_____ and _____, Trustees, or their successors in trust, under the _____ LIVING TRUST dated _____, and any amendments thereto. Social Security number ___-__-____.

and

_____ and _____, Trustees, or their successors in trust, under the _____ LIVING TRUST dated _____, and any amendments thereto. Social Security number ___-__-____.

Both of us, as Trustees, will have authority to sign on the account, but only the signature of one Trustee is necessary to sign on behalf of the account. The checks are to remain the same as they are currently.

We are providing Affidavits of Trust* which evidence creation of our respective trust agreements. Attached to the Affidavits and incorporated in each are selected provisions of the trusts evidencing creation of the trust and the initial Trustees, statement of revocability of the trust, the designation of successor Trustees, powers of the Trustees, and signature pages from the respective trust agreements.

We are relying on you to make this change in account name accurately and as soon as possible, as we are doing personal planning for ourselves and our family.

Thank you for your assistance in this matter.

Sincerely,

_____

_____

* See Form 1201.

Form 1303

Letter to Bank—Individual Trust

Date:
Bank Address:

_____

_____

_____

Re: _____
    Account Number:

Dear Sir or Madam:

Please change the above-referenced account from my individual name to the name of my revocable trust. The name of my trust is as follows:

_____, sole Trustee, or his successors in trust, under the _____
LIVING TRUST, dated _____, and any amendments thereto.

I will have sole authority, as Trustee, to sign the account. The checks are to remain the same as they are currently.

I am providing an Affidavit of Trust* which evidences creation of my trust agreement. Attached to the Affidavit and incorporated in it are selected provisions of the trust evidencing creation of the trust and the initial Trustee, statement of revocability of the trust, the designation of successor Trustees, powers of the Trustees, and signature pages from the trust.

I am relying on you to make this change in account name accurately and as soon as possible, as I am doing personal planning for myself and my family.

Thank you for your assistance in this matter.

Sincerely,

Enclosure

* See Form 1201.

Form 1304

Letter to Bank—Certificate of Deposit

Date:
Bank Address:

_____

_____

_____

Re: Certificate of Deposit Account Number and Maturity Date for:

_____

_____

Certificate No. _____, Maturity Date: _____
SSN No. _____
SSN No. _____

Dear Sir or Madam:

Please change the registration on the above-referenced Certificate of Deposit to the name of our revocable living trust. The name of our trust is as follows:

_____ and _____ , Trustees, or their successors in trust, under the _____ LIVING TRUST, dated _____, and any amendments thereto.

Both Trustees should sign the signature card, but only the signature of one Trustee is necessary to sign on behalf of the account.

We are providing an Affidavit of Trust* which evidences creation of our trust. Attached to the Affidavit and incorporated in it are select provisions of the Trust evidencing the creation of the trust and initial Trustees, statement of revocability of the trust, the designation of successor Trustees, the powers of the Trustees, and the signature pages.

We are relying on you to make this change in account name accurately and as soon as possible, as we are doing personal planning for ourselves and our family.

Sincerely,

_____

_____

Enclosure

* See Form 1201.

Form 1305

ASSIGNMENT TO LIVING TRUST
OF
CERTIFICATES OF DEPOSIT

_____ and _____,
Husband and Wife, do hereby transfer and assign, without consideration and in order to change formal title only, all right, title and interest which they now have in the following Certificates of Deposit to _____ and _____, Trustees, or their successors in trust, under the _____ LIVING TRUST dated _____, and any amendments thereto.

Institution	Account Number	Maturity Date

Dated: _____,

_____
, Grantor

_____
, Grantor

STATE OF   )
) ss.
COUNTY OF   )

On _____ , before me, the undersigned Notary Public, in and for said County and State, personally appeared _____ personally known to me (or presented _____ as identification) to be the persons described who executed the foregoing Assignment, and acknowledged executing the same for the purposes herein contained.

WITNESS my hand and official seal.

_____
, Notary Public

My commission expires:

Form 1401

STOCK OR BOND POWER

Account Number _____

FOR VALUE RECEIVED, the undersigned does (do) hereby sell, assign and transfer to

_____

(Name)

_____

(Address)

_____

(City, State, Zip Code)   (Social Security or Taxpayer Identifying No.)

IF STOCK, COMPLETE THIS PORTION:

_____ shares of the _____ stock of _____ represented
(number)   (type)   (Company)

by Certificate(s) No(s). _____ inclusive standing in the name of the undersigned
(Number)

on the books of said Company.

IF BONDS, COMPLETE THIS PORTION:

_____ bonds of _____ in the principal amount
(number)   (Name)

of $_____, No(s). _____ inclusive standing in the name of the
(Amount)   (Number)

undersigned on the books of said Company.

The undersigned does (do) hereby irrevocably constitute and appoint _____ attorney to transfer the said stock or bond(s), as the case may be, on the books of said Company, with full power of substitution in the premises.

Dated: _____

_____   _____
(Signature)   (Signature)

Form 1402

Letter to Transfer Agent—Individual Trust

Date:

Address:

_____

_____

_____

Re: Transfer of _____ Stock

    Certificate(s): No. _____

Dear

Enclosed is an executed Stock Assignment Separate From Certificate. Title on the stock certificates is currently held in the following name:

        _____

Please reissue the stock in the name of my revocable living trust agreement as follows:

    _____ and _____ , Trustees, or their successors in trust, under the _____ LIVING TRUST dated _____, and any amendments thereto.

I am providing an Affidavit of Trust* which evidences creation of my trust. Attached to the Affidavit and incorporated in it are selected provisions of the trust evidencing creation of the trust and the initial Trustees, statement of revocability of the trust, the designation of successor Trustees, powers of the Trustees, and signature pages from the trust agreement.

I am relying on you to make this change in account name accurately and as soon as possible, as I am doing personal planning for myself and my family.

Sincerely,

_____   _____

Enclosure

* See Form 1201.

Form 1403

Letter to Transfer Agent— Separate Trusts/Tenants in Common

Date:

Address:

_____

_____

_____

Re: Transfer of _____ Stock

Certificate(s): No. _____

Dear

Please transfer the title of the attached stock certificates from our name to the name of our revocable living trust agreement. Title is currently held in the following name:

_____, JTWROS*

Please reissue the stock in the name of our living trust agreements as tenants in common as follows:

_____ and _____, Trustees, or their successors in trust, under the _____ LIVING TRUST dated _____, and any amendments thereto.

and

_____ and _____, Trustees, or their successors in trust, under the _____ LIVING TRUST dated _____, and any amendments thereto.

We are providing Affidavits of Trust† which evidence creation of our respective trust agreements. Attached to the Affidavits and incorporated in each are selected provisions of the trusts evidencing creation of the trusts and the initial Trustees, statement of revocability of the trusts, the designation of successor Trustees, powers of the Trustees, and signature pages from the respective trust agreements.

We are relying on you to make this change in account name accurately and as soon as possible, as we are doing personal planning for ourselves and our family. Please notify us in writing when you have completed this change.

Sincerely,

_____   _____

Enclosure

* Joint Tenancy with Right of Survivorship.
† See Form 1201.

Form 1404

Letter to Transfer Agent—Joint Trust

Date:

Address:

_____

_____

_____

Re: Transfer of _____ Stock

    Certificate(s): No._____

Dear

Please transfer the title of the attached stock certificates from our name to the name of our revocable living trust agreement. Title is currently held in the following name:

_____, JTWROS

Please reissue the stock in the name of our living trust as follows:

_____ and _____ , Trustees, or their successors

in trust, under the _____ LIVING TRUST dated _____, and any

amendments thereto.

We are providing an Affidavit of Trust* which evidences creation of our trust. Attached to the Affidavit and incorporated in it are selected provisions of the trust evidencing creation of the trust and the initial Trustees, statement of revocability of the trust, the designation of successor Trustees, powers of the Trustees, and signature pages from the trust agreement.

We are relying on you to make this change in account name accurately and as soon as possible, as we are doing personal planning for ourselves and our family. Please notify us in writing when you have completed this change.

Sincerely,

_____   _____

Enclosure

* See Form 1201.

Form 1405

Letter to Brokerage Account Representative

Date:

Address:

_____

_____

_____

Re: Brokerage Account Name and Number for:

_____

_____

Account No. _____

Dear

Please change the registration on the above-referenced brokerage account to the name of our revocable living trust. The name of our trust is as follows:

_____ and _____ , Trustees, or their successors in trust, under the _____ LIVING TRUST dated _____ , and any amendments thereto.

We are providing an Affidavit of Trust* which evidences creation of our trust. Attached to the Affidavit and incorporated in it are selected provisions of the trust evidencing creation of the trust and the initial Trustees, statement of revocability of the trust, the designation of successor Trustees, powers of the Trustees, and signature pages from the trust agreement.

We are relying on you to make this change in account name accurately and as soon as possible, as we are doing personal planning for ourselves and our family.

Please send us the appropriate forms for our signatures at your earliest convenience.

Sincerely,

_____   _____

Enclosure

* See Form 1201.

Form 1406

Letter to Stockbroker

Date:

Address:

_____

_____

_____

RE: Name change for the account of _____

Dear

Please change my account, number _____, which is currently in the name of _____ and _____, Husband and Wife, as Joint Tenants, to the name of our Living Trust. The account name should now read:

_____ and _____, Trustees, or their successors in trust, under the _____ LIVING TRUST dated _____, and any amendments thereto.

We are providing an Affidavit of Trust* which evidences creation of our trust. Attached to the Affidavit and incorporated in it are selected provisions of the trust evidencing creation of the trust and the initial Trustees, statement of revocability of the trust, the designation of successor Trustees, powers of the Trustees, and signature pages from the trust agreement.

We are relying on you to make this change in account names accurately and as soon as possible, as we are doing personal estate planning. It is our understanding that there is no charge for this name change.

Please notify us in writing when you have completed this change.

Sincerely yours,

* See Form 1201.

Form 1407

Assignment to Living Trust of Bearer Bonds

_____ and _____, Husband and Wife, Grantors, do hereby transfer and assign, without consideration and in order to change formal title only, all of their right, title and interest in those certain Bearer Bonds, located in their Safe Deposit Box at _____(Bank), _____(Branch), to:

_____ and _____, Trustees, or their successors in trust, under the _____ LIVING TRUST dated _____, and any amendments thereto.

Dated: _____   Witnesses as to both:

_____   _____
, GRANTOR   , WITNESS

_____   _____
, GRANTOR   , WITNESS

STATE OF   )
) ss.
COUNTY OF   )

On _____, before me, the undersigned Notary Public, in and for said County and State, personally appeared _____, personally known to me (or presented _____ as identification) to be the persons who executed the foregoing instrument, and acknowledged executing the same for the purposes herein contained.

WITNESS my hand and official seal.

_____
, Notary Public

My commission expires:

Form 1408

ASSIGNMENT TO LIVING TRUST
OF LIMITED PARTNERSHIP WITH CONSENT

_____, does hereby transfer and assign, without consideration and in order to change formal title only, all of his/her right, title and interest in _____. A copy of the certificate evidencing the limited partnership interest, Certificate No. _____ is attached hereto, to _____ and _____, Trustees, or their successors in trust, under the _____ LIVING TRUST dated _____, and any amendments thereto.

THIS ASSIGNMENT IS EFFECTIVE IMMEDIATELY, AND SAID PARTNERS (OR THEIR SUCCESSORS) SHALL HEREAFTER RECEIVE THEIR SHARE OF PARTNERSHIP PROFITS, LOSSES AND DISTRIBUTIONS, TOGETHER WITH ALL OF THEIR RIGHTS UPON DISSOLUTION OF THE PARTNERSHIP.

Dated: _____.

_____
                                    , Grantor

STATE OF   )
) ss.
COUNTY OF   )

On _____, before me, the undersigned Notary Public, in and for said County and State, personally appeared _____, personally known to me (or presented _____ as identification) to be the person who executed the foregoing instrument, and acknowledged executing the same for the purposes herein contained.

WITNESS my hand and official seal.

_____
                          , Notary Public
My commission expires:

CONSENT TO ASSIGNMENT

The undersigned general partner of _____, a limited partnership, hereby consents to the foregoing assignment and approves admission of:

_____ and _____, Trustees, or their successors in trust, under the _____ LIVING TRUST dated _____, and any amendments thereto

as a substitute limited partner with all the rights, privileges and duties of a limited partner and subject to all the provisions of the partnership agreement.

Dated: _____

_____
, General Partner

Form 1409

Letter to General Partner

Date:
Address:

_____
_____
_____

Re: Transfer of Limited Partnership Interest

Dear

My attorney has recently prepared a revocable living trust for me as part of my overall estate planning. I am currently in the process of transferring all my assets to my living trust. Enclosed is my Assignment of Limited Partnership and a Consent to Assignment for your signature. The legal name of my living trust is:

_____ and _____, Trustees, or their successors in trust, under the _____ LIVING TRUST dated _____, and any amendments thereto.

Please send me notification at your earliest convenience that you have consented to the assignment and my living trust is the legal owner of my partnership interest. Thank you for your cooperation in this matter.

Very truly yours,

Form 1501

For Specific Personal Property for One Trust Maker

BILL OF SALE

_____, of _____, the County of _____, in the State of _____ (herein called the Grantor), for and in consideration of Ten and 00/100 Dollars and other valuable consideration, the receipt whereof is hereby acknowledged, does hereby bargain, sell, grant and convey unto, _____ and _____, Trustees, or their successors in trust, under the _____ LIVING TRUST dated _____, and any amendments thereto (herein called the Grantee), and the successors and assigns of the Grantee, all of my right, title, and interest in and to _____.

Any possession or use by the Grantor of any such property subsequent to the date of this Bill of Sale shall be subject at all times to the authority of the Grantee to claim and take possession thereof. The Grantor hereby covenants that the Grantor has the right to transfer the property subject to this Bill of Sale and will warrant and defend title to the same against the lawful claim and demands of all other parties.

Dated _____.

_____
, Grantor

STATE OF   )
) ss.
COUNTY OF   )

On _____, before me, the undersigned Notary Public, in and for said County and State, personally appeared _____, personally known to me (or presented _____ as identification) to be the person who executed the foregoing instrument, and acknowledged executing the same for the purposes herein contained.

WITNESS my hand and official seal.

_____
, Notary Public

My commission expires:

Form 1502

For Specific Personal Property of Two Trust Makers

BILL OF SALE

_____ and _____, of
_____, the County of _____, in the State of _____ (herein called
the Grantors), for and in consideration of Ten and 00/100 Dollars and other valuable consideration, the receipt whereof is hereby acknowledged, do hereby bargain, sell, grant and convey unto
_____ and _____, Trustees, or their successors in trust, under
the _____ LIVING TRUST dated _____, and any amendments
thereto (herein called the Grantee), and the successors and assigns of the Grantee, the following
personal perperty:

Any possession or use by the Grantors of any such property subsequent to the date of this Bill of
Sale shall be subject at all times to the authority of the Grantee to claim and take possession thereof.
The Grantors hereby covenant that the Grantors have the right to transfer the property subject to
this Bill of Sale and will warrant and defend title to the same against the lawful claim and demands
of all other parties.

Dated _____.

_____   _____
                        , Grantor   , Grantor

STATE OF   )
) ss.
COUNTY OF   )

On _____, before me, the undersigned Notary Public, in and for said County and
State, personally appeared _____ and _____, both of whom are personally known to me (or produced _____ as identification) to be the
persons who executed the foregoing instrument, and acknowledged executing the same for the
purposes herein contained.

WITNESS my hand and official seal.

_____
                        , Notary Public
My commission expires:

Form 1503

For Specific Personal Property of One Trust Maker

ASSIGNMENT OF PERSONAL PROPERTY

For value received I, _____, of the City of _____, the County of _____, and the State of _____, hereby assign, transfer, and convey to:

_____ and _____, Trustees, or their successors in trust, under the _____ LIVING TRUST, dated _____, and any amendments thereto,

all of my right, title, and interest in the following personal property:

Dated _____.

_____
, Assignor

STATE OF   )
) ss.
COUNTY OF   )

On _____, before me, the undersigned Notary Public, in and for said County and State, personally appeared _____, personally known to me (or presented _____ as identification) to be the person who executed the foregoing instrument, and acknowledged executing the same for the purposes herein contained.

WITNESS my hand and official seal.

_____
, Notary Public
My commission expires:

Form 1504

For Specific Personal Property of Two Trust Makers

ASSIGNMENT OF PERSONAL PROPERTY

For value received We, _____ and _____,
of the City of _____, the County of _____, and the State of _____,
hereby assign, transfer, and convey to:

_____ and _____, Trustees, or their successors
in trust, under the _____ LIVING TRUST dated _____, and any
amendments thereto,

all of our right, title, and interest in the following personal property:

Dated _____.

_____   _____
                    , Assignor   , Assignor

STATE OF   )
) ss.
COUNTY OF   )

On _____, before me, the undersigned Notary Public, in and for said County and
State, personally appeared _____ and _____, both of whom are personally known to me (or produced _____ as identification) to be the
persons who executed the foregoing instrument, and acknowledged executing the same for the
purposes herein contained.

WITNESS my hand and official seal.

_____
                    , Notary Public
My commission expires:

Form 1505

General, for One Trust Maker

BILL OF SALE

_____, of _____, the County of _____, in the State of _____ (herein called the Grantor), for and in consideration of Ten and 00/100 Dollars and other valuable consideration, the receipt whereof is hereby acknowledged, does hereby bargain, sell, grant and convey unto _____ and _____, Trustees, or their successors in trust, under the _____ LIVING TRUST dated ____, and any amendments thereto (herein called the Grantee), and the successors and assigns of the Grantee, all household goods, personal effects and tangible personal property of every kind and nature now owned or hereafter acquired by the Grantor, specifically including all furniture and furnishings, collections and objects of art, wearing apparel, jewelry, silverware, china, art and antiques, numismatic or collectible coins, currency and stamps, and sporting equipment, but specifically excluding, however, any property constituting a part of and used in connection with any business enterprise in which the Grantor has an interest. Any possession or use by the Grantor of any such property subsequent to the date of this Bill of Sale shall be subject at all times to the authority of the Grantee to claim and take possession thereof. The Grantor hereby covenants that the Grantor has the right to transfer the property subject to this Bill of Sale and will warrant and defend title to the same against the lawful claim and demands of all other parties.

Dated _____.

_____
                            , Grantor

STATE OF   )
) ss.
COUNTY OF   )

   On _____, before me, the undersigned Notary Public, in and for said County and State, personally appeared _____, personally known to me (or produced _____ as identification) to be the person who executed the foregoing instrument, and acknowledged executing the same for the purposes herein contained.

WITNESS my hand and official seal.

_____
                            , Notary Public
My commission expires:

Form 1506

General, for Two Trust Makers

BILL OF SALE

_____ and _____, of _____, the County of _____, in the State of _____ (herein called the Grantors), for and in consideration of Ten and 00/100 Dollars and other valuable consideration, the receipt whereof is hereby acknowledged, do hereby bargain, sell, grant and convey unto _____ and _____, Trustees, or their successors in trust, under the _____ LIVING TRUST dated ____, and any amendments thereto (herein called the Grantee), and the successors and assigns of the Grantee, all household goods, personal effects and tangible personal property of every kind and nature now owned or hereafter acquired by the grantors, specifically including all furniture and furnishings, collections and objects of art, wearing apparel, jewelry, silverware, china, art and antiques, numismatic or collectible coins, currency and stamps, and sporting equipment, but specifically excluding, however, any property constituting a part of and used in connection with any business enterprise in which the Grantors have an interest. Any possession or use by the Grantors of any such property subsequent to the date of this Bill of Sale shall be subject at all times to the authority of the Grantee to claim and take possession thereof. The Grantors hereby covenant that the Grantors have the right to transfer the property subject to this Bill of Sale and will warrant and defend title to the same against the lawful claim and demands of all other parties.

Dated _____.

_____   _____
                        , Grantor   , Grantor

STATE OF   )
) ss.
COUNTY OF   )

On _____, before me, the undersigned Notary Public, in and for said County and State, personally appeared _____ and _____, both of whom are personally known to me (or presented _____ as identification) to be the persons who executed the foregoing instrument, and acknowledged executing the same for the purposes herein contained.

WITNESS my hand and official seal.

_____
                        , Notary Public
My commission expires:

Form 1507

General, for One Trust Maker

ASSIGNMENT OF PERSONAL PROPERTY

For value received I, _____, of the City of _____, the County of _____, and the State of _____, hereby assign, transfer, and convey to:

_____ and _____, Trustees, or their successors in trust, under the _____ LIVING TRUST dated _____, and any amendments thereto,

all of my right, title, and interest in all of my tangible personal property. My tangible personal property shall include, without limitation, all of my jewelry, clothing, household furniture, furnishings and fixtures, chinaware, silver, photographs, works of art, books, boats, automobiles, sporting goods, artifacts relating to my hobbies, and all other tangible articles of personal property which I now own or hereafter acquire, regardless of how they are acquired or the record title in which they are held.

Dated _____.

_____

_____, Assignor

STATE OF   )

) ss.

COUNTY OF   )

On _____, before me, the undersigned Notary Public, in and for said County and State, personally appeared _____, personally known to me (or presented _____ as identification) to be the person who executed the foregoing instrument, and acknowledged executing the same for the purposes herein contained.

WITNESS my hand and official seal.

_____

_____, Notary Public

My commission expires:

Form 1508

General, for Two Trust Makers

ASSIGNMENT OF PERSONAL PROPERTY

For value received we, _____ and _____
of the City of _____, the County of _____, and the State of _____,
hereby assign, transfer, and convey to:

_____ and _____, Trustees, or their successors
in trust, under the _____ LIVING TRUST, dated _____, and any
amendments thereto,

all of our right, title, and interest in all of our tangible personal property. Our tangible personal property shall include, without limitation, all of our jewelry, clothing, household furniture, furnishings and fixtures, chinaware, silver, photographs, works of art, books, boats, automobiles, sporting goods, artifacts relating to our hobbies, and all other tangible articles of personal property which we now own or hereafter acquire, regardless of how they are acquired or the record title in which they are held.

Dated _____.

_____   _____
                , Assignor   , Assignor

STATE OF   )
) ss.
COUNTY OF   )

On _____, before me, the undersigned Notary Public, in and for said County and State, personally appeared _____ and _____, both of whom are personally known to me (or produced _____ as identification) to be the persons who executed the foregoing instrument, and acknowledged executing the same for the purposes herein contained.

WITNESS my hand and official seal.

_____
                , Notary Public
My commission expires:

Form 1509

Letter to Property and Casualty Agent

Date:

Address:

_____

_____

_____

Re: Property and Casualty Insurance

Dear Sir or Madam:

My attorney has recently prepared a revocable living trust for me as part of my overall estate planning. To complete this estate planning, it is necessary for me to transfer all of my assets, including my personal residence, into my revocable living trust. I shall continue to live in my residence just as before the transfer.

Please make all the changes necessary to continue my property and casualty insurance coverage on this property. The official name of my trust is:

_____ and _____, Trustees, or their successors in trust, under the _____ LIVING TRUST, dated _____, and any amendments thereto.

Please contact me if you need any additional information and send me written confirmation of these changes.

Thank you in advance for your assistance in this matter.

Very truly yours,

Form 1510

Bill of Sale of Motor Vehicle, Mobile Home, Trailer, Recreational Vehicle, and/or Boat

---

Seller:

Seller's Mailing Address:

Buyer: _____ and _____, Trustees, or their successors in trust, under the _____ LIVING TRUST dated _____, and any amendments thereto.

Buyer's Address:

Consideration: Ten and No/100 ($10.00) Dollars

Personal Property:
    Make: _____
    Model: _____
    Year: _____
    VIN: _____
    Type: _____
    Weight: _____

For value received, Seller sells and delivers the personal property to Buyer and warrants and agrees to defend title to the personal property to Buyer and Buyer's successors against all lawful claims.

When the context requires, singular nouns and pronouns include the plural.

Dated _____.

_____   _____
                        , Seller   , Seller

STATE OF   )
) ss.
COUNTY OF   )

    On _____, before me, the undersigned Notary Public, in and for said County and State, personally appeared _____, personally known to me (or produced _____ as identification) to be the person who executed the foregoing instrument, and acknowledged executing the same for the purposes herein contained.

WITNESS my hand and official seal.

_____
                        , Notary Public
My commission expires:

Form 1511

ASSIGNMENT OF AIRCRAFT TO LIVING TRUST

For value received I, _____ of the City of _____, the County of _____, State of _____, hereby assign, transfer, and convey to:

_____ and _____, Trustees, or their successors in trust, under the _____ LIVING TRUST dated _____, and any amendments thereto,

all of my right, title, and interest in my _____ (Make) _____(Model) airplane with registration number ___,_____.

Dated _____.

_____

STATE OF   )
) ss.
COUNTY OF   )

On _____, before me, the undersigned Notary Public, in and for said County and State, personally appeared _____, personally known to me (or presented _____ as identification) to be the person who executed the foregoing instrument, and acknowledged executing the same for the purposes herein contained.

WITNESS my hand and official seal.

_____

_____, Notary Public

My commission expires:

Form 1512

Letter to FAA Assigning Aircraft to Living Trust

Date:

Federal Aviation Administration
DOT/OST/OAA, P-56
400 7th Street SW
Room 6401
Washington, D.C. 20590

RE: Issuance of New Certificate of Registration

Dear Sir or Madam:

I have assigned my airplane to my revocable living trust. Enclosed is a copy of the Assignment and my current Certificate of Registration. Please issue a new Certificate of Registration to:

_____ and _____, Trustees, or their successors in trust, under the _____ LIVING TRUST dated _____, and any amendments thereto.

Please contact me if you have any questions. Thank you in advance for your cooperation in this matter.

Very truly yours,

Enclosure

Form 1513

Letter to U.S. Coast Guard

Date:

Commanding Officer
United States Coast Guard
Documentation Department
Claude Pepper Federal Bldg., 5th Floor
51 S.W. First Avenue
Miami, FL 33130

RE: Transfer of Vessel

To Whom It May Concern:

I wish to transfer my vessel to my recently established revocable living trust. In order to accomplish this transfer I have enclosed the following documents:

1. Application for Documentation or For Surrender, Replacement, or Redocumentation.
2. Bill of Sale completed in duplicate.
3. Certificate of Marking.
4. Application, Consent, and Approval for Surrender of Certificate of Documentation of Vessel covered by Preferred Mortgage.
5. Original Certificate of Documentation.
6. Check in the amount of $_____ to cover change in ownership fee and fee for recording the Bill of Sale.

Please send me a new Certificate of Documentation at your earliest convenience. Feel free to contact me if you need any additional information. Thank you in advance for your cooperation in this matter.

Very truly yours,

Enclosures

Form 1514

MEMORANDUM FOR DISTRIBUTION
OF TANGIBLE PERSONAL PROPERTY OF

Pursuant to the provisions of the _____ LIVING TRUST, dated _____, I hereby request my Trustee to distribute the following items of nonbusiness tangible personal property as follows:

**Description of Tangible
Personal Property**

**Recipient of Tangible
Personal Property**

If a recipient of a particular item of nonbusiness personal property does not survive me, such item shall be disposed of as though it had not been listed in this memorandum. In the event there is a conflict between this memorandum and the _____ LIVING TRUST, the terms of my trust shall control.

Dated: _____   _____
                                       TRUST MAKER

_____
WITNESS

Form 1515

Memorandum of Personal Property in the Form of a Trust Amendment

AMENDMENT TO THE
_____ LIVING TRUST
CONCERNING TANGIBLE PERSONAL PROPERTY

On _____, I, _____, signed the _____ LIVING TRUST, more formally known as:

_____ and _____, Trustees, or their successors in trust, under the _____ LIVING TRUST dated _____, and any amendments thereto.

Pursuant to the applicable provisions of my living trust, which permit me to amend my trust in writing at any time, I now wish to amend my trust to provide for the specific distribution of personal property as follows:

Distribution of Tangible Personal Property

I hereby direct my Trustee to distribute the following items of nonbusiness tangible personal property as follows:

Description of Tangible Personal Property	**Recipient of Tangible Personal Property**

(continued on following page)

If a recipient of a particular item of nonbusiness personal property does not survive me, such item shall be disposed of as though it had not been listed in this amendment.

I executed this amendment on _____.

I certify that I have read the foregoing amendment to my revocable living trust agreement, and that it correctly states the changes that I desire to make in my trust. I approve this amendment to my revocable living trust in all particulars, and request my Trustee to execute it.

_____ , Trustmaker

_____ , Trustee

_____ , Trustee

STATE OF   )
) ss.
COUNTY OF   )

The foregoing amendment to the _____ LIVING TRUST was acknowledged before me on _____, by _____, as Trustmaker and Trustee, and by _____, as Trustee, all of whom personally appeared before me, are personally known to me or presented _____ as identification.

WITNESS my hand and official seal.

_____ , Notary Public

My commission expires:

Form 1601

Request for Change of
Ownership/Beneficiary of Insurance Policy

TO:

RE: Change of Ownership/Beneficiary
      Policy No.:
      Policy Holder:
      Policy Amount:
      Type of Policy:

Gentlemen:

My attorney has recently prepared a revocable living trust for me as part of my overall estate planning. I am currently in the process of transferring all my assets to my living trust. Please make the following changes to the Ownership and/or Beneficiary designation of the above-referenced policy as follows:

_____ I desire that the DESIGNATED OWNER of the Policy be changed to _____ and _____, Trustees, or their successors in trust of the _____ LIVING TRUST, dated _____, and any amendments thereto.

_____ I desire that the DESIGNATED BENEFICIARY of the Policy/Account be changed to _____ and _____, Trustees, or their successors, in trust of the _____ LIVING TRUST, dated _____, and any amendments thereto.

_____ I desire that the FIRST CONTINGENT BENEFICIARY be changed to _____.

A copy of my Affidavit of Trust* is included herewith for your information.

SIGNED AND WITNESSED at _____, [State], on _____.

_____
, Grantor

_____
, Witness

Enclosure

* See Form 1201.

Form 1602

BENEFICIARY DESIGNATION OF TRUSTEES UNDER
REVOCABLE TRUST INSTRUMENT

This form may not be photocopied or otherwise reproduced

ABA

© 1979, Real Property, Probate
and Trust Law Section,
American Bar Association
Reprinted with permission

INSURED'S NAME: _____

INSURANCE COMPANY (HEREIN "THE COMPANY"): _____

POLICY NUMBER(S): _____

ALL BENEFICIARY DESIGNATIONS AND SETTLEMENT OPTION ARRANGEMENTS CONCERNING THE INSURED UNDER EACH CAPTIONED POLICY ARE REVOKED. EACH SUCH POLICY'S PROCEEDS SHALL BE PAID IN A SINGLE SUM TO THE FOLLOWING TRUSTEE(S) [HEREIN "THE TRUSTEE(S)"] OF THE TRUST (HEREIN "THE TRUST") UNDER THE FOLLOWING TRUST INSTRUMENT [HEREIN "THE TRUST INSTRUMENT"]:

_____

NAME OF CURRENT TRUSTEE(S)

OR THE SUCCESSOR(S) IN TRUST, AS TRUSTEE(S) UNDER A WRITTEN INSTRUMENT CREATED BY

_____

NAME OF GRANTOR(S)

DATED _____, AND ALL AMENDMENTS MADE BEFORE THE INSURED'S DEATH.

IF, BEFORE PAYMENT OF THE PROCEEDS, THE COMPANY RECEIVES PROOF SATISFACTORY TO IT THAT THE TRUST HAS BEEN REVOKED OR IS OTHERWISE NOT IN EFFECT AT THE INSURED'S DEATH, THE PROCEEDS SHALL BE PAID IN A SINGLE SUM TO THE OWNER, IF LIVING AT THE INSURED'S DEATH, OTHERWISE TO THE OWNER'S EXECUTORS, ADMINISTRATORS, OR ASSIGNS.

ALL RIGHTS OF OWNERSHIP IN EACH CAPTIONED POLICY, INCLUDING THE RIGHT TO CHANGE THIS DESIGNATION AT ANY TIME, ARE RESERVED TO THE OWNER, REGARDLESS OF ANY CONTRARY PROVISION OF THE TRUST INSTRUMENT.

THIS DESIGNATION INCORPORATES ALL OF THE PROVISIONS ON THE REVERSE OF IT.

_____   _____
DATE   OWNER

TO BE COMPLETED IF ANY COMMUNITY PROPERTY INTEREST EXISTS IN ANY CAPTIONED POLICY

I CONSENT TO THIS DESIGNATION.

_____   _____
DATE   OWNER'S SPOUSE

ATTORNEY'S CERTIFICATION

I CERTIFY THAT I AM AN ATTORNEY AT LAW AND AM FULLY FAMILIAR WITH THE TRUST INSTRUMENT. I FURTHER CERTIFY THAT THE TRUST INSTRUMENT: (1) HAS BEEN EXECUTED AND IS ACCURATELY DESCRIBED, (2) GRANTS NO TRUSTEE ANY POWER TO EXERCISE POLICY RIGHTS IN ANY CAPTIONED POLICY DURING THE INSURED'S LIFETIME, AND (3) IS REVOCABLE BY ITS GRANTOR(S).

_____
ATTORNEY AT LAW

_____   _____
STREET ADDRESS   CITY AND STATE

(Failure to complete this certification may result in the company's requiring submission of the trust instrument before making any policy loan or permitting the owner to exercise any policy right.)

RECORDED BY THE COMPANY:

_____   _____
DATE   AUTHORIZED SIGNATURE

(continued on following page)

1. DEFINITIONS.

    A. PROCEEDS.

      THE TERM "PROCEEDS" INCLUDES ALL AMOUNTS PAYABLE UNDER EACH CAPTIONED POLICY BY REASON OF THE INSURED'S DEATH, INCLUDING THE COMMUTED VALUE OF ANY INSTALLMENT OR DEFERRED PAYMENT PROVISION.

    B. POLICY.

      THE TERM "POLICY" INCLUDES THE TERMS "ANNUITY CONTRACT", "ENDOWMENT POLICY", "GROUP POLICY", "GROUP CERTIFICATE", "RIDER", AND "SUPPLEMENTAL AGREEMENT".

    C. OWNER.

      THE TERM "OWNER" MEANS "POLICY OWNER", AND INCLUDES THE TERM "RIGHTS HOLDER". WHEN THE FACTS AND CONTEXT REQUIRE, THE TERM "OWNER" MEANS "OWNERS" AND "RIGHTS HOLDERS".

    D. INSURED.

      THE TERM "INSURED" MEANS "ANNUITANT" WHEN THE FACTS AND CONTEXT REQUIRE.

    E. GRANTOR.

      THE TERM "GRANTOR(S)" INCLUDES THE TERMS "SETTLOR(S)", "TRUSTOR(S)", "DONOR(S)", AND "CREATOR(S)".

    F. INCLUDES.

      THE TERM "INCLUDES" MEANS "INCLUDES BY WAY OF ILLUSTRATION AND NOT IN LIMITATION".

2. SUBORDINATION.

   THE INTEREST OF THE TRUSTEE(S) UNDER EACH CAPTIONED POLICY SHALL BE SUBORDINATE TO ANY ASSIGNMENT OF THAT POLICY MADE BEFORE OR AFTER THIS DESIGNATION.

3. DISCHARGE.

   THE COMPANY IS NOT RESPONSIBLE FOR THE APPLICATION, DISPOSITION, OR USE OF ANY PROCEEDS PAID TO THE TRUSTEE(S). THE COMPANY SHALL BE FULLY DISCHARGED FROM ALL LIABILITY BY THE RECEIPT OF THE TRUSTEE(S).

4. TRUST IN EFFECT.

   PRIOR TO PAYMENT OF THE PROCEEDS, THE COMPANY MAY REQUIRE EVIDENCE SATISFACTORY TO IT THAT THE TRUST HAS NOT BEEN REVOKED AND IS THEN IN EFFECT.

5. NO EFFECT.

   THIS DESIGNATION SHALL NEITHER AFFECT THE OWNER'S RIGHTS AS PROVIDED IN ANY CAPTIONED POLICY, NOR AFFECT ANY INSURANCE PAYABLE UNDER ANY CAPTIONED POLICY BY REASON OF THE DEATH OF ANY PERSON OTHER THAN THE INSURED.

6. COMMUNITY PROPERTY.

    A. NO NOTICE.

      IF A COMMUNITY PROPERTY INTEREST EXISTS IN ANY CAPTIONED POLICY, THE COMPANY SHALL BE FULLY PROTECTED IN MAKING PAYMENT OF THE PROCEEDS TO THE TRUSTEE(S) EVEN THOUGH, AFTER THE DATE OF EXECUTION OF THIS DESIGNATION:

       (I) THE OWNER AND THE OWNER'S SPOUSE DIVORCE,

       (II) THE OWNER'S SPOUSE DIES, OR

       (III) THE OWNER AND THE OWNER'S SPOUSE SEVER THEIR INTEREST IN THE COMMUNITY,

      AS LONG AS THE COMPANY HAS NO WRITTEN NOTICE OF ANY OF THOSE CIRCUMSTANCES.

    B. NO RESPONSIBILITY.

      THE COMPANY IS NOT RESPONSIBLE TO INQUIRE WHETHER A COMMUNITY PROPERTY INTEREST EXISTS IN ANY CAPTIONED POLICY. THE COMPANY SHALL BE FULLY PROTECTED IN RELYING ON ITS GOOD FAITH BELIEF THAT THERE IS NO COMMUNITY PROPERTY INTEREST IN ANY CAPTIONED POLICY IF THE OWNER'S SPOUSE FAILS TO CONSENT TO THIS DESIGNATION IN THE SPACE INDICATED.

W A R N I N G

THIS FORM IS NOT INTENDED TO BE USED TO MAKE A GIFT OF A POLICY, TO CHANGE OWNERSHIP OF A POLICY, OR TO MAKE A POLICY PAYABLE TO TRUSTEES UNDER A WILL OR TO TRUSTEES OF AN IRREVOCABLE TRUST.

Form 1603

Request for Change of Beneficiary/Disability Policy

Date:

Address:

_____

_____

_____

Re: Beneficiary Designation for Disability Policy:
_____, Insured

    Policy No. _____

    SSN No. _____

Dear

As the insured under the above-referenced Disability Income Policy, I wish to make sure that if I become disabled that the benefits under the plan are paid to my revocable living trust. If I become disabled as defined under the policy, please make all payments to:

    _____ and _____, Trustees, or their successors in trust, under the _____ LIVING TRUST dated _____, and any amendments thereto.

Enclosed is an Affidavit of Trust* which evidences creation of my trust agreement. Attached to the Affidavit and incorporated in it are select provisions of the Trust evidencing the creation of the trust, the statement of revocability of the trust, the designation of successor Trustees, the powers of the Trustees, and the signature pages.

I am relying on you to take all appropriate steps to assure that my Disability Policy benefits are paid to my living trust unless I notify you in writing to the contrary. If you have a form that needs to be signed, please send it to me for my signature as soon as possible. If I do not hear from you, I will rely on the fact that you have agreed to make the payments as outlined in this letter.

If you should have any questions regarding this matter, please do not hesitate to contact me.

Sincerely,

* See Form 1201.

Form 1604

Letter to Life Insurance Company/Lifetime Beneficiary of Annuity

Date:

Address:

_____

_____

_____

Re: Beneficiary Designation for:

_____, Policy No. _____

Annuity—Ten-Year Plan

SSN No. _____

SSN No. _____

Dear

We want to designate our living trust as the lifetime beneficiary of the above-referenced annuity for purposes of estate planning. Payments under the annuity should be made directly to:

_____ and _____, Trustees, or their successors in trust, under the _____ LIVING TRUST dated _____, and any amendments thereto.

We are providing an Affidavit of Trust* which evidences creation of our Trust agreement. Attached to the Affidavit and incorporated in it are select provisions of the Trust evidencing the creation of the Trust, the statement of revocability of the Trust, the designation of successor Trustees, the powers of the Trustees, and the signature pages.

If this letter is not sufficient to change the payments to our trust, please send us the appropriate forms or information needed to accomplish our objective.

If you should have any questions regarding this matter, please do not hesitate to contact us.

Sincerely,

_____   _____

* See Form 1201.

Form 1605

Letter to Insurance Company/Death Beneficiary of Annuity

Date:

Address:

_____

_____

_____

Re: Change of Beneficiary Designation for:

_____, SSN No.

_____, SSN No.

Policy No. _____

Type of Annuity: _____

Dear

This letter is to confirm changing the beneficiary designation for our jointly held annuity to our living trust.

Please change the beneficiary designation of our policy to:

_____ and _____, Trustees, or their successors in trust, under the _____ LIVING TRUST dated _____, and any amendments thereto.

We are providing an Affidavit of Trust* which evidences creation of our Trust agreement. Attached to the Affidavit and incorporated in it are select provisions of the Trust evidencing the creation of the Trust, the statement of revocability of the Trust, the designation of successor Trustees, the powers of the Trustees, and the signature pages.

We are relying on you to take all appropriate steps to assure that our beneficiary designation for our jointly held annuity is changed properly. Please send the appropriate form for our signatures as soon as possible.

If you should have any questions regarding this matter, please do not hesitate to contact us.

Sincerely,

_____   _____

* See Form 1201.

Form 1606

ASSIGNMENT OF PRIVATE ANNUITY

_____, Grantor, does hereby transfer and assign without consideration and in order to change formal title only, all of his/her right, title, and interest in that certain Private Annuity dated _____, between _____ as Payor and _____ as Annuitant, a copy of which is attached hereto and incorporated herein, to:

_____ and _____, Trustees, or their successors in trust, under the _____ LIVING TRUST dated _____, and any amendments thereto.

Dated: _____

_____
, Grantor

_____
, Witness

_____
, Witness

Form 1607

Notification Letter for Private Annuity

Date:

Heading:

_____

_____

_____

RE: Private Annuity dated

Dear

As part of my overall estate planning, I have recently established a revocable living trust. I transferred to my revocable living trust the above-referenced private annuity. Please make all future annuity payments directly to:

_____ and _____, Trustees, or their successors in trust, under the _____ LIVING TRUST dated _____, and any amendments thereto.

Please feel free to contact me if you have any questions. Thank you for your cooperation in this matter.

Very truly yours,

Form 1608

SPOUSAL WAIVER FOR QUALIFIED RETIREMENT PLAN

I hereby consent to the designation made by my spouse. I understand that I am waiving my rights to the benefit described in my husband's/wife's _____ [name] Qualified Retirement Plan if my spouse dies before I do, and I hereby acknowledge that I understand that the effect of the designation is to cause the Retirement Plan benefits to be paid to beneficiaries other than me if my spouse dies before I do. I further understand that if I am *not* the sole beneficiary, then each beneficiary designation is not valid unless I consent to it and that my consent is irrevocable unless my spouse revokes the beneficiary designation. I further acknowledge and approve and consent to the identity of the beneficiaries.

Dated: _____

_____

Spouse's Signature

_____

Signature of Plan Official

STATE OF   )
) ss.
COUNTY OF   )

   On _____, before me, the undersigned Notary Public, in and for said County and State, personally appeared _____, personally known to me (or produced _____ as identification) to be the person who executed the foregoing instrument, and acknowledged executing the same for the purposes herein contained.

WITNESS my hand and official seal.

_____

                                      , Notary Public

My commission expires:

Form 1609

Letter of Notification to Plan Administrator

Date:

Address:

_____

_____

_____

Dear

I have named my revocable living trust as the primary beneficiary of the following plan:

The official name of my trust is:

_____ and _____, Trustees, or their successors in trust, under the _____ LIVING TRUST dated _____, and any amendments thereto.

Attached is a copy of the trust for your files in compliance with Treasury Regulation §1.401(2)(a)-1, D-5(QSA).

Please contact me if you have any questions.

Very truly yours,

Form 1701

Assignment of Promissory Note to Living Trust

_____ and _____, Grantors
and Husband and Wife, do hereby transfer and assign, without consideration and in order to change
formal title only, all of their right, title and interest in that certain Note, executed by _____,
a copy of which is attached hereto, to _____ and _____, Trustees,
or their successors in trust, under the _____ LIVING TRUST
dated _____, and any amendments thereto.

Dated _____.

Witnesses as to both:

_____

, Grantor

_____

, Witness

_____

, Grantor

_____

, Witness

STATE OF   )

)   ss.

COUNTY OF   )

On _____, before me, the undersigned Notary Public, in and for said County
and State, personally appeared _____, personally known to me
(or presented _____ as identification) to be the persons who executed the foregoing
instrument, and acknowledged executing the same for the purposes herein contained.

WITNESS my hand and official seal.

_____

, Notary Public

My commission expires:

Form 1702

Letter of Notification of Assignment of Promissory Note to Living Trust

Date:

_____

_____

_____

RE: Promissory Note dated _____

Dear

As part of my overall estate planning, I have recently established a revocable living trust. I have transferred to my trust your promissory note dated _____, in the original principal amount of $_____.

Please make all remaining payments due under the promissory note payable to:

_____ and _____, Trustees, or their successors in trust, under the _____ LIVING TRUST dated _____, and any amendments thereto.

Please feel free to contact me if you have any questions. Thank you for your cooperation in this matter.

Very truly yours,

Form 1801

ASSIGNMENT TO LIVING TRUST
OF SOLE PROPRIETORSHIP ASSETS

_____, Assignor, does hereby transfer and assign, without consideration and in order to change formal title only, all of his/her right, title and interest in that certain Sole Proprietorship commonly known as _____, a _____ sole proprietorship, to _____ and _____, Trustees, or their successors in trust, under the _____ LIVING TRUST dated ____, and any amendments thereto.

This assignment includes all of the interest of the undersigned in the assets and properties of the sole proprietorship, of whatsoever kind and character, whether tangible, intangible, real, personal or mixed, and wherever located, including without limitation all cash, cash equivalents, bank accounts, accounts receivable, stocks, bonds, notes, cash surrender value of insurance policies, inventories, deposits, goodwill, and all other supplies, materials, work in process, finished goods, equipment, machinery, furniture, fixtures, motor vehicles, claims and rights under leases, contracts, notes, evidences of indebtedness, purchase and sales orders, copyrights, service marks, trademarks, trade names, trade secrets, patents, patent applications, licenses, royalty rights, deposits, and rights and claims to refunds and adjustments of any kind, together with all policies of insurance thereon but subject to any liens thereon.

Dated: _____

_____
, Grantor

STATE OF   )
) ss.
COUNTY OF   )

On _____, before me, the undersigned Notary Public, in and for said County and State, personally appeared _____, personally known to me (or presented _____ as identification) to be the person who executed the foregoing instrument, and acknowledged executing the same for the purposes herein contained.

WITNESS my hand and official seal.

_____
, Notary Public

My commission expires:

Form 1802

POSTMORTEM ASSIGNMENT TO LIVING TRUST

I, _____, of the City of _____, State of _____, the Assignor, do hereby assign, transfer and convey all of my interest in those assets held in Account No. _____ with _____ to _____ and _____, Trustees, or their successors in trust, under the _____ LIVING TRUST dated _____, and any amendments thereto, the Assignee.

I hereby authorize and direct _____ to transfer and convey to the Assignee(s) at my death all of my right, title, and interest in and to said stock without liability therefor.

Dated: _____.

_____
, Assignor

STATE OF   )
) ss.
COUNTY OF   )

On _____, before me, the undersigned Notary Public, in and for said County and State, personally appeared _____, personally known to me (or presented _____ as identification) to be the person who executed the foregoing instrument, and acknowledged executing the same for the purposes herein contained.

WITNESS my hand and official seal.

_____
, Notary Public

My commission expires:

Form 1803

ASSIGNMENT TO LIVING TRUST OF GENERAL PARTNERSHIP INTEREST

_____, Grantor and _____,
Grantor, Husband and Wife, do hereby transfer and assign, without consideration and in order to change formal title only, all of their right, title and interest in and to their interest in _____ [Partnership Name], to _____ and _____, Trustees, or their successors in trust, under the _____ LIVING TRUST, dated _____, and any amendments thereto.

Dated: _____

_____
, Grantor

_____
, Grantor

STATE OF   )
) ss.
COUNTY OF   )

On _____, before me, the undersigned Notary Public, in and for said County and State, personally appeared _____ and _____, personally known to me (or presented _____ as identification) to be the persons who executed the foregoing instrument, and acknowledged executing the same for the purposes herein contained.

WITNESS my hand and official seal.

_____
, Notary Public

My commission expires:

Form 1804

POSTMORTEM ASSIGNMENT OF
PARTNERSHIP INTEREST TO LIVING TRUST

_____ of _____ [address], the City of _____, State of _____, _____ [zip] herein referred to as "Assignor," does hereby assign, transfer and convey, unto _____ and _____, Trustees, or their successors in trust, under the _____ LIVING TRUST dated _____, and any amendments thereto, herein referred to as "Assignee," all right, title, and interest of Assignor in and to the _____ Partnership.

I hereby authorize and direct _____ to transfer and convey to the Assignee at my death all of my right, title, and interest in and to said Partnership without liability therefor.

The Assignee is subject to all the terms and conditions of the Partnership Agreement, including, but not limited to, any applicable purchase options or buy-sell provisions.

Dated: _____

_____
, Assignor

STATE OF   )
) ss.
COUNTY OF   )

On _____, before me, the undersigned Notary Public, in and for said County and State, personally appeared _____, personally known to me (or presented _____ as identification) to be the person who executed the foregoing instrument, and acknowledged executing the same for the purposes herein contained.

WITNESS my hand and official seal.

_____
, Notary Public

My commission expires:

Form 1805

ASSIGNMENT TO LIVING TRUST OF LIVESTOCK BRAND

_____, does hereby transfer, convey, and assign, without consideration and in order to change formal title only, all of his/her right, title and interest in and to his/her exclusive right to use the Brand described on the attached Certificate No. _____, incorporated by reference, to:

_____ and _____, Trustees, or their successors in trust, under the _____ LIVING TRUST dated _____, and any amendments thereto.

Dated: _____

_____
, Grantor

STATE OF   )
) ss.
COUNTY OF   )

On _____, before me, the undersigned Notary Public, in and for said County and State, personally appeared _____ _____, personally known to me (or presented _____ as identification) to be the person who executed the foregoing instrument, and acknowledged executing the same for the purposes herein contained.

WITNESS my hand and official seal.

_____
, Notary Public

My commission expires:

Form 1806

UNREGISTERED LIVESTOCK BILL OF SALE

Date:

Seller:

Seller's Mailing Address:

Buyer: _____ and _____, Trustees, or their successors in trust, under the _____ LIVING TRUST dated _____, and any amendments thereto.

Buyer's Address:

Consideration: Ten and no/100 ($10.00) Dollars

Personal Property:

_____ HEAD OF _____ located at: _____

_____ HEAD OF _____ located at: _____

For value received Seller sells and delivers the personal property to Buyer and warrants and agrees to defend title to the personal property to Buyer and Buyer's successors against all lawful claims.

When the context requires, singular nouns and pronouns include the plural.

EXECUTED and DELIVERED on _____.

_____

, Seller

STATE OF   )
) ss.
COUNTY OF   )

On _____, before me, the undersigned Notary Public, in and for said County and State, personally appeared _____, personally known to me (or presented _____ as identification) to be the person who executed the foregoing instrument, and acknowledged executing the same for the purposes herein contained.

WITNESS my hand and official seal.

_____

, Notary Public

My commission expires:

Form 1807

ASSIGNMENT OF ROYALTY INTEREST TO LIVING TRUST

_____, Grantor, hereby transfers and assigns without consideration, and in order to change formal title only, all of his/her right, title, and interest in those certain rights to royalty payments contained in the agreement between Grantor and _____ company, dated _____, a copy of which agreement is attached hereto, to _____ and _____, Trustees, or their successors in trust, under the _____ LIVING TRUST dated _____, and any amendments thereto.

Date: _____

_____   _____

_____   _____

STATE OF   )
) ss.
COUNTY OF   )

On _____, before me, the undersigned Notary Public, in and for said County and State, personally appeared _____, personally known to me (or produced _____ as identification) to be the person who executed the foregoing instrument, and acknowledged executing the same for the purposes herein contained.

WITNESS my hand and official seal.

_____

, Notary Public

My commission expires:

Form 1808

ASSIGNMENT OF COPYRIGHT TO LIVING TRUST

_____, Grantor, hereby transfers and assigns, without consideration, and in order to change formal title only, all of his/her right, title, and interest in and to the attached copyright, which is registered under Certificate No. _____, dated _____, in the United States Copyright Office to _____ and _____, Trustees, or their successors in trust, under the _____ LIVING TRUST dated _____, and any amendments thereto.

Date: _____

_____   _____
, Grantor   , Witness

_____   _____
, Grantor   , Witness

STATE OF   )
) ss.
COUNTY OF   )

On _____, before me, the undersigned Notary Public, in and for said County and State, personally appeared _____, personally known to me (or produced _____ as identification) to be the person who executed the foregoing instrument, and acknowledged executing the same for the purposes herein contained.

WITNESS my hand and official seal.

_____

, Notary Public

My commission expires:

Form 1809

ASSIGNMENT OF TRADEMARK TO LIVING TRUST

_____, Grantor, hereby transfers and assigns, without consideration, and in order to change formal title, only, of his/her right, title and interest in his/her trademark, a copy of which is attached hereto, which is registered under Certificate No. _____, dated _____, in the United States Patent and Trademark Office to _____ and _____, Trustees, or their successors in trust, under the _____ LIVING TRUST dated _____, and any amendments thereto.

Date: _____

_____
, Grantor

STATE OF   )
) ss.
COUNTY OF   )

On _____, before me, the undersigned Notary Public, in and for said County and State, personally appeared _____, personally known to me (or produced _____ as identification) to be the person who executed the foregoing instrument, and acknowledged executing the same for the purposes herein contained.

WITNESS my hand and official seal.

_____
, Notary Public

My commission expires:

Form 1810

ASSIGNMENT TO LIVING TRUST
OF LIQUOR LICENSE

_____, Assignor, hereby sells, assigns and transfers unto _____ and _____, Trustees, or their successors in trust, under the _____ LIVING TRUST dated _____, and any amendments thereto, Assignee, all of the Assignor's right, title and interest in a certain liquor license issued by the County of _____, State of _____, as License No. _____.

This Assignment shall become effective upon the approval of said transfer by the Board of County Commissioners of _____ County at a duly held meeting and pursuant to lawful notice.

Dated: _____

_____
, Assignor

_____
, Assignor

STATE OF   )
) ss.
COUNTY OF   )

On _____, before me, the undersigned Notary Public, in and for said County and State, personally appeared _____, personally known to me (or presented _____ as identification) to be the person who executed the foregoing instrument, and acknowledged executing the same for the purposes herein contained.

WITNESS my hand and official seal.

_____
, Notary Public

My commission expires:

Form 1901

RECEIPT OF REAL PROPERTY DEED

_____ and _____ as Trustees of the _____ LIVING TRUST dated _____, hereby acknowledge receipt of the Warranty Deed, a copy of which is attached hereto on this ____ day of _____, 19____.

_____

, Trustee

_____

, Trustee

Form 1902

AFFIDAVIT OF SUCCESSOR TRUSTEE
FOR DECEASED TRUSTEE

1. The following Trust (the "Trust") is the subject of this Affidavit:

   _____ and _____, Trustees, or their successors in trust, under the _____ LIVING TRUST dated _____, and any amendments thereto.

2. Section _____ of Article _____ states that in the event of the death of an initial Trustee, _____ shall serve as a Successor Trustee.

3. One of the initial Trustees, _____, died on _____.

4. The Trust is currently in full force and effect.

5. Attached to this Affidavit and incorporated herein by reference are selected provisions of the Trust including the pages naming the initial trustees, creating the trust, trustees' powers, designation of successor trustees, a copy of of the signature pages, and a copy of the Death Certificate for _____.

6. The Trust provisions which are not attached to this Affidavit are of a personal and confidential nature and set forth the distribution of Trust property. They do not modify the powers of the Trustees.

7. The signatories of this Affidavit are currently the acting Co-Trustees of the Trust and they declare that the foregoing statements and the attached trust provisions are true and correct, under penalty of perjury under the laws of the State of _____.

8. This Affidavit was executed in the County of _____, State of _____, on _____.

_____   _____
, Trustee   , Trustee

Form 1903

AFFIDAVIT OF SUCCESSOR TRUSTEE
FOR TRUSTEE WHO HAS RESIGNED

1. The following Trust (the "Trust") is the subject of this Affidavit:

    _____ and _____, Trustees, or their successors in trust, under the _____ LIVING TRUST dated _____, and any amendments thereto.

2. Section ____ of Article _____ states that in the event of the resignation of an initial Trustee, _____ shall serve as a Successor Trustee.

3. An initial Trustee, _____, resigned on _____.

4. The Trust is currently in full force and effect.

5. Attached to this Affidavit and incorporated herein by reference are selected provisions of the Trust including the pages naming the initial trustees, creating the trust, trustees' powers, designation of successor trustees, a copy of the signature pages, and a copy of Letter of Resignation.

6. The Trust provisions which are not attached to this Affidavit are of a personal and confidential nature and set forth the distribution of Trust property. They do not modify the powers of the Trustee.

7. The signatories of this Affidavit are currently the acting Co-Trustees of the Trust and they declare that the foregoing statements and the attached Trust provisions are true and correct, under penalty of perjury under the laws of the State of _____.

8. This Affidavit was executed in the County of _____, State of _____, on _____.

_____   _____
                    , Trustee   , Trustee

Form 1904

AFFIDAVIT OF SUCCESSOR TRUSTEE
FOR DISABLED TRUSTEE

1. The following Trust (the "Trust") is the subject of this Affidavit:

   _____ and _____, Trustees, or their successors in trust, under the _____ LIVING TRUST dated _____, and any amendments thereto.

2. Section ____ of Article _____ states that in the event of the incompetency of an initial Trustee, _____ shall serve as a Successor Trustee.

3. One of the initial Trustees, _____, was declared incompetent on _____.

4. The Trust is currently in full force and effect.

5. Attached to this Affidavit and incorporated herein by reference are selected provisions of the Trust including the pages naming the initial trustees, creating the trust, trustees' powers, designation of successor trustees, a copy of the signature pages, and a copy of Letters from two physicians declaring _____ incompetent.

6. The Trust provisions which are not attached to this Affidavit are of a personal and confidential nature and set forth the distribution of Trust property. They do not modify the powers of the Trustees.

7. The signatories of this Affidavit are currently the acting Co-Trustees of the Trust and they declare that the foregoing statements and the attached trust provisions are true and correct, under penalty of perjury under the laws of the State of _____.

8. This Affidavit was executed in the County of _____, State of _____, on _____.

_____   _____
                        , Trustee   , Trustee

Form 1905

Letter Requesting Permission
to Transfer Cooperative Stock to a Trust

Date:

Cooperative Association
Board of Directors

_____

_____

_____

Dear

My attorney has recently prepared a revocable living trust for me as part of my overall estate planning. I am now in the process of transferring all of my assets to my revocable living trust. The purpose of this letter is to request your approval of the transfer of my cooperative unit to my revocable living trust. This transfer is taking place solely for estate planning purposes and I shall continue to live in the apartment.

Please provide me with any documentation you require to effectuate this transfer. I am aware of the federal income tax benefits that are available to a cooperative association when at least 80% of the apartment owners are "tenants-stockholders" within the meaning of Internal Revenue Code Ù216(b)(2). The Tax Reform Act of 1986 provides that, beginning January 1, 1987, a revocable living trust is included in the definition of tenant-stockholders. Therefore, the transfer of my cooperative apartment to my revocable living trust does not affect the favorable tax treatment enjoyed by our cooperative association.

For purposes of any transfer documentation you may require, the legal name of my revocable living trust is:

_____ and _____, Trustees, or their successors in trust, under the _____ LIVING TRUST dated _____, and any amendments thereto.

Please let me know if you need any additional information in order to transfer my cooperative apartment to my revocable living trust. Thank you in advance for your assistance in this matter.

Very truly yours,

Form 1906

Letter Requesting Permission
to Transfer Condominium Unit to a Trust

Date:

Name and Address of:
Condominium Association
Board of Directors

_____

_____

_____

Dear

My attorney has recently prepared a revocable living trust for me as part of my overall estate planning. I am now in the process of transferring all of my assets to my revocable living trust. The purpose of this letter is to request your approval of the transfer of my condominium unit to my revocable living trust. I am making this transfer solely for estate planning purposes and shall continue to live in the condominium unit.

Please provide me with any documentation you require to complete this transfer. For purposes of any transfer documentation you may require, the legal name of my revocable living trust is:

_____ and _____, Trustees, or their successors in trust, under the _____ LIVING TRUST dated _____, and any amendments thereto.

Please let me know what, if any, additional information you may need at your earliest convenience. Thank you in advance for your cooperation in this matter.

Very truly yours,

Form 1907

Notification Letter to Lender of Transfer to Living Trust

Date:

Address:

_____

_____

_____

Re: Mortgage No. _____

Dear

My attorney has recently prepared a revocable living trust for me as part of my overall estate planning. I am currently in the process of transferring all my assets to my living trust. I am writing this letter to request your permission to transfer my residence located at _____ to my living trust. This residence is encumbered by the above-referenced mortgage. The property would be titled in the following name:

_____ and _____, Trustees, or their successors in trust, under the _____ LIVING TRUST dated _____, and any amendments thereto.

My family and I shall continue to reside in this home and it will continue to be our personal residence.

Please feel free to contact me if you have any questions.

Very truly yours,

Form 1908

Notification Letter to Lender of
Transfer to Living Trust Under Garn–St. Germain Act

Date:

Address:

_____

_____

_____

RE: Mortgage No. _____

Dear

My attorney has recently prepared a revocable living trust for me as part of my overall estate plan-ning. I am currently in the process of transferring all my assets to my living trust. I am now in the process of transferring my residence located at _____ to my living trust. This residence is encumbered by the above-referenced mortgage.

The purpose of this letter is to notify you that I am transferring my residence subject to the mortgage to my revocable living trust officially known as:

_____ and _____, Trustees, or their successors in trust, un-der the _____ LIVING TRUST dated _____, and any amendments thereto.

My family and I shall continue to reside in this home and it will continue to be our personal residence. This transfer is specifically permitted under the Garn–St. Germain Depository Institutions Act of 1982 and the Regulations promulgated thereunder. See 12 CFR §591.5.

Please feel free to contact me if you have any questions.

Very truly yours,

Form 2001

ASSIGNMENT TO LIVING TRUST
OF CERTIFICATE OF INTERMENT RIGHTS

_____, Grantor and _____,
Grantor, Husband and Wife, do hereby transfer and assign, without consideration and in order to change formal title only, all of their right, title and interest in that certain Certificate of Interment Rights, contracted with _____ (Organization), a copy of which is attached hereto, to _____ and _____, Trustees, or their successors in trust, under the _____ LIVING TRUST, dated _____, and any amendments thereto.

Dated: _____   Witnesses as to both:

_____   _____
                       , Grantor   , Witness

_____   _____
                       , Grantor   , Witness

STATE OF   )
) ss.
COUNTY OF   )

   On _____, before me, the undersigned Notary Public, in and for said County and State, personally appeared _____, personally known to me (or presented _____ as identification) to be the person who executed the foregoing instrument, and acknowledged executing the same for the purposes herein contained.

WITNESS my hand and official seal.

_____

                       , Notary Public

My commission expires:

Form 2002

ASSIGNMENT TO LIVING TRUST
OF BURIAL PLOT/MAUSOLEUM

_____, Grantor, and _____,
Grantor, Husband and Wife, do hereby transfer and assign, without consideration and in order to
change formal title only, all of their right, title and interest in those certain Burial Plot(s)/Crypt(s),
located at _____ (Cemetery), a copy of which agreement is attached hereto,
to _____ and _____, Trustees, or their successors in trust, under the
_____ LIVING TRUST, dated _____, and any amendments thereto.

Dated: _____   Witnesses to both:

_____   _____
, Grantor   , Witness

_____   _____
, Grantor   , Witness

STATE OF   )
) ss.
COUNTY OF   )

On _____, before me, the undersigned Notary Public, in and for said County
and State, personally appeared _____, personally known to me
(or presented _____ as identification) to be the person who executed the foregoing
instrument, and acknowledged executing the same for the purposes herein contained.

WITNESS my hand and official seal.

_____
, Notary Public

My commission expires:

Form 2003

ASSIGNMENT TO LIVING TRUST OF MEMBERSHIP

_____, Grantor, and _____,
Grantor, Husband and Wife, do hereby transfer and assign, without consideration and in order
to change formal title only, all of their right, title and interest in that certain Membership in
_____ (Organization), a copy of which is attached hereto, to _____
and _____, Trustees, or their successors in trust, under the _____
LIVING TRUST, dated _____, and any amendments thereto.

Dated: _____

_____   _____
, Grantor   , Witness

_____   _____
, Grantor   , Witness

STATE OF   )
) ss.
COUNTY OF   )

    On _____, before me, the undersigned Notary Public, in and for said County
and State, personally appeared _____, personally known to me
(or presented _____ as identification) to be the person who executed the foregoing
instrument, and acknowledged executing the same for the purposes herein contained.

WITNESS my hand and official seal.

_____
, Notary Public

My commission expires:

Form 2004

ASSIGNMENT TO LIVING TRUST OF JUDGMENT

_____, Grantor, and _____,
Grantor, Husband and Wife, do hereby transfer and assign, without consideration and in order to
change formal title only, all right, title and interest in that certain Judgment, entered in the
_____ (Court), of _____ (State), County of _____
Judicial District, Case Number _____, filed _____ vs. _____
a copy of which is attached hereto, to _____ and _____, Trustees,
or their successors in trust, under the _____ LIVING TRUST, dated _____,
and any amendments thereto.

Dated: _____   Witnesses to both:

_____   _____
                    , Grantor   , Witness

_____   _____
                    , Grantor   , Witness

STATE OF   )
) ss.
COUNTY OF   )

   On _____, before me, the undersigned Notary Public, in and for said County
and State, personally appeared _____, personally known to me
(or presented _____ as identification) to be the person who executed the foregoing
instrument, and acknowledged executing the same for the purposes herein contained.

WITNESS my hand and official seal.

_____
                                        , Notary Public

My commission expires:

Form 2101

ANATOMICAL GIFT

In the hope that I may help others, I, _____, hereby make this anatomical gift, if medically acceptable, to take effect upon my death.

Personal Information

_____

Full Name

_____

Street Address

_____

City, State, Zip Code

_____

Next of Kin

_____

Street Address

_____

City, State, Zip Code

_____

Social Security No.

_____

Telephone Number

_____

Relationship

_____

Telephone Number

I GIVE:

_____ Any needed organs or parts

_____ Only the following organs or parts:

_____

_____

_____

I have previously signed with a medical school. **Yes** _____ **No** _____

Form 2102

MEMORIAL LETTER

_____

[Date]

To My Loved Ones:

General Purpose of This Letter

This letter is written in order to share my feelings with my Trustees and loved ones about my general memorial wishes.

The thoughts which I share in this letter should not be considered to be rigid and binding on anyone. They should be tempered with what my survivors wish done in these areas after they have examined the circumstances existing at my death, and their own wishes, whatever they may be.

Conflicts with My Living Trust or Pour-Over Will

If the feelings I express in this letter are in conflict with any of the provisions of my living trust or Pour-Over Will, the provisions of my living trust or Pour-Over Will shall control and the provisions of this letter shall be void and of no effect.

Funeral and Burial Instructions

I have included in this letter my desires concerning my last rites and burial services. I hope that my survivors will consider them in making those decisions that they deem best.

My Desires for My Funeral and Burial Arrangements

_____

_____

_____

_____

_____

_____

[Signature]

Index

Page numbers in *italics* indicate documents.

Account Agreement–Individual Trust, 128, *129–30*

Account Agreement–Joint Trust, 128, *131–32*

accountants, 22, 25, 26, 38, 39–40, 81, 85, 87, 88, 93
  fees of, 39
  lawyer referrals from, 34, 35

accounts receivable, 174, 178

advisors, *see* professional advisors, team of

Affidavit of Successor Trustee, 115, 198, *237*
  for Deceased Trustee, 198, *298*
  for Disabled Trustee, 198, *300*
  for Trustee Who Has Resigned, 198, *299*

Affidavit of Trust, 114, 115, 133, 136, 138, 145, 215, *235*

airplanes, 150, 152, *269, 270*

American Bar Association, 157

Anatomical Gift, 10, 14, 219, *309*

annuities, 72
  beneficiaries of, 159–60, *279, 280*
  commercial, 158–60
  deferred, 159
  immediate, 159
  private, 160, *281, 282*

apartments, cooperative, 200, *301*

Application for Employer Identification Number, 96, *98*

appraisals, 65

assignment, 148–49, 187, 216
  of Aircraft to Living Trust, 152, *269*
  of Bearer Bonds to Living Trust, 139, *255*
  of Burial Plot/Mausoleum to Living Trust, 215, *306*
  of Certificate of Interment Rights to Living Trust, 215, *305*
  of Certificates of Deposit to Living Trust, 133, *248*
  Consent to, 146, 186, *257*
  of Copyright to Living Trust, 188, *294*
  of Deed of Trust, 166, *169–70*
  general, 149–50
  General, for One Trust Maker, *265*
  General, for Two Trust Makers, *266*
  of General Partnership Interest to Living Trust, 185, 186, *289*
  of Installment Sale Contract to Living Trust, *171,* 172
  of Judgment to Living Trust, 216, *308*
  of Land Sale Contract to Living Trust, 172, *173*
  of Land Sale Contract to Living Trust–Buyer, 209, *210*
  of Lease for Oil, Gas, or Mineral Interests, 209, *211*
  of Leasehold to Living Trust, 212, *213*
  of Lease to Living Trust, 205, *206*
  of Limited Partnership with Consent, to Living Trust, 146, 185–86, *256*
  of Liquor License to Living Trust, 188, *296*
  of Livestock Brand to Living Trust, 187, *291*
  of Membership to Living Trust, 215, *307*
  of Mortgage, 165, *167–68*
  of Private Annuity, 160, *281*
  of Promissory Note to Living Trust, 166, 172, 174, *285*
  of Royalty Interest to Living Trust, 188, *293*
  of Sole Proprietorship Assets to Living Trust, 177, *287*
  for Specific Personal Property of One Trust Maker, *261*
  for Specific Personal Property of Two Trust Makers, *262*
  of Time-Share to Living Trust, 201, *204*
  of Trademark to Living Trust, 188, *295*
  see also bill of sale

attorney, *see* lawyer

Attorney's Certificate, 115, *236*
automobiles, 61, 62, 150, 151–52

bank accounts, 62
    checking, 69, 123, 124, 126–28, 133, 161
    FDIC coverage of, 133–34
    joint, 126
    letters to bank about, *244, 245, 246, 247*
    money market, 128, 133
    payable-on-death, 123, 124, 134
    in personal information checklist, 69
    savings, 62, 69, 123, 124, 126–28, 133
    value of, 65
bank trust officers, 25, 38, 44–45, 87
    lawyer referrals from, 34–35
bearer bonds, 138–39, *255*
beneficiaries, *275, 276–77*
    of annuities, 159–60, *279, 280*
    of disability policies, 158, *278*
    of life insurance policies, 156–57
    of retirement plans, 160, 161–63, 164
Beneficiary Designation of Trustees under
        Revocable Trust Instrument, 156–57,
        276–77
bill of sale, 61, 148–49
    general, 149–50
    General, for One Trust Maker, *263*
    General, for Two Trust Makers, *264*
    for Motor Vehicle, Mobile Home, Trailer,
        Recreational Vehicle, and/or Boat, 151,
        268
    for Specific Personal Property of One Trust
        Maker, *259*
    for Specific Personal Property of Two Trust
        Makers, *260*
    Unregistered Livestock, *292*
    see also assignment
boats, 61, 150, 152–53, *268*
Bond or Stock Power, 136, 138, 179, *249*
bonds, 61, 64, 135, 136, 138–39, 148
    bearer, 138–39, *255*
    Flower, 145
    in personal information checklist, 71
    Savings, 139, 145
brokerage accounts, 136, 138, *253*
brokerage firms, 136–38
brokers, *see* stockbrokers
burial and memorial instructions, 10, 14, 219
burial plots, 215, *306*
Business Account Agreement, 128, *131–32*
business and professional interests, xv, 73, 74,
        177–90
    limited liability companies, 187
    partnerships, *see* partnerships

privately owned corporations, 179–84
sole proprietorships, 74, 177–79, 187, *287*
special business or income-producing prop-
        erty, 187–88
special tax rules for business property, 188–
        190
see also corporations

cars, 61, 62, 150, 151–52
C corporations, 182, 183
cemetery plots, 215
certificates of deposit, 62, 128–33, *247, 248*
    payable-on-death, 123, 124
certified financial planner (CFP), 40
charity, 54–55
chartered financial consultant (ChFC), 40
chartered life underwriter (CLU), 42
checking accounts, 69, 126–28, 133, 161
    payable-on-death, 123, 124
checklist for designing your plan, 24, 46–59,
        77, 85, 86
    distributing children's property, 52–54
    federal death tax savings, 58
    giving to charity, 54–55
    providing for minor children, 52
    providing for your family, 47, 49–51, 58
    providing for yourself, 48
    providing for your spouse, 48–49
    trustee selection, 56–57
    ultimate distribution of property, 55
ChFC (chartered financial consultant), 40
children, 52
    family trust and, 49–50
    property of, 52–54
CLU (chartered life underwriter), 42
club memberships, 215, *307*
Coast Guard, U.S., 152–53, *271*
commercial annuities, 158–60
common trusts, 52
community property, 62, 64–65, 99, 100, 108
    transfer of, to trust, 106–8
Community Property Agreement, 108,
        109–10
computer programs, 18
condominiums, 200–201, *302*
Consent to Assignment, 146, 186, *257*
conservatorship (guardianship; living pro-
        bate), 11, 12, 16, 18, 85, 91, 92
Consumer Account Agreement, 128, *129–30*
control, 4–5, 6, 7, 10, 12, 15, 23, 60, 91, 93
cooperative apartments, 200, *301*
copyrights, 188, *294*
corporations, 73, 177, 183–84
    C, 182, 183

family-owned, waiver of attribution rules for, 189
nominee, 118
privately owned, 179–84
professional, 183–84
S, 182–83
costs, 18
after-death, of living trust–centered plan, 19
court, 4, 6–7
initial, of living trust–centered plan, 16–18
of living trust–centered plan, 15–19
of probate, 16, 17, 19
of will planning, 16, 19
see also fees
credit unions, 128

death, 3–4, 6, 10
burial and memorial instructions and, 10, 14, 219
living will and, 10, 13, 87
deeds, 61, 62, 64, 191
to convert joint tenancy to tenancy in common, 102, *103*
of Conveyance, 201, *202–3*
from joint tenancy directly into separate living trust, 102, *105*
Quitclaim, 192, *193*
receipt of, 195, *297*
tenancy in common, 63
from tenants in common to separate living trusts, 102, *104*
for time-share, 201, *202–3*
of trust, 166, 172
trustee's or fiduciary, 195
types of, 192–96
unrecorded, 195–96
warranty, 192, *194*
deferred annuities, 159
Department of Motor Vehicles, 151, 153
disability (incapacity), 4, 5, 6, 9, 10, 48, 91
and durable special power of attorney for funding, 10, 11–12
guardianship and, 11, 12, 16, 18, 85, 91, 92
and health care power of attorney, 10, 13
disability insurance, 62, 158, *278*
documents, xv, 9–15, 25, 85, 217–26, 229–310
boilerplate, 10, 18, 108
do-it-yourself, 18
drafting of, 38
Location Lists for, 217, 218, 220–24
location of, 10, 15, 217–18
reviewing and signing of, 86–87

see also personal information checklist; *specific documents*
durable power of attorney, 124, 125
general, 12, 158
durable special power of attorney, 87, 123
disability insurance and, 158
for funding, 10, 11–12, 124–25, 158, 159, 160–61, 184, *241–43*
for health care, 10, 13, 87
Joint Property, 122, *238–39*

employee plans:
disability insurance, 62, 158
incentive stock options, 146–47
life insurance, 42–43
retirement, *see* retirement plans
stock ownership, 160
ESOP (employee stock ownership plan), 160
Esperti Peterson Planning Process, xiv, 4, 15, 18, 20–28, 29, 31, 41, 42, 87, 227
from advisors' perspective, 27–28
beginning of, 22–23
planning pyramid in, 20–22
"team" approach to, 37; *see also* professional advisors, team of
from your perspective, 23–26
see also checklist for designing your plan; living trust–centered plan
estate planning, xiii, xiv, 8, 9, 21, 227
as "death planning," 3–4
do-it-yourself, 18
self-education in, 23–24, 37, 43
seminars on, 23, 43, 80
"upside down" approach to, 20, 22
see also Esperti Peterson Planning Process; living trust–centered plan
estate planning, definition of, 3–7, 8, 9, 15, 22, 28, 79–80, 227
control in, 4–5, 6, 7, 10, 12, 15
giving away of property in, 4, 6
incapacity and, 4, 5, 6
as standard of measurement, 7
taxes and expenses in, 4, 6–7
estate planning councils, 35
estate taxes, *see* taxes
evidence of title, 61
expenses, *see* costs; fees

family-owned corporations, 189
family trusts, 47, 49–51, 58
farm and ranch interests, 74
farm equipment, 188
Federal Aviation Administration (FAA), 152

Federal Deposit Insurance Corporation (FDIC), 133–34
federal estate taxes, *see* taxes
federal identification number, 96
fees, 4, 6–7
    of accountants, 39
    of financial planners, 40–41, 81
    of lawyers, xv, 17–18, 31, 36, 87, *232*
    of stockbrokers, 43
    see also costs
fee simple, 62, 63
fictitious and trade names, 178
fiduciary deed, 195
financial planners and advisors, 22, 25, 26, 38, 40–41, 43, 87, 88, 93
    credentialed, 40
    feeas and commissions of, 40–41, 81
    lawyer referrals from, 34, 35
    see also accountants; professional advisors, team of
Flower Bonds, 145
forms, *see* documents
Form SS-4, 96, *98*
Form W-9, 96, *97*, 138
funding, 15, 25–26, 40, 85, 87, 89–227
    durable special power of attorney for, 10, 11–12, 124–25, 158, 159, 160–61, 184, *241–43*
    income taxes and, 93–96
    master tracking checklist for, 93, 94–95
    methods of, 111–25
    overview of, 91–98
    see also property; *specific types of assets*

Garn–St. Germain Depository Institutions Act, 208–9, *304*
gas interests, 74, 209
general assignment, 149–50
    for One Trust Maker, *265*
    for Two Trust Makers, *266*
general bill of sale, 149–50
    for One Trust Maker, *263*
    for Two Trust Makers, *264*
general partnerships, 185, 186, *258*, *289*
grantor trusts, 93, 183
group insurance, 157
    disability, 158
guardianship (conservatorship; living probate), 11, 12, 16, 18, 85, 91, 92

Hand, Learned, 6
health care power of attorney, 10, 13, 87
homes:
    manufactured or mobile, 153, *268*
    primary residence, 198–99
    vacation, 200
homestead exemption, 199

immediate annuities, 159
incapacity, *see* disability
incentive stock option (ISO), 146–47
income taxes, *see* taxes
Income Tax Ramifications of My Living Trust, 96, *234*
individual retirement plan (IRA), 160, 163
installment sale contracts, 166–72
insurance, 15, 62, 65, 156, *280*
    commercial annuities, 158–60
    disability, 62, 158
    group, 157, 158
    life, *see* life insurance
    private annuities, 160
    property and title, 196–97
insurance agents, 85, 88
    lawyer referrals from, 34
interment rights, 215, *305*
inter vivos trust, *see* living trust
investment limited partnerships, 146
investments, xv, 15, 61, 62, 64
    in personal information checklist, 69
    see also business and professional interests; securities; *specific types of investment properties*
IRA (individual retirement plan), 160, 163
irrevocable life insurance trust, 157
ISO (incentive stock option), 146–47

Joint Declaration of Trust Ownership, 119, *120–21*
Joint Property Durable Special Power of Attorney, 122, *238–39*
joint tenancy, xiii, 5, 100, 102, 108
    of automobile, 151
    of bank account, 126
    joint trusts and, 100
    Magic Wand and, 119–22
    with right of survivorship, 8, 62, 63, 64, 100, 102
    separate trusts and, 102
joint trusts, 99–100, 108, 126, 127, *244*, *252*
    joint tenancy property and, 100
    transfers of community property to, 106–8
judgments, 75, 216, *308*

Keydel, Frederick, 119

land sale contracts, 172–74, 209
land trusts, 118–19

Last Will and Testament, *see* wills
laws:
    changes in, 87–88, *233*
    state, 4–5, 11, 50, 99, 100, 151
lawyer(s), xiii, xiv, xv, 10–11, 15, 18, 22, 24–
        25, 26, 27, 29, 37, 38, 40, 43, 45, 47, 77
    advisors as sources for, 34
    being your own, 18
    confirming first meeting with, 36, *231*
    contacting of, 29, 30–33
    Esperti Peterson Planning Process used by,
        29, 30
    estate planning council as sources for, 35
    fees of, xv, 17–18, 31, 36, 87, *232*
    financial products and services and, 83–84
    finding of, 29–36
    first meeting with, 24
    friends as sources for, 33
    funding and, 92–93, 111
    lack of promptness in, 33, 36
    law changes and, 87–88, *233*
    meeting with, before meeting with other
        advisors, 77–80
    National Network of Estate Planning Attor-
        neys and, 17, 29, 30, 32, 33, 227
    real estate transfer and, 102, 191
    review sessions with, 88
    second meeting with, 84, 85–88, *232*
    sources for, 33–35
    that you do not know, meeting of, 35–36
    that you have used before, contacting of,
        32–33
    that you know but have not used, contact-
        ing of, 30–32
    trust officers as sources for, 34–35
leases, 201–5, 212
lettered stock, 138
letters:
    to Bank–Certificate of Deposit, 133, *247*
    to Bank–Individual Trust, 127, *246*
    to Bank–Joint Trust, 127, *244*
    to Bank–Separate Trusts/Tenants in Com-
        mon, 127, *245*
    to Brokerage Account Representative, *253*
    about Changes in the Law, 88, *233*
    to Confirm Appointment with Your Attor-
        ney, 36, *231*
    to Confirm Your Fee and Second Meeting,
        232
    to FAA Assigning Aircraft to Living Trust,
        152, *270*
    to General Partner, 146, *258*
    to Insurance Company/Death Beneficiary
        of Annuity, 160, *280*

to Life Insurance Company/Lifetime Bene-
        ficiary of Annuity, 159, *279*
    Notification, for Private Annuity, 160, *282*
    Notification, to Lender of Transfer to Liv-
        ing Trust, *303*
    Notification, to Lender of Transfer to Liv-
        ing Trust Under Garn–St. Germain Act,
        208–9, *304*
    of Notification of Assignment of Promissory
        Note to Living Trust, 166, 172, 174, *286*
    of Notification to Plan Administrator, 163,
        284
    to Property and Casualty Agent, 198–99,
        267
    Requesting Permission to Transfer Condo-
        minium Unit to a Trust, 200–201, *302*
    Requesting Permission to Transfer Cooper-
        ative Stock to a Trust, 200, *301*
    to Stockbroker, *254*
    to Transfer Agent–Individual Trust, *250*
    to Transfer Agent–Joint Trust, *252*
    to Transfer Agent–Separate Trusts/Tenants
        in Common, *251*
    to U.S. Coast Guard, 153, *271*
licenses, 188
life insurance, 17, 62, 65, 156–57, *279*
    beneficiaries of, 156–57
    in employee benefit plans, 42–43
    group, 157
    in personal information checklist, 72
life insurance agents, 22, 25, 38, 40, 41–43,
        44, 65, 87, 93
    CLU-designated, 42
    lawyer referrals from, 34, 35
limited liability companies, 187
limited partnerships, 185–86, *256*
liquor license, 188, *296*
livestock, 187–88, *291*, *292*
living probate (guardianship; conservator-
        ship), 11, 12, 16, 18, 85, 91, 92
living trust(s), 8
    Affidavit of, 114, 115, 133, 136, 138, 145,
        215, *235*
    amendments to, 88, 155, *273-74*
    designing of, 1–88
    document, 10–11, 47
    duplicate originals of, 86–87, 217
    funding of, *see* funding
    joint, 99–100, 106–8, 126, 127, *244*, *252*
    probate avoided by, 91–92
    separate, 52–54, 99–100, 102, 106, 108,
        126, *245*, *251*
    sold by companies, 18, 108
    subtrusts of, 47, 48–55

living trust(s) (*cont.*)
  taxes and, *see* taxes
  transfer of property to, xv, 15, 17, 40, 99, 100, 102, 106–8
  trust maker and, 99
  types of, 99–110
  see also trust
living trust–centered plan, xiii–xiv, 7, 8–19, 227
  after-death cost of, 19
  Anatomical Gift Form in, 10, 14, 219, *309*
  burial and memorial instructions in, 10, 14, 219
  costs of, 15–19
  defined, 8–10
  documents in, *see* documents
  do-it-yourself, 18
  durable special powers of attorney for funding in, 10, 11–12, 124–25, 158, 159, 160–61, 184, *241–43*
  follow-up in, 26
  health care power of attorney and, 10, 13, 87
  initial costs of, 16–18
  living will in, 10, 13, 87
  Memorandum of Personal Property in, 10, 14, 153–55, *272, 273–74*
  planning process in, *see* checklist for designing your plan; Esperti Peterson Planning Process; professional advisors, team of
  pour-over will in, 10, 11, 14, 87, 112, 217
  preparation for, 24
  "team" approach to, 37; *see also* professional advisors, team of
  see also personal information checklist
living will, 10, 13, 87
loans, 165
  see also receivables
Location Lists, 15, 217, 218, 220–24
location of important papers, 10, 15

Magic Wand, 119–22, 128
marital trust (pocketbook trust), 47, 48–49, 50, 51, 58
master funding tracking checklist, 93, 94–95
mausoleums, 215, *306*
Medallion Guarantee Program, 136
memberships, 215, *307*
Memorandum of Personal Property, 10, 14, 153–55, *272*
  in the Form of a Trust Amendment, 155, *273–74*
memorial and burial instructions, 10, 14, 219
Memorial Letter, 219, *310*

mineral interests, 74, 209
mobile homes, 153, *268*
money market accounts, 128, 133
mortgages, 73, 165–66, 172, 207
  due-on-sale clauses and, 207–8
  refinancing of, 197
Motor Vehicles, Department of, 151, 153
mutual fund accounts, 145–46

National Association of Estate Planning Advisors, 39
National Network of Estate Planning Attorneys, 17, 29, 30, 32, 33, 227
nominee, 116
nominee corporations, 118
nominee partnerships, 116–18, 119, 128, 178
notes:
  in personal information checklist, 73
  promissory, 166, 172, 174, *285, 286*
  U.S. Treasury, 139
Notification Letter for Private Annuity, 160, *282*
Notification Letter to Lender of Transfer to Living Trust, *303*
  Under Garn–St. Germain Act, 208–9, *304*

oil interests, 74, 209

partnerships, 73, 177, 185–86, *290*
  general, 185, 186, *258, 289*
  investment limited, 146
  limited, 185–86, *256*
  professional, 186
payable-on-death (POD) accounts, 123, 124, 134
personal information checklist, 14, 24, 42, 59, 60–76, 77, 85
  property titles and, 61–62
  property values and, 65
  types of ownership and, 62–65
personal property, 65, 71, 148–55
  airplanes, 150, 152, *269, 270*
  automobiles, 61, 62, 150, 151–52
  boats, 61, 150, 152–53, *268*
  intangible, 188
  manufactured or mobile homes, 153
  Memorandum of, 10, 14, 153–55, *272, 273–74*
  without registered title, 148, 149–50
  with registered title, 148, 149, 150–53
  in sole proprietorship, 177
  tangible, 148–49, 177, *272*
  trust amendment and, 155

planning, *see* checklist for designing your plan; Esperti Peterson Planning Process
planning pyramid, 20–22
pocketbook trust (marital trust), 47, 48–49, 50, 51, 58
POD (payable-on-death) accounts, 123, 124, 134
Postmortem Assignment, 123–24, 166, 184, *240, 288*
    of Partnership Interest, 186, *290*
pour-over wills, 10, 11, 14, 87, 112, 217
power of attorney, *see* durable power of attorney
private annuities, 160, *281, 282*
privately owned corporations, 179–84
probate, xiii, xiv, 3, 8, 9, 11, 18, 30, 32, 60, 85
    annuities and, 159
    avoidance of, with living trust, 91–92
    costs of, 16, 17, 19
    living (guardianship), 11, 12, 16, 18, 85, 91, 92
    living trust funding and, 25, 26
    promissory notes and, 174
    receivables and, 165
    simplified, for small estates, 125
professional advisors, team of, xv, 7, 15, 18, 20, 22, 23, 24, 26, 47, 59, 64, 65, 77, 87, 218, 225
    accountants, *see* accountants
    creation of, 24–25, 36, 37–45
    Esperti Peterson Planning Process from perspective of, 27–28
    financial planners, *see* financial planners and advisors
    first meeting with, 24, 82–83
    funding and, 92–93, 111
    lawyer referrals from, 34
    lawyers, *see* lawyers
    life insurance agents, *see* life insurance agents
    limited perspectives of, 38
    making list of, 10, 15
    meeting with, 25, 77–84
    meeting with, before meeting with lawyer, 80–82
    meeting with lawyer before meeting with, 77–80
    National Association of Estate Planning Advisors and, 39
    reasons for using, 37–38, 45
    review sessions with, 88
    and second meeting with lawyer, 85–86
    stockbrokers, 34, 38, 40, 43, 61, 64, 87
    three approaches to meeting with, 77–82

trust officers, 25, 34–35, 38, 44–45, 87
    which advisors to use, 38–39
professional corporations, 183–84
professional partnerships, 186
promissory notes, 166, 172, 174, *285, 286*
property, xv, 214–16
    assignment of, *see* assignment
    business, tax rules for, 188–90
    cemetery plots, 215
    of children, 52–54
    community, 62, 64–65, 99, 100, 106–8
    control of, 4–5, 6, 7, 10, 12, 15, 60, 91
    fee simple ownership of, 62, 63
    giving to whom you want at time of your choosing, 4, 6
    information about, 10, 14–15; *see also* personal information checklist
    insurance for, 196–97
    joint tenancy of, *see* joint tenancy
    judgments, 75, 216, *308*
    locating titles to, 61–62
    memberships, 215
    safe-deposit boxes, 214–15, 217
    sale of, *see* bill of sale; receivables
    special business or income-producing, 187–188
    special use valuation, 189–90
    tenancy-by-the-entirety, 62, 63–64, 102–6, 108
    tenancy-in-common, 62, 63, 100, 108, 127
    titles to, 5, 64
    transfer of, to trust, xv, 15, 17, 40, 99, 100, 102, 106–8
    types of ownership of, 62–65
    ultimate distribution of, 55
    value of, 65
    see also funding; living trust; living trust–centered plan; personal information checklist; personal property; real property; trust

Quitclaim Deed, 192, *193*

ranch and farm interests, 74
real property (real estate), xv, 61, 102, 191–213
    condominiums, 200–201, *302*
    cooperative apartments, 200, *301*
    land trusts and, 118
    leasing of, 212
    mortgage refinancing and, 197
    out-of-state, 207
    in personal information checklist, 75
    rental, 201–7

real property (real estate) (*cont.*)
  residences, 198–99
  subject to indebtedness, 207–12
  successor trustees and, 197–98
  time-shares, 201
  transfer of, to living trust, 191–97
  types of, 198–207
  vacation homes, 200
  value of, 65
  see also deeds
Receipt of Real Property Deed, 195, *297*
receivables, 165–76
  deeds of trust, 166, 172
  installment sale contracts, 166–72
  land sale contracts, 172–74
  mortgages, 165–66, 172
  in personal information checklist, 73
  promissory notes, 166, 172, 174, *285, 286*
  security interests in accounts receivable, 174
rental real estate, 201–7
Request for Change of Beneficiary/Disability Policy, 158, *278*
Request for Change of Ownership/Beneficiary of Insurance Policy, 156, *275*
Request for Reissue of United States Savings Bonds/Notes in Name of Trustee of Personal Trust Estate, 139, *141–44*
Request for Taxpayer Identification Number and Certification, 96, *97*
residences, 198–99
retirement plans, 15, 17, 62, 156
  beneficiaries of, 160, 161–63, 164
  nonqualified deferred compensation, 164
  in personal information checklist, 71
  qualified, 160–63, *283*
revocable living trust, *see* living trust
revocable trust accounts, 133–34
royalty interests, 188, *293*

safe-deposit boxes, 214–15, 217
sale of property, *see* bill of sale; receivables
savings accounts, 62, 69, 126–28, 133
  payable-on-death, 123, 124
Savings Bonds, 139, 145
S corporations, 182–83
Section 1244 stock, 181–82, 183
securities, 135–47
  bonds, *see* bonds
  brokerage accounts, 136, 138
  investment limited partnerships, 146
  mutual fund accounts, 145–46
  stock, *see* stock
  U.S. Treasury, 139–45
  value of, 65

security interests in accounts receivable, 174
seminars, estate planning, 23, 43, 80
separate trusts, 52–54, 99–100, 106, 108, 126, *245, 251*
  joint tenancy property and, 102
simplified employee pension plan (SEP), 160
Small Estates Act, 151
sole proprietorships, 74, 177–79, 187, *287*
Specific Personal Property Assignment for One Trust Maker, *261*
Specific Personal Property Assignment for Two Trust Makers, *262*
Specific Personal Property Bill of Sale for One Trust Maker, *259*
Specific Personal Property Bill of Sale for Two Trust Makers, *260*
Spousal Waiver for Qualified Retirement Plan, 161, *283*
spouse, 48–49
  family trust and, 49–50
  trust types and, 99–110
  types of ownership and, 63–64
SS-4 Form, 96, *98*
state laws, 4–5, 11, 50, 99, 100, 151
stock(s), 61, 64, 135–38, 148, 177
  attribution rules and, 189
  employee incentive, 146–47
  lettered, 138
  in limited liability company, 187
  in personal information checklist, 69–70
  in privately owned corporations, 179–84
  restrictions on transfer of, 179–81
  Section 1244, 181–82, 183
stockbrokerage firms, 136–38
stockbrokers, 38, 40, 43, 61, 64, 87, *254*
  fees of, 43
  lawyer referrals from, 34
stock certificates, 61
Stock or Bond Power, 136, 138, 179, *249*
Stock Power, 135–36, *137*, 179, 184
Street Name Account, 136
successor trustees, 115, 197–98
  affidavits of, *237, 298, 299, 300*

taxes, xv, 4, 6–7, 17, 21–22, 31, 49, 50, 51, 93–96
  annuities and, 159
  boilerplate forms and, 108
  and businesses in trust, 179
  C corporations and, 182, 183
  charitable contributions and, 54
  federal estate, installment payment of, 188–190
  federal estate, saving on, 58

Flower Bonds and, 145
homestead exemption and, 199
installment sale contracts and, 172
joint property and, 100
land sale contracts and, 174
limited liability company and, 187
Magic Wand and, 122
and residence transfer to trust, 199
Savings Bonds and, 145
S corporations and, 182, 183
Section 1244 stock and, 181, 182, 183
special rules for business property, 188–90
state transfer, 196
and transfer of rental real estate to trust, 205–7
Tenancy Agreement, 100, *101*
tenancy by the entirety, 62, 63–64, 102–6, 108
tenancy in common, 62, 63, 100, 108, *245, 251*
  of bank accounts, 127
time-shares, 201
title(s), 5, 64
  evidence of, 61
  insurance, 196–97
  locating of, 61–62
  in name of trustee, 112–13
  registration, property with, 148, 149, 150–153
  registration, property without, 148, 149–50
trade and fictitious names, 178
trademarks, 188, *295*
transfer on death (TOD) of securities, 124
Transfer to Living Trust–Shareholders or Buy-Sell Agreement, *180,* 181
Treasury bonds, bills, notes, and direct accounts, 139–45
Treasury Direct Transaction Request, 139, *140*
trust(s), xiii, 4, 29
  changes in laws of, 87–88
  common, 52
  family, 47, 49–51, 58
  grantor, 93, 183
  joint, 99–100, 106–8, 126, 127, *244, 252*

land, 118–19
pocketbook, 47, 48–49, 50, 51, 58
separate, 52–54, 99–100, 102, 106, 108, 126, *245, 251*
see also living trust
trust companies, 44
trustee(s), 10, 85
  establishing authority of, 113–15
  selection of, 56–57
  surviving or successor, 115, 197–98, *237, 298, 299, 300*
  title in name of, 112–13
trustee's deed, 195
trust maker, 99
trust officers, 25, 38, 44–45, 87
  lawyer referrals from, 34–35

Uniform Commercial Code (UCC), 174
  Financing Statement, 174, *175,* 178
  Statement of Change, 174, *176*
Uniform Probate Code (UPC), 154, 166, 184, 186
Unregistered Livestock Bill of Sale, 188, *292*
U.S. Coast Guard, 152–53, *271*
U.S. Treasury bonds, bills, notes, and direct accounts, 139–45

vacation homes, 200

W-9 Form, 96, *97,* 138
Warranty Deed, 192, *194*
  to convert joint tenancy to tenancy in common, 102, *103*
  from joint tenancy directly into separate living trust, 102, *105*
  from tenants in common to separate living trusts, 102, *104*
  for time-share, 201, *202–3*
wills, xiii, 3, 4, 5, 8, 9, 11, 29, 30, 31, 32, 86–87, 88, 155, 217–18
  costs of, 16, 19
  Memorandum of Personal Property and, 154
  pour-over, 10, 11, 14, 87, 112, 217